Praise for *Temple Stream*

"Bill Roorbach is a brilliant guide to the natural world. Gracefully combining deep knowledge, lyrical description and wry humor, his writing draws you out of your chair and into a world of streams and meadows and trees and bugs and beavers. And it makes you want to stay there."
—*Seattle Times*

"*Temple Stream* is nature writing at its best....There's no preaching, no politics or philosophy. Just terrific storytelling."
—*Cleveland Plain Dealer*

"While genuine in his appreciation of Nature, Roorbach is the antithesis of the smug and self-absorbed Naturalist. . . . *Temple Stream* is a moving book: thoughtful, precise, about much more than flora."
—*The Believer*

"There are other autobiographical books about Maine, but Roorbach's writing is so compelling, his eye for the human condition so keen, that this is in a class of its own."
—*Library Journal* (starred review)

"A celebration of life...deft and evocative, making small adventures loom large."
—*Kirkus Reviews*

"With a voice as pure and true as the stream itself, Roorbach limns a lyrical yet precise portrait of the life teeming along one deceptively simple yet richly essential part of the natural world."
—*Booklist*

Praise for Bill Roorbach

"Roorbach falls, for me, into that small category of writers whose every book I must read, then reread."
—Jay Parini, author of *The Apprentice Lover*

"Here is a narrator who makes you glad to be alive, giddy to be in his presence, grateful to love friends and family and dogs with generosity and abandon, to show tenderness and thus be saved by strangers."
—Melanie Rae Thon, author of *First, Body*

"Roorbach is a master of capturing and expressing joy."
—*Hartford Courant*

"Roorbach has a knack for tapping into deep undercurrents and bringing them to the surface with the least amount of fanfare or fuss."
—*L.A. Weekly*

Also by Bill Roorbach

FICTION:

The Smallest Color
Big Bend

NONFICTION:

A Place on Water
(with Robert Kimber and Wesley McNair)
Into Woods
Summers with Juliet

INSTRUCTION:

The Art of Truth (ed.)
Writing Life Stories

TEMPLE STREAM

A RURAL ODYSSEY

Bill Roorbach

DIAL PRESS TRADE
PAPERBACKS

TEMPLE STREAM
A Dial Press Trade Paperback Book

PUBLISHING HISTORY
Dial Press hardcover edition published August 2005
Dial Press Trade Paperback edition / June 2006

Published by The Dial Press
A Division of Random House, Inc.
New York, New York

Book design by Glen Edelstein
Map illustration by Kenneth Batelman
Title page photo by Ed Frank
Cover photo © Alvis Upitis/Panoramic Images
Cover design by Belina Huey

The author wishes to acknowledge Furthermore: a program of
the J. M. Kaplan Fund, for grant assistance during the research
and writing of this book.

A portion of this book originally appeared in *Harper's Magazine*.

"The Town That Ends the Road" Copyright © 1966, 1999, 2003
by Theodore Enslin.

"Eros at Temple Stream" by Denise Levertov, from *Poems 1960–1967*, copyright ©
1966 by Denise Levertov. Reprinted by permission of
New Directions Publishing Corp.

Library of Congress Catalog Card Number: 2005045493

ISBN-10: 0-385-33655-1
ISBN-13: 978-0-385-33655-0

Printed in the United States of America
Published simultaneously in Canada

www.dialpress.com

10 9 8 7 6 5 4 3 2 1
BVG

For Juliet and Elysia,
and for my mother, Reba, who started me looking.

Man is a stream whose source is hidden.
—Ralph Waldo Emerson

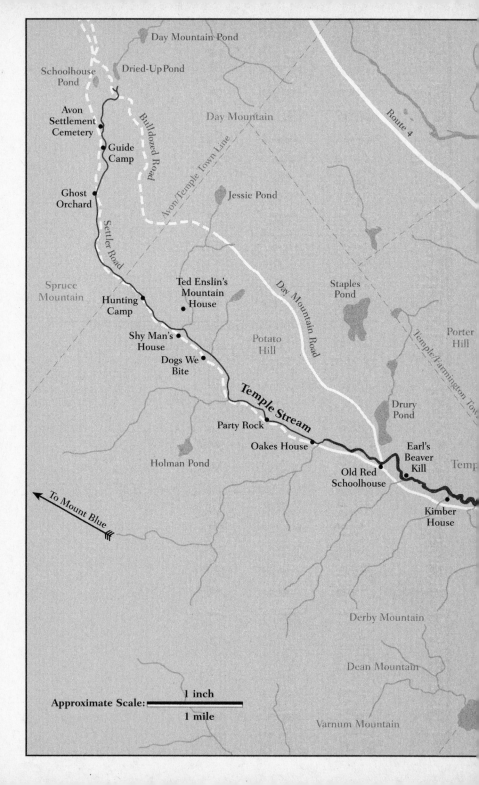

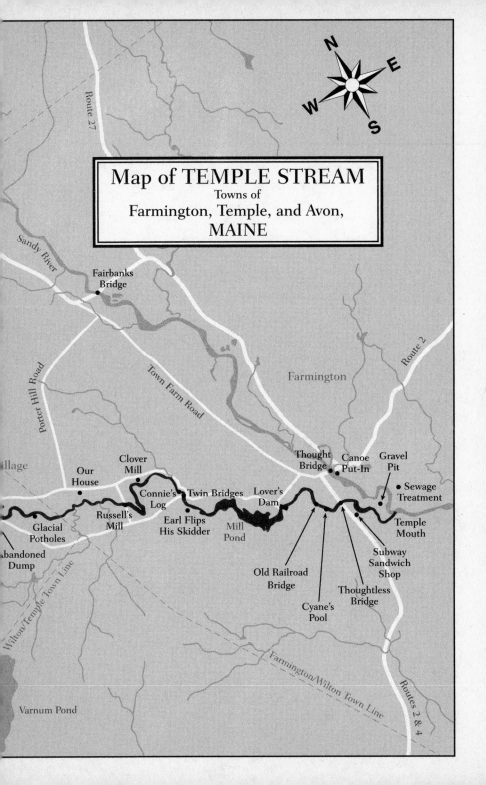

Map of TEMPLE STREAM
Towns of
Farmington, Temple, and Avon,
MAINE

Summer Solstice

THE MOST DIRECT ROUTE FROM OUR PARLOR TO TEMPLE Stream is out the deck doors and down the steps, alongside the barn and down some more, following the slope of our scruffy backyard past the gardens, past the hollow apple tree, through the milkweed meadow to the ever-thickening bramble of raspberries. From there it's a bushwhack into a boggy stand of balsam fir and white birch, then over a tumbled and moss-claimed stone wall, across the neighbor's first hayfield, finally through tangled streamside alders to the water, four hundred paces altogether, a thousand feet due south, thirty-four feet of altitude down. The stream there moves slowly through beaver flats, its course marked by silver maples and black cherries and yellow birches leaning. It's a pocket paradise—birdsong and beaver work, no roads near, no houses in sight, large hayfields on both sides, a broad swath of sky above.

Our house was built in 1874 by Mary Butterfield and W. F.

Norcross, newly wed, and was positioned not quite across the street from her parents' house and on their land (which had been Abenaki territory). Mary's husband and infant son died just three years later. She must have walked down to the stream sometimes to try and think, grief-struck. Her parents' house burned down about the same time, more sorrow. They came to live with Mary in her place, which was tiny, if still new.

By the time my wife, Juliet Karelsen, and I bought it—October 2, 1992—the house was considerably bigger, having grown addition by addition at the hands of a succession of owners in the hundred twenty-five years since Mary mourned. Juliet and I have put in endless hours of repair and remodeling, but it's still a modest house, well worn. The floors slant sharply, the porch roof leaks chronically, the bedrooms are hot in summer, the dirt-floor basement is wet in March and April, the mice come in from the fields in fall.

We heat with wood in winter, and the heat expands to every corner. Sunlight fills the house always, and if the rooms are eccentric they're cozy, too, and after more than a decade they are our own, so much so that the house and grounds seem the very structure of our marriage. Knock on our door and you knock on our lives.

The high ground around here is Mount Blue, modest in montane terms at thirty-two hundred feet, but impressive when viewed from the Sandy River, which flows through our town—Farmington, Maine—at just three hundred sixty feet above sea level. Atop Mount Blue on a clear day, after a steep hike on a frank New England trail, one clambers over broken chain-link, climbs what's left of the old fire tower, looks west, sees Mounts Washington, Jefferson, and Adams—the highest northeastern peaks—and endless other humps and hills and mountains, all blue and purple with distance, sometimes white with snow. One feels oneself well atop the rugged world. The closest peaks north and west (many of them mounted by the Appalachian Trail) make the Longfellow Range, named for the poet.

Eastward, there is diminishment: Day Mountain smaller than Blue, Derby Mountain less, a glint from Varnum Pond to orient the view, Porter Hill just there (our house nestled near it somewhere indistinct), Voter Hill unmistakable with its tall radio tower, then the Farmington hills smaller, and smaller yet: Perham, Titcomb, Powderhouse, Cowen. One's world-eye peers down a short, primordial slope, following Temple Stream southeast to Farmington, where it makes an unhurried confluence with the Sandy River. The Sandy continues east till it meets the mighty Kennebec in meanders at Norridgewock. The Kennebec meets and absorbs the Androscoggin yet further east at Merrymeeting Bay near the city of Bath, flows on in estuary past revolutionary Fort Popham and finally to thorough (yet continual) dispersal in the Gulf of Maine and the Atlantic Ocean.

The Temple is our point of contact with all the waters of the world.

I MEANT TO MARK OUR FIRST SUMMER SOLSTICE ON TEMPLE Stream with a little hike and a swim. The day was all southerly breezes and unseasonably hot, every green thing taking hold, the sky blown with popple fluff and soaring hawks.[1] Juliet was at Clearwater Veterinarian with our dog, Desmond, and the new puppy, Wally: Wally had to get his shots.

I'd spent the morning rough-wiring our gutted bathroom— our only bathroom—the third room to go under the hammer in nine months of hard do-it-yourself remodeling. The steel tub balanced loose on bare floor joists, soon to be replaced by an antique claw-foot (found, like Wally, in the classified ads), twenty dollars, a hundred-mile drive. Juliet and I had been bathing by candlelight under broken plaster for two months, not an altogether unpleasant fate.

I shook the old vermiculite insulation and sawdust out of my hair, dropped my electrician's belt on the kitchen table, hurried through the attached barn and out into the day—sky like blue heaven, white butterflies floating purposefully over everything. I fairly dove down the lawn. You could hear the stream roaring through the fields below, that's how high the water was after a week of rain. I'd strip down and jump in quick no matter how cold, wash the frustration of the morning's work away, slough off every dead cell of winter, emerge a new man, baptized for a new life in this new house, this new town, this new world. I gamboled down through the tall grass and hawkweed flowers, playing wild.

At the raspberry brambles I pulled up short. I had distinctly heard a low grunt just beyond the olden stone wall and five or ten yards into the dense foliage of Lulu's woods. I'd cleaned up an old farmstead dump just there, taken out a wringer-washer, several mysterious boilers, a bedframe, maybe a hundred bot-

---

1. Popple is the common name for white poplar, or eastern aspen.

tles of no interest, but I'd had to leave the cars, four rusted old beauties heaped upon one another, no engines, no tires, grown over nicely and camouflaged by Virginia creeper and wild grapes.

That grunt. My dairying neighbor's Holsteins had been pushing their way through his faulty electric fence as a matter of course, but this wasn't a cow. I pretended to forage in the brambles, thinking not to scare whatever beast it was before I could get a glimpse. My neck prickled with the distinct sensation of something watching me, something very large. There'd been coyotes all winter, singly and doubly and in a large, loose, howling pack. We'd had a bear for several weeks that spring, a nervous and scrawny but formidable yearling that repeatedly visited the compost pile back up the hill behind the blackberries, closer to the house. But my gut guess was moose, because the presence I felt was that size, and moose were common enough, if not in this exact spot. I turned my head incrementally, picked as if at berries, looked slyly into the trees. Back behind the stone wall something moved distinctly, shuffling in the litter of the forest floor. I peered into the shadows. Nothing. I stepped closer, pretended to examine raspberry leaves, all the while scanning the thick foliage of the wood sidewise.

Then the creature *spoke,* in a booming voice: "Berryin'?"

I jumped, shouted a curse.

The voice said, "I'd not expect many berries this time of year!"

"Who's that!" I demanded.

"Didn't mean to scare you," the loud voice said.

I spotted him then, a huge figure in the leafy dark.

One prefers to minimize one's fear: "Startled me, is all."

"I hate a start," he said, pronouncing it *stat,* and stepped into the light.

He was enormous, wide beard untrimmed, two streaks of gray in it, thick mustache that fell over his mouth, flannel shirt, top button ripped, thermal-underwear shirt beneath despite the heat, massive shoulders, massive arms, massive hands black with engine grease, massive chest pressing the bib of a huge pair of Carhartt overalls, legs like tree trunks, big leather shoes that looked to be shaped by a chain saw, unlaced, heavy rawhide dangling, one pant leg rolled up high showing *long johns.*

It's the first day of summer, I wanted to tell him. It's ninety degrees.

His gaze was not unfriendly, exactly, more like wild. He *was* a moose. He said, "I couldn't help but notice you have some cars here." *Caz,* he said. Couldn't help but notice? He was deep in our space. He took a couple of long strides toward me, climbed nimbly up on the jumbled stones of the old wall, displacing them noisily with his weight, eyed me but briefly from my skinny ankles to my tattered gym shorts to my Field Gallery T-shirt, cast his gaze on the closest of the old cars.

He said, "This one here is a '36 Ford coupe. That one there is a '32. This chassis under here is from a Model A, *yessuh!* These wheels must be older yet. That under there is a Volkswagen Bug, 1959." My visitor didn't smile, didn't make eye contact, but looked at the car bodies fondly.

I relaxed as best I could, tried for an affable tone, said, "I kind of inherited all these."

He looked at me hard. He said, "Where is it you're from? I can't place that *accent.*"

"We moved here from New Sharon," I said, which as an answer to his exact question was a lie, as was the covering concoction of a Maine accent I'd thrown in for good measure. Juliet and I had only rented in New Sharon, ten miles downstream on the Sandy River, a tentative first year in the area after I'd taken my first teaching job, at the University of Maine at Farmington. But for the moose man, I wanted to be from Maine.

"New Sharon? Not *our* New Sharon. You're from Connecticut, yes?"

He had me pegged exactly.

"True enough," I said.

"Lotsa money down they-uh," he said, exaggerating his Maine twang.

"I prefer it here immensely," I said.

"*Immensely,*" he said. He jumped down off the wall easily, clatter of rocks, tugged at all the vines, put his hands on the roof of the nearest car, rocked the formerly unmovable thing a few times. I stepped up too, struggling in the tangle of vines. We stood there with the car between us. I'd never really looked at it, was surprised to see how whole it was, elegant lines of another era, some of its chrome parts still gleaming, junk nevertheless.

The moose man said, "I know a feller who would like this-here one."

I was speechless: was the moose man casing cars?

"He's got one in restoration just like this, see—and could use a few of these *pats*. See how clean the dash is here—you've even got the glove-box door and that gutta-percha knob there." He talked fast, where my stereotyping would have had him slow and laconic, and it was as if he were speaking a foreign language, or possibly Old English.

I said, "It's a '36?"

"The last good year for the American automobile," he said, and seemed to see me again. He couldn't hold my eye (nor I his), but checked my outfit again, clearly found it wanting. The last blackflies of the season began to appear. Several crawled up his arms, but he didn't seem to notice. I tried not to swat at mine, either, waited uncomfortably for them to bite.

He said, "So you bought the Moonrobin place...."

"From Pete Johnson," I told him.

"Pete Johnson. He's the schoolteacher?" *Teach-ah.*

"I reckon so, over in Anson."

"You *reckon* so."

And he'd pegged me again, caught me imitating him. He rocked the hulk of the '36 coupe, the last good car made in America, a thousand pounds of rusted metal.

"The old places are trying," he said, and "We do like it when people from away take care of our older homes."

I took offense: "We love this place."

"You love it, we live it. How long will you plan to stay?"

One knows when one is being baited. Others of our rural neighbors had said similar things about the evanescence of flatlanders, and I knew that long explanations weren't going to get me anyplace useful with the moose man. I just stood there in my dashing gym shorts, didn't say a word, slapped a blackfly on my neck, couldn't stop myself.

"Fairies got your tongue?" Now he really did look at me.

And the fairies did have my tongue.

His eyes softened. "Going for a nature walk, Professor Rawback?" He had my name and my job title in his files, some-how—and this was unsettling.

I said, "Tell me *your* name again?"

"Down to the brook to have look, carrying your crook and a book?"

I grew unaccountably heated: "Listen, Big Guy, I'm down there every day. I grew up in nature. I know my way around the woods, okay?"

He was taken aback, or maybe just acted taken aback, that particular Yankee brand of joke born of Yankee irony. His eyes glittered. He shook his head. Suddenly gentle, he said, "You maybe know *your* little bit of the woods. And that is the thing, isn't it, with you yuppies. Well, I ought not say *you*. But these yuppies coming into the woods know maybe Mount *Katahdin*, and they surely know Acadia Park, and they have been up to Moosehead in their BMW 320i's, and thus, you see, they think they have been in the *forest primeval*. And you, Professor, you walk back and deposit micturants in the stream and that's your nature for you. What do you know about *nature*? 'In *wild-ness* is the preservation of the *world*,' that's what you know, and it's horseshite, hagwash, manure of chickens to be spread on the fields."

He knew Thoreau. My wheels spun, trying to catch up to this moose-mannered social critic who wouldn't say his name.

He minced a little, said singsong, *"Oh, I go forth unto the woods and I'm feeling spiritual now. Think I'll quill me a poem!"*

Abruptly then he became furious, and I started again to feel afraid, this on top of my own rising anger. Who was he to lecture me, standing here on *my property*? There was just the junked body of a '36 Ford coupe between us, and he was rocking the thing like he might pick it up and put it on my head.

"Easy," I said.

"Easy," he repeated.

We stood there examining the old car and "feeling our feelings" (as my wife the former art therapist would say). His showed in his posture. Mine must have shown in my neck, which pulsed uncomfortably. I didn't want him to see the heat in my face. At length, in modulated tones, and by way of peacemaking, I said, "It's awfully good to meet you."

The moose man spat. But slowly he relaxed. The hatchet was buried. Conversationally again, humorously even, he said, "It's not so bad to meet you, a-neither." He rocked the car a little. "Just don't get to thinking you own these woods, *Professor.*"

Abruptly he turned, vaulted the stone wall, and tromped off through the trees, fast, a moose all right, thrashing its enormous antlers, pushing aside saplings, gone in a flash toward the water.

THE FARMINGTON PUBLIC LIBRARY IS HOUSED IN A HANDsome if diminutive stone building graced with the only dome in town. Under the dome, armchairs and town fathers, ornate arches. The stacks are circular, too; the floor of the top story is made of glass to let light filter down to the shelves below. I like to sit in one of the armchairs in the Holman Reading Room—

tall windows, high ceiling—put my feet up on the andirons of the large stone fireplace, read a rainy afternoon away.

Spurred by the moose man's anger, I went down to the library to learn what I could of the stream from books. Jean Oplinger, the cheerfully mordant town librarian, took an interest, and together we rifled the stacks for scant references. While I read, Jean kept coming by with more books and maps and tattered old tracts, slipped out of the room silently when there were no more to be found.

According to Thomas Parker's *History of Farmington, Maine, from Its First Settlement to 1846,* which I noted was written barely a half century after the events at hand, Stewart Foster and Ephraim Allen, a pair of trappers, were the first "whites" to spend a whole winter around here. They camped through the season on the Sandy River "200 rods" from what is now a deep, popular swimming hole under the Fairbanks Bridge just west of Farmington. Come spring, they hollowed a log to make a dugout canoe and returned home downstream via the Kennebec, rich with furs and full of news of an extended intervale (as it's still called here), or interval land—what elsewhere is sometimes called bottomland—a flat valley stretch of excellent crop soil where the Sandy River widens in its own floodplain, leaving rich, rocky New England earth already stripped of trees by constant flooding and icing, and where Indians had farmed for generations. They noted mill seats, too, places where they thought the power of water might successfully be harnessed to run a grain- or sawmill: Temple Stream had a number of quality sites.

And a man named Pierpole was said to have kept a secret

lead mine on Day Mountain, up at the top of Temple Stream, a lode of pure ore from which he fashioned his bullets. Tradition has it that Pierpole was the last Indian in these parts (after the devastation of the many tribes in the hundred years of so-called Indian Wars before the American Revolution, and by smallpox). But he wasn't last: the 2000 census for Franklin County (of which Farmington is the county seat) records a Native American population of some eighty-six souls. Maybe what's meant is that he was the last wilderness Indian here. In any case, the man had settled to cultivate the land in what is now Farmington Falls, east of town. His departure was used by historian and poetaster alike as a convenient marker for the end of an era of romantic burbling over the state of the "savage" in New England. He stayed till about 1800, was last seen floating out of sight on the Sandy, which he called the Mussul Unsquit.[2]

As Francis Butler reports in his 1885 *A History of Farmington, Maine*:

> Pierpole is described by those who have seen
> him, as of medium height, broad in the shoul-
> ders, straight, strong and lithe. His features
> were comely, his eyes black and glowing. He
> always wore the dress of the aborigines—a
> blanket and silver medal. Many attempts were
> made to induce him to adopt a European cos-
> tume, but in vain. Once he progressed so far

---

2. Vincent York in *The Sandy River and Its Valley* says this means Great Carry Stream and that the name refers back to the presettlement use of the river as a major carry and float between the Kennebec and what would later be Montreal.

as to put on a pair of buckskin breeches, at the
earnest solicitation of his friends, but the re-
straint was too great. "Too much fix um," said
Pierpole.

The first Europeans, whom the Indians called sun-men
and red-beards and fire-builders and liars and worse, also de-
pended on the rivers and the streams for simple transportation
and reliable guidance through unmarked forest, at least at
first, later depending on them for the movement of logs and
fibers and grains to mills downstream, and when mills finally
got built here, for moving the milled goods straight to market.
Over the course of the nineteenth century dozens of mills
bloomed and fell on diminutive Temple Stream, all of them
gone now, utterly gone, washed away, or neglected and lost.

The earliest was a rudimentary sawmill making boards for
houses, barns, and fences: first things. Quickly thereafter a
gristmill, ground grain being infinitely more valuable than
whole, which rots in storage.[3] Fulling mills did better on the
Sandy, exactly at the site of Pierpole's last camp in fact, turning
out fulled wool cloths (meaning cleansed and thickened), but
washing away in twenty-year floods, washing away almost
predictably, their owners salvaging what could be rescued from
downstream and trying again, or giving up and heading downstream themselves, to gentler civilizations. Further up the Temple, very near our house, another sawmill saw fifty years' use;
near that, an oddity: a clover mill, in which the difficult seeds

---

3. In fact, at a time when very little cash was in use, ground grain was money. The first
bridge across the Temple was built by one Moses Starling for the price of 150 bushels,
circa 1790.

of the European import were separated from their hulls for planting to grow dairy feed and bee flowers. All that clover in my lawn is the work of people intent on milk and honey.

The goods made by mills or processed by mills at the onset of our town were meant for local consumption. But as the stagecoach roads developed, a growing amount of product could be sent downstream. Upstream came the wealth the products represented: manufactured goods; fresh-strain livestock; exotic foodstuffs (oranges, bananas); new settlers; minted, then printed, monies. Growth benefited everyone. More people meant more production, which meant more surplus, which meant more trips for the four-horse stagecoach to Hallowell. And then the railroad came—about 1850, abandoned now—and raw mill stuffs could be shipped economically and in huge bulk by central buyers to central mills supplying central manufacturers who could afford centralized sales forces: gently down the stream (merrily, merrily, merrily), the true down-trickle of economics, like the sap of a thousand Day Mountain sugar maples ending up in one tank, there to be boiled and further condensed for its sweetness.

Our streams and rivers bequeathed their pervasive metaphor of flow to the discussion of economies, but the actual streams and rivers are no longer engines of commerce. In this way they are abandoned, but this is no bad thing. In being abandoned they are saved. The millstreams, once the prized locus of all things human, have turned invisible.

JULIET AND I SPENT THE FIRST YEAR OF OUR MARRIAGE IN Montana, a kind of extended honeymoon during which we hiked a great deal and went broke. On the way back to our cramped rental in Helena from a day in Yellowstone country we stopped at the Bozeman animal shelter—we'd been looking for a puppy—and fell for a funny little fellow who seemed to pick us out too. He was part of a bizarre litter whose mother was a full-bred Boston terrier, father a full-bred Border collie. Two of the seven pups could have passed for Boston terriers, two could have passed for Border collies, but the three in the middle had found their own original ways to mix the legacy. Desmond, as we called him, was one of these, a handsome and sensitive soul, black and white with expressive ears and good posture. He had a terrier's wide jaw but a Border collie's long snout. He claimed us by coming to lean on my leg while his siblings rumbled. We took him home and felt a family.

A year later we moved him to New Sharon—me with my new job—and a year after that to Temple Stream. Desi liked the water, but needed canine company, we thought, so once the winter was done Juliet went in search of ... Wally. Who turned out to be another curious mix, his mother half Border collie, half basset hound, his wayward dad a springer spaniel, I'm afraid. From the spaniel come the freckles and the webbed paws. From the basset hound come the mighty chest and expressive howling. From the Border collie come the long fur— black and white—and the great flag of a tail. Despite the odds, he was a handsome puppy and a good match for Desi, and the two of them played for hours on end, racing with teeth clamped at each end of a long stick, for example, or splashing endlessly in the stream in a game of chase the minnows, and wrestling, always wrestling.

Wally was much bigger than Desi at a year and a quarter, solstice 1994, exactly one year after I met the moose man. By then it was the kitchen I was remodeling. The first morning of summer found me sweating pipe, bringing water to the new sink and to the house's first-ever dishwasher: copper elbows and tees and sleeves, shut-off valves and faucet set, solder and flux, tape dope and trap nuts, my favorite kind of work. About noon, the dogs began to bark, and then barked louder and whined and ran in circles, pandemonium as a loud knock came at our disused front door. I wiped my hands, turned off my torch, waded through the dogs to the door, eyed the hunched figure out there—a tall fellow in an ironed white shirt and bolo tie, mouth set, an altogether formal demeanor, the sort who'd have been a tax collector in the old days, or a funeral man. This dour presence and I gazed at each other through the bubbly old windows until I pointed at the porch door, where I met him, holding Desi and Wally by their collars as they clamored sniffing and snorting, Desi with his back up, theatrical growling.

Our visitor was unimpressed: "Earl Pomeroy says you have a '36 Ford coupe down here and I wondered what you wanted for it."

He'd taken me by surprise. I'd expected a message about God's angry love (or abiding love, depending on the sect). I said, "I don't know. What's it worth, do you think?"

"Well, it's worth what someone will pay for it."

We just stood there. He kept his face perfectly blank. If he was friends with the moose man—Earl Pomeroy, a name I was happy to have learned—he'd get no quarter from me: "Well, just hypothetically, what do you think someone *would* pay for it?"

"Maybe a couple hundred if it's usable at all, but that's just maybe."

After a long silence I asked his name and he told me: Fred Ouellette. He said he liked a close-to-the-road house like ours, meaning that he didn't, just a little convoluted Yankee small talk. Then the dogs and I led him at an amble down the yard to the old junk pile.

Mr. Ouellette brightened at the sight of the coupe. "Jeezum," he said. "This is fine, this is. See, I can use these spurs, and this latch here—and I need this glove-compartment door, and here you've got the original gutta-percha knob. Oh, this is something!" He wasn't going to resell the thing, but was going to use it to finish the restoration of a beloved car of his own, same year, same make, a project he'd been on ten years. He showed me where the convertible top would have gone, and showed me a pair of cleats he was missing, two of the many chrome bits I'd seen shining through the undergrowth from as far away as the house.

I said, "The last great car made in America."

And he said, "Oh, you sound just like that oddball Earl. The last great American car, sir, is the '65 Mustang, preferably in blue, or possibly the '66 Shelby GT, *yessuh*."

We stood over the derelict coupe a long time, talking. Mr. Ouellette lived in Auburn, an hour away. He just shrugged when I asked how he knew Earl, seeming to say, How does anyone know Earl? In the end, I gave the car to him for the towing, gave it away on impulse, since it didn't really feel like

mine to sell. He was neither grateful nor ungrateful, but said
he'd come by to pick it up "terrectly." The dogs were abject
when he just simply left: they'd expected at the very least a
swim in the stream and a long walk. That's what visitors were
for.

A few weeks later, Mr. Ouellette pulled up in a sleek
wrecker, brand-new—one of those long, tilting, stainless-steel
flatbeds, equipped with a big cable winch. On the door was a
professionally painted sign in black, red, and gold:

FRED OUELLETTE
VINTAGE CARS AND TRUCKS
BOUGHT—SOLD—SWOPPED

Well, I still felt good about finding the old hulk of a car a
life, whether or not Mr. Fred had skinned me, and howsoever
he believed the word *swap* to be spelled. He backed past the
house and down the yard in an expert flurry, never mind
the grass and brush and barking dogs, hooked his chain onto
the old frame in an uncannily exact place, started the winch
(*wench,* he said). The carcass turned and skidded on bare,
rust-frozen wheels right to the ramp the truck bed made, slid
perfectly into place as the dogs marked the truck's big tires.
Fred secured the car with nylon web straps, cinched these
down. The whole operation took less than ten minutes. Proto-
col required that we talk a little after, so we leaned on the truck
bed and admired the coupe. He showed me its one best fea-
ture—a fender with plenty of metal left. "Even still got some
paint," he said.

I said, "Well, I'm happy you'll be able to use it."

He said, "I'll have to thank Earl Pomeroy," which was as close as he got to thanking me.

I said, "Will you see him?"

"Oh, sure. I suppose so."

"Where does Mr. Pomeroy live, anyway?"

"Oh, you know, I find him at the diner."

And then he just drove off. It was up to me to take Desi and Wally swimming, and so I did, down to the stream, all of us carrying sticks.

BY THE TIME OF THE NEXT SOLSTICE, 1995, I'D BEEN RE-cruited away from the University of Maine at Farmington by Ohio State: double the pay, half the classes. Juliet, meanwhile, had been accepted by the School of the Art Institute of Chicago for an MFA in painting, her longtime dream. While we people took a crash trip to search for separate housing in two new cities, longest days of the year, the lucky dogs got to stay in Farmington with friends. Two apartments arranged, Juliet and I came back to enjoy the rest of the summer near the stream: soon enough we'd be moving.

For the next several years, summer solstices came rich with meaning: we were home again after a school year away, having survived a maelstrom of housesitters and landlords, grad students and city parks, homesick dogs on leashes. But no matter what wiles the Midwest used to ensnare us, we always extri-cated ourselves when the school year was done and made our way home to Maine by the first day of summer.

... Summer solstice 1999, and I'm down by our bend in the stream, sitting on the big rock (a glacier-tumbled and farmer-dragged chunk of layered Pleistocene-era metamudstone, as I'll later learn), thinking what to do with the block of grant time I've got coming: we've got the fall in Maine. I've been here on the rock all morning alone—bird watching, plant watching, bug watching, streamside omphaloskepsis—after an early quarrel with Juliet. She wants me to quit Ohio State altogether so we can move back here. Quit a tenured position? No other job in sight? Impossible. I've had a swim. I'm shirtless, barefoot. There's an unaccountable smell of grapes in the air, wine on the breath of the stream.

I know this stretch intimately. Over the years I've waded and swum and explored extensively, skied or skirted the changing ice, canoed in high water, tried a little fishing, spotted moose and deer and fisher and mink. I know the fast water directly upstream, too, boulders and white water, deep hemlock glades. I know the narrow beaver pond downstream, fifteen feet deep, steep woods on one side, wide flats cultivated to hay on the other, a wonderful swimming hole, deep water from bank to bank, the spot where wading stops and skinny-dipping begins: Shangri-la.

Suddenly, in a thundering flash of huffing, black-on-white ecstasy, big dog Wally is there, then Desi. Juliet can't be far behind, and isn't. She shuffles along in the leaves, thinking hard, sits right beside me, pushes me with her hip, upsets my balance.

"Sorry about this morning," she says, still truculent.

"No, it was me. I was wrong," I say, no better.

She puts an arm around my shoulders, connubial silence in

the forest bedlam: kingfisher, chipmunks, chickadees, blue jay, ravens overhead, the stream rumbling over the rocks of the washed-out beaver dam below us. A rust-killed balsam is dropping its needles, filling the air with that citrus scent; we hear each needle hit every branchlet on its way to the ground, an infinitesimally quiet proceeding, but a racket nonetheless. The dogs lay themselves down in the leaves behind us like library lions, play lookout.

At once we say the same phrase: "I've been thinking."

"You first," Juliet says, following a mosquito with her eyes.

"Well," I say slowly. "I've got the whole summer and fall coming here, and I would really like to finally explore this stream."

Just then, exactly then, there's a frantic scrabbling in the grapevines in the dead elm across the water. It's a gray squirrel, working the remains of last year's grapes. The dogs leap to action, hurtle down the high stream bank, plunge into the water. Alarmed, the little creature gives a curious leap. The grapevines shake. Our squirrel races up the trunk to the highest branches, then races down, then back up, then down again, all the way to the ground and right into the dogs' frantic faces, scrambles in front of them through the leaves, makes two big, screaming loops all the way around the dogs like its brain is on fire, then tumbles down the embankment and *crosses the stream,* leaping athletically rock to rock where the beaver dam's been washed away. But he misses the longest leap—a squirrel!—misses and lands in the water with a splash, frantically swims in the current to the gnawed point of a beaver stick, climbs upon it in a hurry, leaps again, grasps a slippery rock with his long-claw forepaws, tail in the water, finally scrambles rock to rock and out of there, dripping. Is the little monkey drunk?

The dogs are way behind, still sniffing at the dead roots of the elm.

"Okay, it's my turn," Juliet says, oblivious.

"Squirrels don't *swim*."

"I've been *thinking*."

And suddenly I know just what she's been thinking—it's nothing new, but something has changed—and in my mind sperm meets egg and cells divide and fetus takes shape and babe is born and grows in elapsed time from child to teen to parent itself to old age.

"I'm thirty-seven," Juliet says.

Upstream One
Temple Mouth to Cyane's Pool

THE FOURTH OF JULY CAME AND WENT BEFORE I MANAGED TO start my exploration of the Temple. I'd been studying various maps and knew where to find its mouth: on the Sandy River just east of town, where blue lines meet. I intended to start there and work my way uphill, section by section, till I found the stream's source, the beginning of everything. Finally, after a day of hopelessly trying to meet a deadline for a magazine article, I threw my beat-up canoe on my truck and made my break, drove toward town, every curve in the road reflecting a bend in Temple Stream. That is, until asphalt abandoned water for a straight shortcut to West Farmington, once a little mill town in its own right, now something of a student ghetto for the kids who don't want to live on campus at UMF.[1]

---

1. And home to a nice post-office branch and a few fringe businesses: video rental, convenience store with gas, tack shop, beautician and tanning, performance car parts, chain saws.

I crossed what used to be called Middle Bridge but what is now known—at least in some circles—as the Thought Bridge, named by an ardent fellow who changed his last name to Bridges when the state condemned part of his property to build the span in question. This Joel Bridges also installed a billboard-sized letter-sign on the front of his house—free speech in foot-high letters—which that day held a message for me, two meanings:

CHANGE YOUR MIND

With that as inspiration I drove down onto a rough dirt road (paved now), bounced past the agreeably ragtag Mother's Pizza (gone now, replaced by the new Department of Human Services building), and parked on what was a mud track (parking lot now, picnic tables) high on the bank of the Sandy River (still the same, always the same).

Quickly, I unloaded the boat, a Mad River Explorer, that workhorse of canoes. I bought mine in Montana. It's built for streams, good for expeditions, handles heavy loads, almost no keel (it's terrible in the wind), very slow, very stable, cane seats, ash gunwales, dark green ABS plastic of the sort that molds over rocks and obstructions: no dents, only scratches, lots of scratches.

I was breathless, felt like an interloper about to be caught in a net by some gruff caretaker from the past, one of Earl's forebears: the mud track was on the site of an old steam sawmill that failed in its bid to beat waterpower, later the location of a "corn shop," where cow cobs were husked and hulled by hand and in season by phalanxes of local women and schoolboys.

Canoe poised over my head, I minced barefoot down a raccoon path through thick poison ivy. Another squirmy trip for paddles and gear, a pause to rinse feet and calves in the cold river, and I was off in search of the mouth of Temple Stream, a sweet ride down the Sandy, just enough current in that particularly dry July to get my displaced weight through the riffles, those shallow stretches of white water between pools. The late-afternoon sunshine slanted bright into the flow and illuminated the bottom: waterlogged tree trunks, insistent veins of clay, ten thousand rocks in every conceivable size and shape, swaying riparian grasses, a school of white-lipped suckers, one large brown trout holding behind a boulder, the fish revealed despite perfect camouflage by his own treacherous shadow.

Thinking of Pierpole, I made the next riffle standing—good fun, though my paddle wasn't long enough to actually pole, and there were plenty of rocks to land on headfirst if the boat flipped. Back to my knees. Over the lip of the high, eroded bank to port, the newly tassled tops of corn slid past. Tree swallows joined cliff swallows and wheeled above the high mud banks. Crows called and chattered, diving, playing. They didn't think about how different they were from crows two hundred years ago: they weren't different, not a feather. A hidden bird sang an imperious short song, repeated it: chestnut-sided warbler. A single spotted sandpiper flew ahead of me. The canoe could have been a log, for all he was worried.

Lines on a map don't translate into anything in nature: I watched the starboard shore intently, looking for a nicely inked and labeled confluence in all the tangled vegetation. Which opened suddenly into an enormous sandbar printed sinuously with machinery treads and the runtier ruts of ATVs—a giant sandbox, someone's gravel pit, backing up a long series of puddles. Suddenly, I was struck by rare intuition: this was the Temple, if only a flood fork. And all the sand and gravel was the delta of the Temple, much bigger than I would have thought, if I'd thought of it at all.

Mussul Unsquit made a wide turn to skirt the Temple's delta, so I followed it, paddling into a small stench. A little investigation turned up the Farmington sewage-treatment plant, hidden up in the trees to port, doing a disagreeable task well, its outflow pipe drooling into the river, faint redolence of chlorine, the town anus perfumed.

But where was our stream? Evening was upon me, the light growing golden. What if the flood fork I'd passed was the only fork? But no, after another hundred yards or so, I spotted an opening in the forest. The Temple entered at a turn before a stretch of real white water, entered flat and deep, a lost lagoon stained golden black with leaf tannins, strong current.

Mussul Unsquit drank this Temple Stream as nothing, a cup of blood, and rushed onward. I was tempted to ride on down, make my way to the sea. Instead, with two long sweep strokes, I turned into our stream, paddled over fallen tree trunks into quietude, switched from downstream (that is, downhill) on the Sandy to upstream on the Temple, working against the stream's flow. The feeling came over me of visiting an ancestor's hometown, the portentous and melancholy feeling I associate with reading lichened gravestones bearing familiar names in cemeteries far away, a stream's debouchment being last things too. I was inordinately excited by this meeting of the end. This was our Temple Stream, all right, but a stranger, as well, and no stream of its own as it flowed on after that spot, absorbed by the Sandy.

Pierpole had been here.

I pulled the boat over a submerged breakwater, huge cut blocks of granite that protected the gravel-pit ford, and carried on. Suddenly, the stream looked like the stream I knew: dense vegetation, clearest water coming in a succession of lovely pools and shallow riffles. The paddle around the delta and gravel pit had taken up a full half hour of my evening light. I hurried, wanting at least to get as far as the next Routes 2 and 4 crossing, a no-name bridge one barely noticed when driving on it, but which, from my perspective down on the stream, had begun to assume the proportions of a gateway to sublime knowledge. Call it the Thoughtless Bridge. It couldn't be far. Already, I was close to the road, paddling parallel to it behind Subway, a chain sandwich shop where I'd bought at least a dozen grinders over the years. And I could smell egg rolls frying: Jade Palace, a Chinese restaurant just down the road from Subway.

Around the next bend appeared the bole of an enormous fallen maple, nicely propped on its own thick branches in the streambed, furniture-smooth above from rushing flood-time baths in sand-laden water, bristling below with broken branches. A tree like this is called a sweeper and would catch you in its arms and drown you fast if you were shooting downstream in high water. I climbed onto it in a gap between branches, balanced awkwardly, pulled the boat over in a clean sliding motion, then onward.

A delivery man from Jade Palace passed silently in a leaky bateau, poling his way along under a handsome rice-paddy hat: an order of General Tso's chicken for folks living on a sandbar downstream. No, not true. No one passed.

I was alone down there.

Except for old car parts, which I suddenly noticed studded the banks—radiators, axles, headlights, transmissions, and then a group of outsized truck parts standing up like sculptures. Squashed under a boulder was one entire car the exact cerulean blue of heaven, so damaged I couldn't identify the make. No matter, it was riprap now. And farm stuff: harrowing disks, plow frames, grader bars, plenty of other items I'd seen in my brief career as a Nebraska farmhand nearly thirty years back.

Despite the junk and the propinquity of Subway and the sure knowledge that farmers and hunters and loggers and tomboys had preceded me, I got the feeling of being where no one had gone before. The water was dark, the shade was deep, the basswood trees and the silver maples and the lone butternut were thick in the trunk, misshapen, leaning. The road was right there, loud. But I was invisible, private, alone, even paddling just below Ryan's, a sports bar in a sheet-steel box building, so close I could have exchanged one wild place for the other, expending no more effort than a minute's scramble up the steep bank.

In *A Week on the Concord and Merrimack Rivers,* Henry David Thoreau writes: "by one bait or another, Nature allures inhabitants into all her recesses." He means you'll find something living wherever you look. But it's hard now to look at, say, a Dunkin' Donuts shop in its strip mall and realize that something about nature (or "Nature") has allured it there: roads have always followed streams, and commerce requires traffic.

A robin, bless him, poked the gravel bar, no lawn bird he. Rusty blackbirds probed the mud, bright yellow eyes focused on their feed, then heads cocked to check me out: benign, boys, so back to work. Pretty hubcaps lay in deep sand, smooth-edged bricks too, bull-broken china, beer bottles of more recent vintage. Wild-cucumber vines climbed and wound through a copse of red osier dogwood, last year's spiny fruit dangling and dry.

Where was that miserable Thoughtless Bridge? I didn't really want to find myself paddling upstream back on the Sandy in the dark, paddling hungry among Mussul Unsquit shades to my takeout at the Thought Bridge.

Catbird in sumac.

Black-eyed Susans.

I thought, I will build a sandbox if Juliet and I make a child. I'll dig away the sod in the dog yard, make a nice rectangle, excavate a pit a foot deep, treat four heavy boards for walls, spike them together nicely, fill the thing with a couple of pickup loads of Sandy River sand. The girl, the boy, whoever it is who comes, will play in there once she's two, and play in there with friends at three and four and five, and older too, more elaborate games and castles and bigger ideas as the wood gives in and the grass reclaims the sand, and one day she'll walk back there or he will and point to the spot and say to some special visitor: that's where my sandbox was. And then walk down through the woods to show that person something that hasn't changed much at all: the stream.

FARMINGTON, MAINE, POPULATION SEVEN THOUSAND, IS AN isolated place in some ways. There's been no public transportation since the demise of the narrow-gauge railroad (not even bus service anymore). Of a quiet night sometimes I think of the Metropolitan Opera, Yankee Stadium, Central Park, Indian food, people of color, Film Forums I and II, our many city friends, my old haunts in SoHo and the Village, and I want to scream. And deep winter nights Juliet thinks of hip galleries, the Santa Monica promenade, outdoor swimming pools, funky clothing stores, yoga classes, movie stars, and admits she's ready to kill me, burn down the house, and drive nonstop to Los Angeles, where her lucky sister lives.

Still, much has changed since the early nineties, when we first landed in Farmington. The *New York Times,* formerly three days late, gets to stores here daily by nine A.M., thanks to digital-remote printing. The twice-weekly *Franklin Journal,* formerly an echo chamber for town government, has become a lively reporter and interpreter of local events and attitudes. (Its offices, coincidentally, are on Routes 2 and 4 just beyond the Thoughtless Bridge—there's even a regular column called "Across Temple Stream.") The one fuzzy television station available when we first arrived is now pretty clear most of the time, and there are three fuzzy new ones to be had by means of our ancient roof antenna. The cable truck has yet to come down our road, but frequent kind letters remind us that for mere dollars a day we could get DirecTV, which apparently comes from outer space *really cheap.* And suddenly there's the Internet—the world's with us, even here.

The owner of the old one-screen theater in the former Elks Lodge downtown took a chance and a big loan a few years ago and built a seven-screen theater, also downtown—a continuing success. The Elks Lodge has been sold to a famous Boston stage company, who will use it to put on summer plays mixing inner-city kids with locals. For grown-up theater, there's the Sandy River Players. The University of Maine at Farmington, part of the Maine university system but a top liberal-arts college in its own right, brings music to town, and dance and lectures and poetry readings, gives us contact with scholars across the disciplines, provides access to a good library (excellent now that millions of volumes are available through the Internet), and offers a swimming pool and gym, not to mention the almost unbearable vigor of two thousand college kids.

The hospital has been expanding, both physical plant and staff (and a lot of our friends are doctors). For aid in our work there is FedEx, as well as cell phones, faxes, and e-mail, none of which were available when Juliet and I first arrived (and we have much better cars now, in which we can get to New York in seven hours, Boston in four, Portland in two. The Portland International Jetport gets us to anywhere at all). Wal-Mart has appeared and metastasized in only a few years to a Superstore, but for all its possible negatives (sprawl, unseen owners, cheap goods, unfair competition, ugly labor practices), Superness saves a trip to Augusta or Waterville when I've been made to want something no one else in Farmington sells. And our downtown is healthy, every storefront occupied, churches well attended, all the bars you'd need, bookstores, clothing stores, doctors and lawyers, pets, hardware, music, money, coffee, art, pleasantly dowdy department store, on and on. Every trip you see twenty acquaintances, a dozen friends.

There's the Farmington Diner, too, its parking lot always full of pickup trucks and big American cars from the seventies. The place is a classic, magnificent in stainless steel and broken signage, a holdout against standardization, not a hundred yards east of the Sandy River (and often flooded by her), not a hundred yards west of its own slow assassin: McDonald's. Inside, there's a constant, whirling social scene that affords a look into the heart of Farmington's humanity, a cross section of appetite and style (absent, perhaps, a good many vegetarians).

In the weeks after Fred Ouellette drove off with our inherited '36 Ford coupe, I kept thinking about him—had he taken me? I leafed through *Uncle Henry's*, which is a voluminous weekly compendium of classified ads, and searched out vintage car bodies. The going price was "You tow." So my heart softened. Still, I wondered about Fred's relationship to the moose man, Earl Pomeroy. Were they a team?

Earl had assumed mountainous proportions in my psychic landscape: I couldn't stop thinking about him. Somehow, I had gotten the idea—not fully formulated—that Earl had something useful for me, some bit of knowledge to impart, some sort of wisdom, perhaps even a backwoods version of something like *grace*. This was a mistake, of course, yet true in its own way, in the way of delusions: Earl did have something to offer, just not what I thought.

One morning late in July of 1994, a flicker woke me at twenty till five, banging on the tin roof exactly over our bedroom to announce his territory in the rosy-fingered dawn. I got up and ran outside naked—this bird with his handsome speckled breast and red bib had been torturing us for some weeks—and flung pebbles at the roof around him till he flew off. Fully awake, I decided to get dressed and take advantage of the early hour to go dry-flying for a couple of brown trout. Of course, the diner was on the way to the Sandy River, where I meant to wet my line.

I walked in the door at five-thirty, and there was Earl, taking up a whole booth, the table pushed all the way to the further bench to accommodate his enormity. I was weirdly excited to see him, still angry with him in some dark corner of my heart. But I walked right up to his table: take him by surprise, ha. Earl looked up and, not the least bit startled, said, "Hello, Professor."

"Hello, Mr. Pomeroy." If he was puzzled as to how I might know his name, he didn't let it show, not at all.

I said, "Mind if I join?"

Coolly he said, "Buy my breakfast?"

Trying for jocular, I said, "Well, why not?"

I found a loose chair, sat at the head of his booth. Pretty soon my favorite waitress, Zimbabwe (who had modeled for a painting by Juliet and who—don't ask her where the name came from—was not from devastated Africa but from Starks, Maine, auburn hair to her waist, hurt brown eyes), brought his food: one western omelet with home fries, toast and sausage, one stack blueberry pancakes with bacon, one double-hamburger platter mounded with french fries and onion rings, a triple-sized fruit salad, and four large glasses of orange juice.

"Buy mine?" I said.

"Nup," said Earl.

Zimbabwe took my order, disappeared.

My oversized companion ate with the utmost delicacy,

started with a little fruit salad, picked out the half grapes one at a time with his fork, chewed each one, nodded his head with private pleasure. He picked up the ketchup dispenser then and made the laciest, prettiest webbing of red across his omelet, used knife and fork to carve off a modest bite. He held his beard down below the table, carefully pulled to one side. He didn't look up at me but worked his plates, a bite from each item in turn. He'd barely dented his breakfast when Zimbabwe dropped mine in front of me, huge platter: eggs over, home fries, toast. It looked like a snack.

I ate. Earl ate. But we weren't exactly eating together.

When every bite was done—and Earl was not fast about it—he finally cast his cold blue eyes upon me. "You're out and about powerful early," he said.

Suddenly I felt exhausted.

He said, "Did Fred get his car?"

"Fred did."

"What'd he pay for it?"

"I don't know. Nothing. I told him he could have it. I mean, that's good work he's doing, recycling old wrecks."

"So he'll tell you. The noble work of salvage. He's a sharp one, that Fred. You might have got some ready cash there."

"I could have used it to buy your breakfast!"

No response at all to the joke. Just this, in the same bemused tone: "You might have got five hundred bucks for that cah."

"Nah."

"Oh, yes."

Defensively: "Well, I feel good about it. He's got his car. I've got it off my property. There'll be a nicely restored coupe to look at one day. I can't sit here and worry about whether I got ripped off by Fred Ouellette."

Earl wiped the corners of his mouth with his napkin, inspected his beard for food. His hands were like blocks, monstrously wide, but he used them tenderly, wiping the table, stacking his plates. He said, "You're one to talk about ripping people off."

Jocular: "What's that supposed to mean, Mr. Pomeroy?"

Dead serious: "Oh, you know what I'm talking about. You think I don't read the paper? We all know the professor scam. Pretend to teach what can't be taught. Set your sails to the prevailing wind. Let your graduate students do all the heavy lifting while you sit around home in your gym shorts, mowing the lawn and *fatting* when the rest of us are working!"

Under sudden attack, I grinned fiercely, said, "That's not fair, Earl. And it's not true. We don't even have grad students at UMF."

"Oh, you can't tell me that! And you can't tell me you've been to work one day this *summah!*"

"In summer I study! I write! That's my job!"

His eyes glittered, but not with humor. He said, "That's not a job. That's grinding your stump."

Zimbabwe arrived just then to pick up plates. Kidding, she said, "You fellas take it outside, you."

"This one's a professor," Earl said.

"That's what I hear," Zimbabwe said wryly. "Now you keep your voices down, you two, or I'll have to take you over my knee!"

I laughed, picturing Earl in that position.

Earl did not laugh. He struggled out of the booth, rose to

his full height, looked down upon me, shook his head in elaborate disgust, turned and lumbered to the door, emphatically leaving the check.

MUSKRAT. HE DIDN'T SEE ME RIGHT AWAY, DIDN'T HEAR ME with all the bridge-traffic white noise up ahead; he just calmly swam in front of me carrying a big leaf and stem from a weed I recognized from my childhood bog adventures but couldn't name—swamp smartweed, as it turns out. He paddled calmly, trailed his food, became aware of me only slowly, perhaps because of the telegraphing ripples of my bow. And casually he turned his head, made frank eye contact with me, held it a second, then simply picked up his pace.

My speed was slightly greater than Muskrat's (Musquash, the Abenaki called him, and so Thoreau), and I gained on him. Bridge brat. What's a canoe to he who's seen a hundred eighteen-wheelers an hour his whole life? When I got too close, he dropped his leaf and hurried faster—still no panic, no dive—and twenty feet further ducked easily into the mud bank.

I pulled up at the next riffle, which flowed under a fallen oak, sat poised a minute holding a dead branch to keep me steady against the bole. At the fat end of the oak a gravel bar had formed. And right there I spied two baby muskrats, about one-third adult size, clearly new in the world, darling. They saw me at the same moment I saw them, bumped into each other in surprise, then rushed headlong *toward* me along the gravel bar, only to duck suddenly under the oak trunk, where at last they were hidden. I thought hiding had been the plan, but soon here they came a-swimming, screwing their tails, matter-of-fact glances back at me. They paddled tandem across the stream and under the overhang of earth, rock, and root carved out by the current.

As I climbed out of the canoe at their gravel bar, one curious little face peered out from the lair across the stream and investigated. I ought to have thrown something or hissed or even howled like a monster to teach him about the danger of people, but couldn't bring myself to be the bad example. Instead I went about pulling the canoe over the log, making as much noise as possible. Even so, when I got to the upstream side I looked back to the cut bank, and there was that little head peering out, and then his sidekick next to him, gawping.

It is nice to be of interest.

Sunset was upon me. The Thoughtless Bridge was just ahead, one more corner, my portal to a new world. I could see it through the leaves and, of course, hear the traffic. It's a relatively new structure, functional, hundreds of tons of concrete, steel railings, four lanes (one in honor of each horse of the old coaches, I suppose), its job to carry traffic over the Temple to the commercial strip, a mile of Burger King, Wal-Mart, movie rentals, donuts, and doctors.[2]

I knew I ought to be turning around, but the world on the upstream side of the bridge beckoned: the *non*commercial strip. And anyway, the gravel bars were spotted white and red

---

2. And from there to the White Mountains of New Hampshire and on, three thousand miles across the country. Route 2 is the old road from Maine to Oregon, a kind of northern Route 66.

and orange with crockery and brick, and suddenly bright green: a telegraph insulator, circa 1850. This I picked up for the collection in our barn window. In the exposed roots of a yellow birch I spotted a bottle, intact, lovely light green with a pleasing, pregnant shape to fit in the hand, thick lip for cork or stopper, delicate seam up to the edge of the neck, the whole somewhat sandblasted by life in the stream. The raised lettering said *Julius Lieber, Petersburg, VA* (a seltzer bottle, according to later research, made in a mold, with the top blob added by the breath of a glassblower, mid-eighteenth century).

These treasures at my feet, night coming down, I paddled sharply and reached the Thoughtless Bridge. And though a reasonable voice claiming good sense told me to turn around right there, I passed under the span in dark shadow. Pigeons clucked from their roosts in the I beams. Cars, logging trucks, UPS vans, RVs, motorcycles, that whole other world zipped overhead, drivers intent on the forward. Dozens of people a minute rushed twenty feet above—weird to contemplate— more people than I'd been that near in weeks. Still, I had the feeling of isolation. I was sitting in an old place that lived on like a troll under the new place, growing happier by the second: I would leave the hurly-burly behind. I emerged into the numinous twilight as from a cave, paddled into the deep pool I'd gazed down on for so many years driving above, such a smooth, long pool that I couldn't resist, night or no. The other side of the bridge: that's where the answers are.

And on the other side, caught up against the logjam-breaking steel prow of the structure, I found this: a beaver stick. I have always loved a stick. This one was a popple sapling twelve feet long as measured against the canoe, gnawed sharp at both ends, tapered from two inches at the butt, blanched and ghostly pale, almost glowing in the dusk, perfectly stripped, almost polished, the bare wood tooled subtly by long teeth.

I knew that beavers like the chlorophyllous bark of the poplars—aspens, cottonwoods, popples—it's sweet and nutritious.[3] My popple stick had been stripped for its food value. I thought of something I'd witnessed once in Montana, a week deep in the Bob Marshall Wilderness, spying out of a tent flap (having awakened in alarm to the sound of carefree splashing): a fat beaver felling a thick-boled, moonlit aspen, start to finish. Only a hundred feet from my vantage point, and perhaps fifty from the bank of a small meltwater pond, the animal shrugged and peered and sniffed cautiously my way for two or three minutes, then hugged the tree, turned its head almost upside down, bit methodically all the way around the trunk with its specialized equipment (front teeth protruding through the upper lip such that the animal could attack the tree with its mouth closed, keeping dirt and wood chips and water out of the throat), always attentive to my position—frequent pauses to sniff—but utterly careless of the probable direction of fall, chewed and ripped, froze as the tree gave a crack, then hustled comically to the water and dove. When the tree hit the ground, the beaver surfaced and circled in the quiet water, peering at his work. Back on dry land, it waddled in a hurry to the upper branches of the fallen giant and began to eat, stripping bark contentedly, pausing to chew. Presently the first beaver was joined by two more, who, keeping their distance from their

---

3. Along the stream the animals had made do with many other species, as well: apple, ash, willow, silver maple, black cherry, white and yellow birch, buckthorn, alder.

benefactor (and wary of me in my tent), methodically trimmed their own branches and dragged them down to the water. Despite my interest I fell back asleep. In the morning the tree trunk was all that was left, barked and limbed, ready for a new life as a campfire bench.[4]

I leaned from the boat and snagged my trophy. The next thing I knew, I was on my feet poling. The stream bottom was good for pushing, and my control of the boat actually improved. The noise of cars and trucks behind me faded, caught up in the leaves of the trees, and faded from my consciousness in any case, caught up in the leaves of my brain, those crucial mechanisms that filter out continuous noise. My pole thumped the rocks, the stream rippled on my prow. I heard my own breathing, the evensong of peepers, the chittering of a score of swallows, the beeping of bats.

At the middle of the long pool I encountered what I can only call a brick bar—thousands of red-orange bricks making their own red-orange gravel, legacy of the West Farmington Brickyard, a goodly nineteenth-century operation located on the bluff just above the cornfield adjacent to the pool: dense-walled beehive kilns producing bricks and gutter pipe and roofing tiles for the area, every project local, every economy your neighbor's.

My pole tapped along a brick-bottomed stream, detritus hardly counting for pollution: the stream's clay had merely been

---

4. One thinks of termites when it comes to the digestion of wood, but beavers can do it too, and some researchers think it happens in the same way: through the use of friendly microorganisms in the stomach that help digest cellulose. In the end there's beaver shit, which is wooden too, coarse chips bonded into balls that one sees deposited on sweepers and stream rocks or sometimes floating in the water of a quiet morning, the original composition board.

baked. Veins of it would be there always, at least in human terms. But the bricks the clay had made possible were moving downstream like any old throwing rock, moving a millimeter here, a foot in flood, giving up molecule after atom to the flow, getting polished round, in a thousand years to be completely disassembled and rolled to the Gulf of Maine as reddish sand, rolled to the sea and pounded and washed and ground and digested, broken down to raw materials for some scruffy hunk of life.

The pool ended abruptly ahead at a broken beaver dam that backed up a higher pool. A continuous mount of water poured smooth through a slot not five feet wide, too fast for the boat. By paddling hard I managed to hold the nose of the canoe in the fast water, bounced there puzzling at the clean edges left in the gap. Someone, a devoted beaver adversary, had been at work with a chain saw. But it looked as though the beavers had been at work since, a gentle insurgency. A few new alder branches, leaves attached, had been laid in, and these were held in the gap by the strong current itself, a bare beginning at repairs. Fiddled into interstices, linking new and old, was something odd, which in the dusk looked like rope. I fell off the current, backed the boat up against the structure to have a closer look: the ropy stuff might be Japanese knotweed, an alien that people around here call bamboo. I used my beaver stick to dislodge a little, and noticed *cobs*. The mystery material was cornstalks, and lots of them. And now that I looked, I could see that a path had been beaten into the adjacent corn-field, a prodigious swath of corn pulled down.

Stick it to the man!

The pool beyond was still but for the quiet rising of a single fish to invisible insects. I thought of Cyane, the Sicilian nymph in Ovid's *Metamorphoses,* who "rose from the ripples / That circled at her waist" to cry: "No farther shall you go!"

A veery, that eerie songbird, sang descending, fuzzy notes: *turn-around-go-back-fix-dinner-like-you-promised.* Not wanting to cross Cyane, I began to turn, meaning to paddle hard, fly back to my truck, but in the water in orange light—and indeed because of the light—something caught my eye: caddisfly nets, silken, finger-size tubes blowing full in the current, attached to the bricks by caddisfly nymphs to strain the water for nutritious plant matter.

I'd seen these nets before—true of so many things in the stream—in fact, I'd studied them closely when I was a boy, named them *windsocks.* Forty years had passed, and here those windsocks blew again. And here was the boy again, late for dinner, all alone in his canoe, drifting homeward.

Autumnal Equinox

BEAVERS IN SUMMER AREN'T BUSY. THEY SLEEP THROUGH THE day to avoid predators and nuisance humans, come out after sundown, groom and goof around, invent swimming games, enjoy wrestling matches, mark territory. Yearlings, especially those in more crowded colonies, or where food has gotten scarce, may make adventurous forays further and further from home looking for mates, but until fall all this activity is desultory, playful.

In September, beavers get to work, primarily night shift, with three goals: shelter, enough food for winter, and deep enough water to keep their swimways open under ice. Colony beavers work to repair and expand lodges and dams and build food caches, swimming far upstream and sometimes waddling into the woods (but not out of their home watershed) to cut and carry endless loads of popple branches.

Unmated yearlings often leave home altogether at this time,

intent on sexual fulfillment. When potential mates meet, a rough courtship ritual takes place, the female trying for dominance over the male, much pushing and shoving (always short of injury), sometimes involving several rematches, until an agreement is reached and the bond is secure. Beavers mate for life, or at least until death do they part.

Out in the world, some young beaver couples find derelict beaver works to restore. The old lodge will be covered with weeds, the old dam will be gapped and broken, rotted, overgrown. The old flowage, perhaps abandoned when food got low, perhaps trapped out, will have seen its vegetation renewed, and the fur men looking elsewhere.

Nothing against trappers—I've done some trapping myself, years back, pocket money during my Nebraska sojourn—but I've grown fond of beavers, and know how trusting and gentle they are. I also know that the beaver was extinguished in Europe during the eighteenth-century craze for its fur and oil, and extirpated in most of its range in prerevolutionary America, sought out and killed colony by colony till the animal was simply gone. After that, farmers and hunters and fishing people missed beavers—water retention, flood control, wetlands. So, late in the nineteenth century and continuing into the twentieth, a prodigious effort was mounted to restore the beaver to its habitat using stocks from remote ponds in Wisconsin. This effort has been successful, especially with beaver hats and castoreum perfumes out of vogue: the beaver is back.

Water means safety and life itself in winter, so the first fall project is the dam. Where there is no abandoned beaver works to rebuild, the young couple must start from scratch. After finding a suitable territory, the pair will scout it for several days, looking for the best spot, usually at a place in the brook or stream that already constricts the flow of water.

Sometimes animals work side by side (if not in particular concert), more often singly. In addition to the usual stripped sticks, almost any material will do: rocks and fallen branches and waterlogged chunks of wood, even the milled lumber that so often turns up after flood, usually bristling with nails (once in Upstate New York, I even spotted a toilet seat embedded among the sticks in a tall dam). It's theoretically possible that the beavers could block the whole Temple Stream valley at Russell's Mill and make a lake for us to live on: the record length for a beaver dam is almost a mile. Some much shorter dams have record heights of fifteen feet or more.

Once the dam is built and the water level regulated, the new beaver couple builds its lodge, either the familiar pond-centered mound or the less visible bank lodge. The mound lodge starts with the beavers piling the sticks and branches until there's an enormous heap standing in water. When this is big enough, the beavers gnaw tunnels into it from the very bottom of the pond, and then chew out a modest chamber, leaving a raised platform inside for sleeping, this about six inches off the water surface, and a lower, wetter platform, for eating and grooming. The excess wood is pulled out through the tunnels, which are built with no sharp, snagging bends. Mud carried against beaver chests from the pond or stream bottom is daubed inside the chamber until the walls are plastered and every gap in the roof well filled, except for air vents. The tunnels become the household plunge holes, the only access to the lodge, all but predator-proof.

Beavers are rodents, and they are as good at tunnels as

squirrels or mice, their cousins. In the woods around active ponds one often steps into a plunge hole, a tunnel entrance as far as a hundred feet back from shore. Beavers are clumsy on land and could never outrun, say, a coyote, were they caught at work on trees far from the water's edge. But they're never far from a plunge hole and instant escape. (Native Americans used to trap beavers by blocking off such tunnels at the water, then breaking through the tunnel roof till they found their quarry, which was gentle enough to be caught by hand.)

All rodents have just two incisors, and wide gaps called diastemata between the incisors and the molars. A squirrel could probably beaver a small tree down if he put his mind to it; certainly squirrels gnaw through plenty of lumber to gain entry to attics and basements and wood sheds. (One of my homesteading neighbors had flying squirrels soaring onto her bed at night from a hole they'd gnawed through a fourteen-inch beam.) A gray squirrel's nest is sticks piled high in a tree and dressed with leaves, insulated chamber inside: a tree-fort beaver lodge. The chipmunk and red squirrel both nest in the ground, digging long beaver tunnels. Mice, rats, gophers, groundhogs, the jaculiferous porcupine: they're all more or less miniature beavers—just add water. Musquash is the closest beaver relative, and has been known to share a beaver lodge in winter, odd bedfellows.

Beavers are the biggest rodents outside South America. They can reach the size of large dogs—forty to sixty pounds is about average for an adult, from Desi's size to almost Wally's. Bigger than that, the old trappers call a "blanket beaver." The record blanket beaver is one hundred ten pounds. The Pleistocene beaver was a true giant: fossil bones have been found that show the animal was about the same as now in the details, but eight feet long, with incisors to match. The Indian tribes of New England and the Great Lakes regions tell stories of enormous beavers—beavers as big as islands—some, in fact, that became islands, and are still there to see in almost any lake, hundreds of yards or even many miles long.

In late August, more emphatically in September, our gardens begin to die. First frost in our valley location is generally within a week or two of Labor Day, and follows the olden wisdom: beware the full moon. The first hard freeze (a full night at twenty degrees or lower—as opposed to mere frost) might wait till the next full moon, but then again, it might come any night at all, starting late August. One looks to the evening sky after a perfect, clear day as the stars emerge and can almost see the heat flying up and up and gone. The cold drops in. I throw old sheets over the tomatoes the way my elderly neighbor Isabel Hammond showed me before she died, pull a tarp over the basil and over the cucurbits (cucumbers, squashes, pumpkins). If there's been no rain, I turn the sprinkler on, something I learned from an orange-growing acquaintance down in Florida: above freezing by definition, the water warms a circular area, leaves a horizon of wilted leaves where the spray can't reach. Some years I do nothing but mourn: you can't stop winter.

One laments the hundred tomato blossoms—too late for them to fulfill themselves—trims them back cruelly. One develops a love of green tomatoes: deep-fried, sautéed, pickled as chutney, built into pasta sauces (they melt in the pan, making a lovely, silken medium). I make pickles and dilly beans, admiring how thoroughly Isabel's heirloom recipes use the garden's most shocking abundance: cukes, peppers, onions, coriander seed, garlic, dill. It's all waiting out there, all ready at once, most of it in danger. I always like the look of our kitchen counters at that time, a cornucopia of tumbled vegetables overflowing a dozen mismatched baskets: squashes, carrots, grabbed bouquets of herbs, three kinds of potatoes, a head or two of broccoli, the last ears of corn, edamame soybeans, red cabbage, piles of wax beans, a nosegay of nasturtiums, twenty gourds, the first little pumpkins to turn orange, mounds of lettuce: food to process, food to store, food to give away, food to eat fresh.

Tomato sauce, tomato soup, tomatoes sliced on plates, tomatoes falling on the kitchen floor, crunching and squirting underfoot. I love a big old heirloom sliced thick and spread with mayonnaise or layered with basil leaves and the neighbor's fresh goat cheese. I love to stand in the garden in the lowering sun and eat a handful of Sun Gold cherry tomatoes, then another and another till my lips burn with the acid of them. I love the fragrance of tomato plants, carry a leaf around just to crush at odd moments and sniff.

Apples! Our trees are rangy, but the fruits, no matter how distorted, are sweet and make good cider or apple butter. In town, the McIntosh man parks his truck at Gifford's, our beloved ice cream place (soon to close for winter). "Had and tat," he intones, offering a sample, "had and tat," and fills you up a half-peck bag, hard and tart indeed. Year to year, I develop different pyrian enthusiasms: apple pie, apple crisp, apple bread, baked apples, applesauce.

Cherries! I love our little suffering Montmorency, which I planted the fall we moved in, absolutely the wrong spot, middle of the field, edge of the garden, windy, lonely. Its partner died in its first winter, chewed and girdled at the ground by starved subnivean mice, tiny beavers. The survivor is now a lovely, shapely tree, bent away from the wind, a spot of shade for summer lettuce. Two dozen cherries in its record year, sour as venom but when cooked in a pot with a little sugar, heavenly.

Plums! Again I planted a pair of young trees, again one died, though I'd learned and had planted them out of the wind in a warm spot near the barn with metal sleeves at the base against mice. For nine years the widowed tree grew bigger and bigger, but no plums. I thought the problem was frost during the bloom, but then learned that plums need pollinating partners close by, preferably of a different species. I duly bought two Japanese breeds, planted them to interbranch with my champion. The taller of the two, nothing but a whip and a twig, produced three blooms its first year. I played bee, buzzed as I stuck my finger in each blossom's face. There was no frost that spring, no big blow, and the fruit set, a plum for every flower. I made jam by the pint, filled the basement with jars. At our equinox party a dozen kids crouched under the laden branches as I shook the tree's trunk and plums rained down to little waiting hands.

And in our woods grow oyster mushrooms and king boletes (also known as porcini, which my Quebecois neighbors call *cèpe*). Sautéed in a little butter, the oysters really are like shellfish, rich and labial on the tongue. The porcinis are crisp and flavorful, divine, though few but Juliet and my mother will eat them with me. My old morel patch gave out: someone cut down the apple trees they grew among. A friend brings two grocery bags of chanterelles from a secret spot she knows: she'll share the bounty but not the location.

Steve at the hardware store gives an appraising look, asks the ritual question: "Got your wood in?" Orion creeps into view after midnight. Old sweaters migrate out of the closets. The sky has never been so blue. The hummingbird goes missing, but the college kids are back, a thousand beats per minute.

RAIN FELL EVERY DAY FOR A WEEK IN MID-SEPTEMBER 1999. The Temple watershed, already full from previous storms, backed up into its drainage, then overflowed the drainage, too. In our soggy woods fungi burgeoned: fly agaric, irregular earth tongue, lobster claw, puffball, sulphur shelf, turkey tail, bleeding milk cap, some poison, some delicious. Soaked song sparrows perched on twigs, seemed to watch the sky in desolation. The changing leaves, barely into fall color, matted on the forest floor unheralded. Fire newts lurked under every rock and rotting log, wriggling when exposed. Our sump pump bumped in our stone basement, coughed water in gouts into the dog yard. The porch roof leaked, filled joint-compound buckets fast. My rain gauge filled daily—nine inches in six days, and more coming. The radio warned of flood: our big rivers were expected to crest sometime Saturday night. Temple Stream would crest earlier, of course.

I splashed down there first thing, dogs puddle-jumping cheerfully ahead of me. Desi heeled when we got close. Wally pulled up short as we rounded the corner: our bluff was under a foot of water. He splashed to where the edge would be, but even he knew not to go in. The stream, normally a brook at that time of year, was flowing ten feet deep. Desi pressed against my legs in fear as we waded to the lookout rock, usually high and dry, now an island. Temple Stream had left its bed, was coursing across my neighbor's wide hayfields, still rising in whirlpools and eddies, carrying all that would float. The familiar streamside trees—basswood, yellow birch, popple, silver maple—stood tall in the torrent, breaking the water. The thick alders were part of the flow, plucked by fast eddies. A whole black-cherry tree, size large, arrived from somewhere upstream and blocked the channel as I watched, then became a filter for detritus: two wooden pallets, a little blue wading pool, a tractor tire, two coolers, a dozen odd boards and branches.[1]

I was thrilled.

I'd had the idea to send messages in bottles during the previous major flood, a whim I'd not followed up, with the idea simply to see how far a bottle could get, and who, if anyone,

---

1. Farmington has had floods in the hundreds since settlement, a surprising number coming in early autumn and not only in spring. In September 1784, all the local mills were lost, including those on our stream. In October 1859, a Sandy River flood got a name—the Pumpkin Freshet—because the fields were flooded before the last crop could come in. Downstream, good neighbors salvaged floating pumpkins by the thousands for the farmers to divide. In 1987, the Farmington Diner—along with three gas stations and Gifford's Ice Cream and McDonald's—found itself eight feet deep in the waters of the Mussul Unsquit.

might find it. At times of normal flow, I knew, a bottle might get to the millpond dam and no further, even if it missed every snag along the way. In water like this, though, it was not impossible that a bottle could make it all the way to the sea. Excited, I raced upstairs to my office under the eaves and typed the following note on my most formal letterhead, added an eye-catching title in large font:

> HELP (ME STUDY RIVER DYNAMICS AND PO-
> ETRY).
> To the Finder of this Note:
> Greetings. You are part of an experiment in
> flood dynamics. And also the poetry of
> streams, particularly the Temple Stream, orig-
> inating in Avon, Maine. This bottle was tossed
> in the water below my house in Farmington,
> just at the Temple line on the above date.
> What I'm hoping is that you will return a copy
> of this note with your information. Even if
> you're only a hundred yards downstream, and
> even if the date is just tomorrow.

The bottom half of the note comprised a questionnaire:

> 1. As exactly as you can: where did you find
>   your bottle?
> 2. On what date?

3. In what circumstances? That is, what were
   you doing when you happened on your
   bottle?
4. Who are you? Your name and address and
   phone are optional.
5. Add any notes or information or anything at
   all you'd like.

I self-addressed ten envelopes, put stamps on them in a
flurry. In the loft of the barn, with the dogs milling and whining at the foot of the ladder, I dug out my beer-making equipment (beer-making a hobby that had run its course, and good
riddance: far too much temptation, daily). I folded each of ten
notes in half lengthwise, added the envelopes, rolled each
packet tight as a Greenwich Village street reefer and such that
the phrase "HELP (ME STUDY RIVER DYNAMICS AND POETRY)"
showed on the outside of each roll. I secured the rolls with ten
colorful hair ties, stuffed the packets into ten Newcastle
Brown Ale bottles (clear glass), and capped each bottle nicely
with my abandoned capping tool, efficient as a brewmaster.
The top shopping bag on the hook happened to be pink and
from Victoria's Secret (a shopping trip had been just one of
Juliet's many steps toward the goal of pregnancy). The bottles
fit tightly in there.

Just then I heard the horrendous roar of Earl Pomeroy's orange GMC pickup truck. And my heart sank. Somehow he always knew when I was up to something embarrassing. Last
time I'd seen him I'd ordered a couple cords of seasoned firewood to cover me through the fall . . . so that would be the pur-
pose of his visit. The dogs barked until they saw who it was

and stopped abruptly (they don't bark at coyotes or bears, ei-ther). Earl slogged right back to the barn, a wet giant covered in mud. I wasn't unhappy to see him, exactly—we'd become less wary of each other in the six years since I'd first met him over my junked cars, and had had considerable coincidental contact—but here I was stuffing English beer bottles with quixotic notes. He was dressed exactly the same as ever, gave me his most serious look.

I said, "Hi, Earl."

"Could not work in this deluge," he said. "Puddles in the woods neck-deep on a tall *hippie*!"

I gave him a laugh, though I'd heard all his insulting gags before.

"And here you are making bee-uh."

"Not exactly, Earl."

He pulled his beard. "Uh-oh."

I pulled a bottle out of the shopping bag preemptively, showed him what was inside.

"You are putting notes in bottles, Professor!"

"Quite so."

"You are putting the bottles in an underwear bag, Professor!"

"This is a hell of a time to deliver cordwood, Mr. Pomeroy."

"I knew you'd be up to something or other on the taxpayer's ticket."

"And I'm in a hurry, too. I have to catch the flood just right."

"Notes in bottles," he said to himself, shaking his head: something to tell the raccoons, as if I hadn't offered enough over the years. The rain was still coming hard, pounding the barn roof. Earl and I stood in the wide doorway side by side, filling it.

He said, "Wet enough to bog a snipe." He said, "The Lord has surely pulled the cork." He said, "You'll be a-paddling back to Ohio!" And: "Well, at least those rich folks out there in the promised land will steam-heat some plush towels for you while you suck the cash outta their butts!"

"So, Earl, what do you think? Maybe just drop my firewood when it's a little drier out?"

"That product is one hundred percent waterproof," he said. "And I see you have a blue tarp sitting right there on the garbage cans."

"I just don't want ruts in the yard, you know?" *Yad,* I said, unconscious imitation.

"Oh, that's right, you got your grass farm here."

My personal ogre wasn't going anyplace, so I left him standing there in the doorway. I clutched my Victoria's Secret bag and clinked and splashed down through the streaming woods to the center of the flood. Earl, laced up to his high, thick knees in some kind of medieval footgear, was already ankle-deep at the bluff when I got there: shortcut. He wouldn't miss this for all the rock maple in Rumford.

"I will now toss the bottles," I said ceremoniously. I climbed up on the tall rock, which made me the same height as Earl.

His eyes narrowed, but he surprised me: no jab, no quip. In fact, he grew solemn. I felt I had to give him a role in the exercise, but planned a quick exit when it was over (maybe even get in the car and head downtown, let him dump the firewood on his own), wanting to avoid any of his angry lectures about the wasteful habits of professors or the multitudinous ways my yuppie associates had ruined the world. I said, "Hold this, Monsieur Pomeroy."

"Gladly, Herr Doktor," he said.

And I presented him with the pinkly feminine shopping bag. He held it open by the handles (these looked tiny in his fingers), offered the bottles to me in earnest, as if we had planned all this together, as if we were friends on a mission. I drew the first bottle out, suddenly glad that Earl was there as witness, lifted that clear, sleek vessel by its fragile neck, gave it a delicate toss end-over-end into the center of the raging current.

"*Bom dia,* Portugal," Earl said without the slightest trace of a smile. I felt sober, too. The bottle chugged fast downstream, staying to the center nicely, rounded the bend hundreds of yards away and out of sight. We waited thirty seconds, threw the next, then thirty seconds again, bottle by bottle till the bag was empty.

Earl called out formal imprecations and advice for each, getting into it, all irony and judgment and fury suspended, his head tilted back, his voice even and strong, almost loving, barely audible under the roar of the torrent: "Float, float, little boat, till ye cain't float no more!" and, "Bring us news from the place you go!" When the bottles were all under way, we watched the stream together, arms folded over our chests, eyes on the far bend, an unmistakable, warm surge of comradeship between us.

That, as it turned out, was the closest I would ever feel to Earl Pomeroy.

Upstream Two
Cyane's Pool to the Lover's Dam

THE MILLDAM AT WALTON'S MILL PARK (A HALF MILE BY WATER from the Temple's mouth, less than two by road from my house) was all black with mosses and molds, the great granite blocks of it set on a natural stone waterfall: one builds a dam where nature has already started the job.[1] October light: a clear, warm morning of long shadows. I watched the water slipping over the dam's rock lip, just the top layer of the old millpond roaring out over the sudden void and falling. I have always found the site spooky, lonely: men worked here, died here. Ground grain flowed like water into the beds of wooden wagons pulled by oxen and horses. Elaborate buildings filled

---

1. As I write there's a proposal before the town to rebuild the dam (at an estimated cost of $160,000) before it gives way. This could be seen as a sentimental gesture, since the dam serves no commercial function anymore. Then again, dam repairs could be seen as the crucial preservation of a well-established pond habitat. Of course, sooner or later, ten years from now or ten thousand, repairs or no, that dam is going to come down and the stream find its way again.

with powerful machinery stood here once (well, no, the stream was powerful—without it, all the machinery would be inert). Dozens of buildings had been washed away, the remains scavenged or abandoned, rotted and rusted down to nothing, disappeared for good along with the people who'd built them. Of what had once been, there was little to see—only a few stones like grave markers, a crushed millrace, the block foundation of the gristmill itself filled in and neatly graded over, the faint remains on the other side of the stream where a series of sawmills had rough-ripped the boards for nearly all the barns around here and many of the houses—surely my own—for more than two centuries. My friend Bob Kimber remembers mountains of sawdust here as recently as the early 1970s, but those were gone too, not a trace. A wide stone monolith, lone remnant of the original Morrison Hill Road Bridge, loomed midstream, sixteen feet high, monument to a lost way of life, holding up nothing that afternoon but a squirrel on break pressing its belly to the warm rock.

The red maples were explosive that fall, woodpecker-head red, red cut from sunsets, and orange from forest fires, dynamite bright against all the trees still caught up in summer and green. The general bird chorus had been modified by recent migration. No more songs of summer visitors—now it was mostly blue jays complaining, businesslike chickadees, crows somewhere distant, the low hooting of the mourning dove's plaintive paean to fall. The stream water pounding on the rocks below the dam filled the air with the biotic, somewhat chthonic smell of pond and freed oxygen—a rich breath like that of its parent rain, the redolence of lost summer. In the tight gravel parking lot I quickly took off my pants and put on my old gym shorts and a worn-out pair of hiking shoes, quickly stuffed the long pants and a warm shirt into my wetbag (a rubber backpack with an opening sealed by multiple folds) just in case. Finally ready, tense as a trespasser, I closed up the truck, grabbed paddles and life vest, hefted the wetbag (heavy with field guides, extra clothes, emergency rope, water bottles, and lunch), crossed the park's well-kept lawn, and quietly slipped down the stout ramp to the roiling stream.

Down there, life was gorgeous. Water squirted between dam blocks. The sun caught the margins of the spray in a psychedelic aurora refracted along the edge of the sheet of falling water. The riverbed stone was sinuously carved, scooped, and pocked. Huge boulders stood where they had since the days of the glaciers. Atop the least of these, in the shadows, a great blue heron posed, October surprise. He picked himself up at eye contact and flew effortfully toward the leaking dam, building speed, adding just enough lift so that his feet, still dangling, grazed the lip of the waterfall.

Then a quick trot back and forth to the truck for the boat, which I flipped over the ramp railing and onto a flood-fresh mud bar. I loaded up quickly, standing in the cold stream, breathing hard, putting the wetbag in the bow as counterweight. I want to say how commerce always ruins the beautiful places, but that dam was so old it looked like nature.

The first fifty yards of stream below the dam were narrow and rocky and, that day at least, *fast.* I climbed a rock to have a look, spotted another mud bar down the way. Back in the boat, I pushed off and rode the torrent, knocking rocks. In seconds, puffing, I bow-jammed into the mud I'd targeted, perfect, and climbed out beside sixteen feet of devastated thirty-inch-diameter galvanized-steel ducting with little trapdoors built in—some kind of grain system from the last gristmill. Nothing but water could have placed it so. And water had dropped a dozen huge boulders delicately atop two massive chestnut timbers notched and pegged in olden times.

I climbed another rock for a long look. Was the next stretch worse? Yes, it was. I gazed upstream once more, thinking about retreating. But I couldn't retreat, because just then a striking couple in matching bicycling outfits came smooching down the ramp, clearly looking for solitude. What they got when they looked around was *me,* standing half hidden among boulders and mill wreckage in my tattered gym shorts. She, I noted, was nearly as tall as he and maybe a little older, dark hair cut to her shoulders and pressed down by bicycle helmet recently shucked, round face, palest skin. He was attractive, too, tall and muscular, sharp haircut.

I pegged them for bankers: she middle management, well ensconced, he just getting started in the mortgage division, small-town branch, soon to move on. They had fallen in love in the previous six weeks or so, had bought bicycles together in the first flush of romance. All this nonsense the impression of seconds. All this and the fact that I didn't think the relationship would last: there was some ineffable reserve in her gestures, something I could see even from fifty yards downstream.

They saw me, too.

I waved, friendly, moved out of their view, pushed the boat over the mud bar and into position to start my next run, held it in place in a sandy slot between a pair of force-blasted boulders. The water was full of detritus from the flooding: potsherds, stream glass, beavered branches. New-fallen leaves floated orderly past, a flotilla of curling, brilliant leaves drifting by on their backs with hands behind their heads, coming one by one in the order they dropped from the flaming maples upstream, stacking up on every rock and stick like love letters tied in ribbon. I studied them and especially the light on them for some time, losing some of my self-conscious trepidation.

But not all, so I looked back upstream, ducking under branches to see my couple. In the short time since I'd looked away she'd already gotten her hands in the back of his bicycle shorts, which molded to her fingers as he pushed against her, and they were kissing. They'd decided I was gone, that strange ponytail man standing in gym shorts on his boulder in the water. But then, Modigliani neck offered to his emotional kisses, she opened her eyes. Before I could look away, she found me down among the rocks and branches. And she held my eye as she pressed into her man, pulled his pants down a notch with the squeezing motion of her hands on his butt. She kissed his shoulder, even licked it, looking me square in the eye. Then she gave a little smile, acknowledged me in some way I couldn't place (all this in two seconds), like, *Too bad, sucker,* or, *This could be you if you weren't scrabbling around the rocks,* or, *You're almost fifty, pal, and married quite happily with sex suddenly all about procreation, whereas I'm not yet thirty and desperately want what you've already got,* or just, *Yes, watch— watch me.* She smiled distinctly for *me* (this with dozens of yards of rushing stream and aurora light and waterfall song and every shadow of every tree in the air between us). His hands . . . I didn't know where they were, but his shoulders ducked and rolled with his project. The very forest seemed tumid suddenly, pent. The young woman smiled at *me* and pulled his hips down into hers and closed her eyes lan-guorously.

When she opened them again, I'd be gone. I shoved the ca-noe into the current and leapt in, crashed the next hundred yards through standing waves, boulders, and bubbling foam, kept the bow straight, scraping and cracking the whole way on assorted rocks the size of dogs and cows, thumped under the Morrison Hill Road bridge and down into the long, deep pool after, suddenly gliding. On the bank above me lurked the im-probable hulk of an Edsel, another casualty of history, distinc-tive chrome radiator grille, a sturdy silver maple growing up out of the hole where the car's windshield had been.

Temple Stream carried me along briskly through the Edsel pool, then hard over the bump of a drowned beaver dam—jab paddle, jog left—and into a sudden, three-way rapids.

Those lovers!

I thought of a poem I knew by Denise Levertov, who had lived on our stream back in the sixties:

EROS AT TEMPLE STREAM

> The river in its abundance
> many-voiced
> all about us as we stood
> on a warm rock to wash
> slowly
> smoothing in long
> > sliding strokes
> our soapy hands along each other's
> slippery cool bodies

> quiet and slow in the midst of
> the quick of the sounding river
>
> our hands were
> flames
> stealing upon quickened flesh until
>
> no part of us but was
> sleek and
> on fire

And I thought of Phoebe, a girl I'd met when I was fifteen and spending two weeks at a rustic coed church camp in my uncle Bill's wild Montana. She was fourteen. We locked eyes in the milling kid-throng right off the buses, and by the conclusion of evening mess (and strictly on her initiative) the two of us had conspired to skip our activity group the next morning to hike on our own. And that meant no one missed us at activity group for the duration. Love at first sight, we said. We made a ritual of sitting by the Boulder River each long morning, talking and kissing and touching experimentally, also pondering the big questions (What is the nature of love? Why shouldn't a river flow uphill?). One day about a week into our deepening romance, we took the excuse of wading the awesome sandy-beach eddy we had found—a churning eye in the river's storm—to strip out of our blue jeans. That callipygian cowgirl wore a pair of kid's white underpants, a long rip opening up in the saddle-worn seat. She crossed the Boulder thigh-deep ahead of me singing the latest Crosby, Stills and Nash ("Suite: Judy Blue Eyes"), perhaps not so oblivious of her effect on me as I thought at the time. Of course, on the other side of the river, the lack of pants changed the quality of our familiar making-out. The sand we lay on was silky, damp, warm. We stripped out of our camp T-shirts, too, couldn't get enough of each other's *skin*. The Boulder River tumbled through its rocks: rhapsody.

I picked the center chute in the two seconds I had to make the call, went crashing into the rapids and around a slight bend. Ahead there was sweeper, a large balsam fir fallen in, dense branches. The only gap was six inches too narrow, but no choice, I pulled hard starboard to find the hole, bumped over the tree trunk full speed, leaned hard to tip the canoe so it would fit, shot through frisked by branches. At last I exhaled. But relief was brief: the pool below was full of rocks, the stiff current humping over them leaving holes downstream. The nose of the canoe caught a boulder before I could react and we spun backward into another rock, spun again sideways, tipped, took on water. I back-paddled with a shout, escaped the next big rock by inches, found the channel by luck, shot through to the head of the next pool, soaked and dripping, a brief hiatus before the next fall and field of rocks. After that, the trip was pool-fall, pool-fall, a quick descent through natural locks on seething water.

At the far end of a long, fast straightaway I was startled to see an old railroad trestle high overhead—the massive thing had been completely hidden by its own rust and black-paint geometry amid the mass of changing leaves and exposed branches around it. No time to admire the scene or read the graffiti—under the span was a small waterfall, the current tightened to a waist by the bridge's bulwarks. We dove in, bow first. The boat flexed under me, slowed to a stop, took on more water, popped up out of the hole with a lurch. I steered hard to clear the next great boulder, but could not. The canoe reared up the face of the thing, dove back, spun clear around.

I rode backward in a fury of spray between the next set of boulders and into Cyane's pool, breathing hard in the sudden calm. I paddled to the cornstalk beaver dam, bumped the boat against it, drooped. I'd come a half mile in minutes. If I'd still smoked cigarettes, that would have been the time to light up.

THE FIRST MILLER ON THE STREAM WAS MAJOR REUBEN Colburn, whose big moment came when he was asked to supply General Washington's brilliant if only partially successful plan to take Quebec by surprise, an overland trek of heroic dimension headed up by Benedict Arnold, not yet famous. Colonel Arnold needed boats to take his army of fifteen hundred men up the Kennebec and thence to the many linked lakes that would bring him to Canada. Major Colburn took the contract, built two hundred bateaux, even accompanied the army on the impracticable trek.[2]

After the war, Colburn helped form a speculative group

2. Robert P. Tristram Coffin tells it in *Kennebec, Cradle of Americans* (circa 1937): "Arnold put up at Major Colburn's. The major had been building two hundred bateaux on order for Arnold. He had them ready. Each would carry six or seven men. They were propelled by four paddles and two poles. They were made of pine, ribbed with oak. But the pine was green, and the 'crazy things' were a great disappointment to the men later on. They were heavy as sin to tote, and they went to pieces with astounding ease. Major Colburn came along with his boats. Everybody cursed them. But it was looking a gift horse in the mouth, for the major never got a red cent for building them."

called the Proprietors of a Township on the Sandy River, which was assigned supervision of a new town by the proprietors of the million-acre Kennebec Purchase. The township was surveyed in 1780, and the intervale land divided into large, narrow farming lots stretching a mile and a quarter back from the river, with even larger lots up on the hills.[3]

The policy of Reuben Colburn and his fellow proprietors was to freely admit all applicants for settlement, subject to the condition that each man make specific improvements on his lot: a house at least twenty feet square and "seven foot in the stud," five acres cleared within three years. Reuben Colburn alerted his hometown of Dunstable, Massachusetts, and a great many of the original settlers of the Farmington intervale were from that town, including one Samuel Butterfield, whose great-granddaughter and her ill-fated husband would build my and Juliet's house many years hence. A steady influx of other settlers arrived from Martha's Vineyard and Cape Cod—beautiful places, but to a farmer's eye already crowded.

Here is historian William Allen's "settler formula," as reported by Vincent York in *The Sandy River and Its Valley*:

> [F]irst year, cut down trees on five or six acres,
> and burn ground over in preparation for plant-
> ing; second year, after planting is done, build
> log house, cut more trees, move family in be-
> fore the harvest; third year, build small barn,

---

3. One lot was left for the state, another for a school (and a school is on the lot to this day), two lots for a minister they hoped to attract (one is now a graveyard and the site of the sewage-treatment plant), and one lot for the town itself, this called the Town Farm, where debtors and indigents and orphans could work for their keep.

increase stock; fourth year, raise English hay, rye, wheat and corn and begin living more comfortably; fifth year, clear more land, increase flocks and herds; sixth year, start pulling stumps and preparing land for the plough; seventh year, build self a framed house if you can.

According to the Allen formula, the seventh year is the crucial one in terms of mills. The family, if still on the ground, was prosperous enough to take the next step. In response to demand, sawmills began to appear around 1790 in the lower [Sandy River] valley and 1800 in the upper.

The first mill was a sawmill on the Temple Stream.

The town ceded the mill privilege to Major Colburn, and with the help of his new townsmen and their teams of oxen, the would-be war profiteer dammed Temple Stream at a small waterfall (the spot from which I'd launch my canoe a bicentennial later). The mill buildings were thrown together quickly, again with community help, and soon the mill was making a private profit that came in the form of a sixth share of the sawn boards. Another of the proprietors, a Mr. Pullen, built a gristmill on the other side of the stream, and earned grain.

A few years later, Jacob and Joseph Eaton, brothers in from the coast, bought the already dilapidated mills from Colburn and Pullen and rebuilt them. But Jacob got the sea itch and built a boat called *Lark,* which he actually floated down the Sandy to the Kennebec, then sailed successfully to the ocean and clear up to the frigid Bay of Fundy, where he foundered on rocks and was drowned.

The next miller was Captain Sylvanus Davis, a businessman who profitably combined the saw and grain operations. On early maps, Temple Stream is generally marked as Davis Stream, perhaps because of the captain's untimely death.

York explains:

> On Christmas Day 1831, Captain Davis down
> in the undercroft of his mill, failed to give this
> spur-wheel a wide enough berth. An oaken
> spur crashed on his head and shoulders and
> he died promptly.

Davis's son Ebenezer, a harness maker, perhaps would have taken over, and certainly would have had a lot of mill business savvy, growing up to it, but on December 30, 1831, just five days after his father's accident, he leaned out through the railings on the covered Center Bridge between Farmington and West Farmington—on the site of the present Thought Bridge—and "slipped and fell to the ice below, and broke his neck."

Like all good historians, Vincent York has a theory: "We suspect retreating Abenakis placed a curse on the mill-site."

PHOEBE AND I WROTE LETTERS BACK AND FORTH ALMOST daily at first, but after a couple of seasons of long-distance mooning, the romance petered out painfully. I thought of her as I ate my lunch on a rock over Cyane's pool, but trying so hard I could only vaguely picture her. So I thought of other things till a breeze rattled the leaves of a stand of young popples up on the bank behind me, and that sound and the movement of the air along with the fragrance of the stream called Phoebe's laugh to mind perfectly, then something of her scent, that spot behind her ear. Perfect recall faded quickly to a pang, and the exact quality of the pang made me think of Marybell Walkingbird, who was my girl later on.

Marybell and I fell in love during a Johnny Winter concert at the Capital Theater in Port Chester, New York, our first date. I recall a bottle of Mateus rosé wine, which I thought very classy. (Drinking age in New York State was eighteen back then—and I, at least, was close to that.) Marybell and I found most of our subsequent privacy in her car or in the deep climax forest behind my parents' house, a steep hill descending to a swamp. In a fort of big rocks she and I could throw my old sleeping bag down after school on warm fall afternoons. The young lovers needed props to leave the house, so we brought our schoolbooks.

This Temple Stream vision was brief again, and specific, a particular moment: her smiling above me in a ray of sunlight, leaves floating by—just that—her black hair falling in my face, me on my back in the crackling forest litter with her tweed skirt as a pillow under my head (thoughtful young woman). And I heard a certain song, one of the dumb ones of the era ("You Make Me Feel Like Dancing"), sung in a comical falsetto that accompanied me unshakably the rest of the Temple Stream day.

The sharp, unbidden memory passed, and I was left with

vaguer images from the voluntary-recall catalog as I ate: Marybell and I conspired to make love nearly every day, this way and that, trying everything we could think of, everything we'd heard of, positions from Japanese books (she collected these), and in nearly every imaginable place, but especially in the woods. There was a mossy rock under hemlock trees, a slab that caught a spot of sun. We practiced lover talk self-consciously, unaware of our essential selfishness. (What's it like for you? What will we name our kids? You make me feel like *me*.) The words *I love you* required a response in kind and revealed in repetition our staggering insecurity, one of the sources of our bond. I remember her voice well. I remember her body, too. She was a field hockey star, liked to squeeze me with her legs. I had to leave her to go to college, and, of course, during the year apart we both found new steadies.

Thirty years later under hemlocks I pine. But briefly: that boy in the woods with Marybell couldn't conceive of the sort of love he'd later find, abiding love, and bedrock: Juliet.

A kingfisher flew past, chattering, station to station and away, upstream. Good to know they stayed as late as October. Perhaps the heron and he were pals. In the warm sun on my mossy rock I ate my sandwich and felt such a wave of well-being that I laughed out loud. Milkweed silks floated in the air, and I was reminded that what Americans call Indian summer was called goose summer in old England (also Saint Martin's summer), the season of geese, that is, when down was in the air: *gossamer*.

On my knee landed a glamorous red damselfly. I dug in the wetbag for my bug book, and for once the identification was definite: *half-banded toper*. And then there was another. They seemed to take a liking to the skin of my leg. One actually let me touch its wings with a fingertip and stroke them lightly. When I touched the top of its head, it jumped back in the air, but hovered only briefly and returned, let me touch more. This, I wanted to explain, was dubious survival technique. The book said that topers are rare because of pollution and loss of habitat, that they need marshy land near deeper water, which, of course, the Temple afforded in that spot. Brightest red twig of a body, a living ruby pin, wings veined like leaves (dark spots at the front edges), orange hairs where wings met body, two white spots atop vermilion head, maroon eyes, the insistence on staying with me.

A *toper* is a drunk, of course.

Juliet and I met in a bar on Martha's Vineyard. It took me weeks to persuade her to go out with me. Finally, I enticed her: a whole day on one of the nude beaches, then waterskiing with a maniacal acquaintance and his overpowered boat, then a cozy dinner of farm-stand vegetables and stolen lob-sters. (Our brazen captain had pulled buoys and pilfered traps; this seemed like fun at the time, as did many other life-threatening behaviors. Now I can only cringe. Also, I owe some Menemsha salt five lobsters, size medium. Whoever you are, many thanks.) We ate it all cozily at home with my five roommates and a dozen other friends, then spent an affec-tionate night in bunkbeds (up and down the little ladder giggling)—I'd gotten the children's room in the rented house. Juliet's hair was sun-bleached nearly white. She had a tan all over. Her eyes were blue as sea-worn mussel shells.

Seventeen years later and we were getting ready to make a kid.

Back on the stream, I paddled up the length of Cyane's pool, a half-banded toper on each knee. Under the railroad bridge (TRUMAN SUCKS BIG DICK), sheer cement bulwarks rose to a height of forty feet. I had to get out and bash my way through alders, line the boat like a dog on a leash through the rocky white water to the next pool. And onward, upstream. One of my half-banded toper pals sat up on the prow of the canoe unmoving, a diminutive figurehead.

The butt of a drowned log floated toward us. I made a couple of strong paddle strokes to avoid it before I realized the object was a beaver swimming calmly. Fifteen feet from our prow it dove. Beaver breath bubbled up under the canoe as the invisible creature slipped beneath us. A minute passed, no sign of the animal upstream or down, then another minute, then the bubbles were back, first on one side of the boat, then the other.[4]

I skulled in the stiff current, waited. Eventually my strategy paid off: two beavers, one to starboard, one to port, surfaced to have a look, audibly taking breaths. The second animal was smaller than the first, and more cautious, watched me closely, made myopic eye contact, paddle-paced back and forth. It inched closer, got to within ten feet, staring, sniffing. The bigger creature sank, disappeared momentarily, then came up right alongside. My surprise must have sent shock waves: the

---

4. Beavers can stay alive underwater as long as fifteen minutes in an emergency (or doomed in a trap). Eight minutes is just a normal dive. By comparison, four minutes with no breathing and the human brain begins to die. But beavers have disproportionately large lungs. The beaver liver is also huge, to process toxins as the breath is held. And in a final adaptation, the beaver heartbeat slows down so that less oxygen gets consumed.

beavers slapped their tails—a single sharp report—and dove as if into the noise they'd made. I hung on, chilled in the shade of the high hillside there. Those brown eyes! Those wet-log faces! I saw my dogs in them, dogs without affection.

The next riffle was very strong, with no firm footing to line from, just knobs of grasses and sedges—so I paddled as hard as I could, putting a burn in my once-mighty biceps, letting my prow nudge and bump along the plentiful rocks to keep us straight. Those beaver faces stayed in my mind, a kind of beaver energy propelled me. Toper One urged me forward, the two of us making about three feet per minute, minute momentum. I puffed and sweated and lost my chill, made my way over the back of someone's drowned and broken Adirondack chair, made the top of the riffle in about the time the entire ride down had taken, then a pool's worth of easy paddling before I reached the three-split rapids, where—nothing for it—I was forced to climb out thigh-deep and pull the canoe, anything for progress back to the dam. I picked the left fork this time, avoiding the sweeper that had almost grabbed me on the way down, forged ahead on the slippery rocks, lost my footing halfway up the course and . . . fell in, dropping first to my knees and grabbing at the canoe to keep from falling the rest of the way, but missing the gunwale and dunking myself face-first. I felt my heart seize, gasped for breath, leapt up out of the cold, slipped again, fell in once more.

Sputtering, I lurched to my feet, pulled the canoe up into the next pond, leapt into it all gooseflesh, doused and dripping, paddled ferociously to warm myself, paddled as far as the riffle below the Morrison Hill Road Bridge, which was as far as I was going to get. The rest of the way to the dam was a torrent. But the explorer must try! I put the paddle to the water, making the fastest strokes I could manage, began to sweat, stabbed at the receding flood till I was under the Morrison Hill Road Bridge once again (there is a large iron mill-gear submerged just there), paddled till Temple Stream and my strength reached stasis, a perfection of stalled canoe and paddler frenzy atop the purest urging flow, and that was as far as our spunky little spermatozoon was going to get.

AT LENGTH, I STOPPED THE FIGHT AND JUST LET THE BOAT flow backward downstream through all the rocks I had passed so laboriously, drifted backward into the head of the cold, black pool. I skulled there in the waning afternoon, soaked to my skin, and felt a terrible chill coming on, wishing for fur (lucky beavers have two kinds of fur, forming insulating and waterproof layers: beaver skin stays dry). That night there'd be a hard frost, and so much for goose summer.

I nudged the boat up into the weeds and dragged it on a fishing path up to Route 43, Temple Road—only a matter of a dozen yards, the familiar road that close to an effective wilderness—flipped it onto my shoulders and walked the road's edge. Just before the mill park, a kid came shredding down the hill on his skateboard, warp speed. I tipped the canoe back to get a look at him, gave a nod that he returned: *Guy with canoe on Route 43, nothing out of the ordinary.* Once the boat was safely in its rack on the truck, I shuffled back for the wetbag and paddles, growing chilly again. Standing in the weeds, I dug out my dry clothes and towel, dressed happily, packed up, strapped the heavy wetbag over my shoulders like a backpack, and, eschewing the road, scrabbled through weeds and alders and over treacherous boulders along the banks of the stream, crossing back and forth twice through the scant and over-washed remains of a dozen destroyed mills—all I could do to keep from falling—and finished my day's adventure next to water.

Near the dam I found myself looking ahead for the kissing couple, though of course by that hour they would have long come and gone. On the ramp, instead, four teenage boys, look-ing like they'd just said yes to drugs. One of them was the skateboard kid—so light and high he'd apparently been able to roll back uphill. The dam was dark in the evening light, had none of the permanence it had assumed at noon. Trudging ex-hausted up the wooden ramp, I tried to imagine the water pressure above and behind those stones in a flood. Unbidden, my bottles came bobbing to mind. A blue jay darted into the brush beside the wooden access ramp, drew my eye six or seven feet down into the darkness below, where a pair of silken panties had draped themselves over a mossy stone. They were black, piped with pink, had been expensive, lay lost. I thought to climb down and get them, but that's just not the kind of thing a man can bring home. And in any case, they were now the property of Temple Stream.

Winter Solstice

STARTING AS EARLY AS OCTOBER, BUT MORE LIKELY NOVEMBER
in a given year, and certainly by December, Temple Stream begins to freeze. Every day the ice changes, grows, shrinks back,
advances.

And every morning, as my research leave from Ohio State
counted down to its conclusion, I hiked down there to have a
look, and hiked down again each evening, just to see what had
changed. Ice paved the way: the muddy parts of the path were
thrown up in frost castles, delicate keeps and crenellations of
dirt and ice that collapsed with a satisfying crunch underfoot.
The kingfisher was quietly gone, no more red-eyed vireo's
song—all the late stayers had quietly moved on, no fanfare,
only absence.

In the stream, pellucid lace formed up around rocks and
alder roots, around the branches of sweepers. Alder tips that

had dipped into the water with the weight of summer collected balls of ice that grew to knobs, crystal as fine as
Victorian chandelier glass. In the extended cold snap we'd just
suffered—a week or so with nighttime temperatures in the
single digits—the knobs morphed into globes and rare plat-
ters, nymphs on dolphins, grew until they touched, the edge
lace spreading till the filigree and figurines and beadwork of
one branch or rock met that of the next, thinnest sheets of ice
growing out into the quiet parts of the stream like etched
panes.

Wally, his winter coat coming in sleek and long, his bull's
chest thrust forward, his tail wagging high, was first to try the
ice. He rushed down, saw that the stream had hardened,
balked. After some expressive barking, he put a mighty paw
down, tapping his claws where water had been. The offending
ice didn't break immediately, so he scraped and scratched in
outrage until it did, flipping up chunks that turned out to be
textured underneath, intricate relief sculptures carved by hy-
draulic friction and the water's slight heat. Path cleared, heed-
less of the chill, exultant Wally splashed in among his own
floating shards till he was up to his chin, drank as from a
smashed chalice.

Desi was next. With his senior citizen's hard-won disdain
for lesser minds, he found a place Wally hadn't sullied, tried
the ice gingerly. Finding it suitable, he proceeded, mincing
toward free water on tippy-tippy claws untrimmed. The ice
sighed and he pulled up short, listened a long minute before
his next brief steps right to the fine edge at the flow, where he
took a cautious drink. The ice out there popped and his ears
flew up in alarm. He retreated, slow steps in reverse. The ice

crackled and broke along miniature fault lines, and the good dog looked back to me for courage, straining every muscle skyward in an effort to make himself lighter.

Night by cold night, the ice sheet thickened. Breezy conditions would have made a rippled surface, but we'd had days of cathedral stillness: window glass. And no snow: the ice was gemstone black, a portal to the bottom, stream grasses still flowing under there, the familiar rocks and sands of summer arranged as in a display case or aquarium, one torpid minnow finning past, then another. I stared into that world daily and lingered, thinking of the time long since that I'd had the luck of seeing a muskrat cruising under the ice. I was thinking, too, that soon I'd have to leave, wouldn't get to see how the story of winter turned out.

By mid-December the stream was nothing but a channel, the thickening ice sheet closing in from both sides. I ventured out upon it behind the test dogs, sliding one foot then the other, listening like Desi for any sound of cracking, lingering over an ice-trapped oak leaf encrypted by the warmth of the sun in a perfect oak-leaf-shaped jewelry case, oak-leaf-shaped lid on top, oak leaf itself nestled several inches down, where it would sunbathe itself clear to the water, leaving just its shadow in ice.

THE SOLSTICE WAS UPON US, ALMOST TIME TO HEAD BACK TO Columbus, a thousand highway miles west and south. The previous spring I'd been awarded tenure—a pale prize, I was

beginning to understand, since it had come in the wrong part
of the country. Juliet had long since finished her program at
the School of the Art Institute of Chicago, and would be
teaching a drawing class at Ohio State. That we'd be colleagues after a fashion was no consolation: we had to leave
Maine, and six months had been enough time for our roots to
sink down again, take hold.

Ms. Bollocks, our long-term housesitter (the only one we'd
ever been able to find, despite repeated attempts to replace
her), would arrive in the morning. Juliet and I packed the
house and put our essential belongings in the old Subaru
wagon, leaving just enough space near the ceiling in back for
the dogs, who we knew would ride like agreeable suitcases no
matter how cramped their space. Juliet glowered at me, carrying boxes; I snapped at her. This living in two places was better
than living in three, but it wasn't working out as the jolly toggle
we'd pictured. Our efforts at pregnancy weren't working either,
and we were up against our last chance for a conception in
Maine. At least that was the rueful joke—last chance—which
we didn't find the right moment to act upon. Outside, the
wind blew, frosty night. A great pile of firewood lay in the yard,
had been drawing wry commentary from the neighbors ("Will
you burn it right *they-uh*?"). Ms. Bollocks had had it delivered,
four cords to add to my three.

I hated her woodpile. This kept me from hating her. Because I had to admit, she was awfully good at taking care of the
house and grounds. And I knew somewhere in me that if anything, she ought to be the object of my compassion. She was
age indeterminate, somewhere between thirty and fifty,

shaved-head bald, five foot one, sunken-chested, affable till questioned or held to her word, devious in all things, the only person who'd answered our ad in the *Franklin Journal* that first year of the great commute. But we had to keep her: who else could accommodate moving in and out at our whim, year after year, always with a cheerful insult?

Overnight, the temperature had fallen to three degrees, a crystal-sharp solstice dawn.[1] I couldn't sleep, so got out of bed. Downstairs, I built up the fire to take the chill off the house, ate a little, dressed warmly, and slipped out into the cold, leaving even the dogs snoring. As always on a last walk, I looked for omens. A male hairy woodpecker, flash of red, landed hard on the bole of a dead popple tree not five feet from my face and knocked at the dead bark for grubs: not an omen. Continuing on, I was joined by a familiar mixed flock of chickadees and white-breasted nuthatches. A kind of tinkling like tiny bells in the height of the flock alerted me to the busy presence of golden-crowned kinglets, good cheerful company, but no omen.

At the stream, a thin sheet of new ice reached out from the thicker veil at the edges, bloomed toward closure of the channel. I contemplated the transformation for a while, still caught

---

1. On the day of the winter solstice, sunrise at our house comes at 8:07. Sunset over the Varnum Pond Hills (as viewed from our kitchen window) comes at 3:41, painfully early, and leaving something less than eight hours of insolation and a long night. The deepest cold, however, doesn't come until the end of January or beginning of February: the face of the planet only slowly gives up the heat of summer. After solstice, daylight gains a minute a day, then incrementally more till mid-January, when it's two minutes a day, then more again till it's three minutes a day at the beginning of February, the most of the year, a noticeable lengthening of afternoons that lifts a certain psychic weight, the weight of darkness. Winter, in contrast to fall, should be called *rise*.

up in the night's tossing discontent, tried to lose myself in looking.

And looking, of course, is when one sees: at the bottom of the steepest of the defunct beaver ramps, the ice had been disturbed, broken up, then thinly refrozen. I thought the breakage might have been caused by a coyote or fox searching out a drink, or even by Wally. But as I looked and puzzled, the thin ice creaked—a strange sound—not the usual popping or groaning. Then it creaked again and visibly bulged, crackling then breaking with a splash around the inquisitive head of . . . a large beaver.

The animal sniffed a few times, looked vaguely in my direction, tipped its nose up, and, perhaps noting that I was there (smells of wool, wood smoke, bread and banana, stress), slipped back under. In a moment, the ice shield bulged again and cracked. The beaver, it became clear, was standing on the bottom and pushing up with its shoulders. It continued to break ice using that method till a hole the size of a car door had been opened, then stood higher in the water to gnaw at the ragged edge, all the while using its forepaws to push down and break off further chunks, working its way clear out to the newer, thinner ice in the channel. Methodically, then, the creature waded all around the hole, pushing the broken pieces under the remaining ice cover and out of the way.

The result of all this effort was a good, clear exit to the mud ramp, which was not defunct after all, an exit that wouldn't refreeze during the relative warmth of the day, and that would be easy to open again the next morning, and perhaps for a few mornings hence as the beaver and his colony mates brought little popple trees down to the water to add to their food cache, a great pile of sticks carefully sunk near their lodge.[2]

Finished with its project, the beaver turned and swam out toward the center of the stream, breaking the thin shelf of newer ice, head held high, tail turned bladewise, then proceeded downstream in the narrow open channel, sank in a dive, and was gone.

Beavers are gentle, I thought, continuing my game. So the omen before me must be gentle too. And a beaver coming up through ice to look around? That must presage some sort of freedom.

---

2. To eat in winter, a beaver slips out of the lodge through plunge holes that exit deep underwater and under ice, swims to the feed bed, and retrieves a preserved stick. Back in the lodge, the animal eats the bark, then shreds the shiny-bare stick for bedding, or adds it to the structure of the dwelling. Winter trips aren't limited to the feed bed, and aren't always brief—danger, sex, supplemental food, voiding, just plain exercise—all may send a beaver swimming far under the ice. To breathe on these long, roofed forays, beavers make use of naturally trapped air bubbles, which the water continually oxygenates. It's also possible to rebreathe an initial breath. The animal blows it out, waits as the bubbles climb in the water, reoxygenating, then breathes it in again where it pools under the ice. A more drastic tactic is to drop the water level of a whole pond a few inches by biting a spillway through the top of a dam. The ice stays high, leaving breathing and swimming room beneath it.

Upstream Three
Lover's Dam to the Twin Bridges

IN DEEP WINTER, TEMPLE STREAM IS A RIBBON OF ROCK-studded ice, liquid only in the deepest parts of its deepest pools, where fish hold and frogs burrow. The beavers have retreated to their lodges, never hibernating. They swim daily under the ice in deep pools of their own creation, eat the bark from stashes of poplar branches, groom one another mewling happily. The fast water behind their dams has closed as slowly as a wound, leaving black ice as textured as scar tissue. There's a gurgling to be heard, no more than that, but it's a welcome sign of life, the stream running cold-thickened through frost pipes and ice tunnels. The rest of the free water is underground as always, flowing through the stream's own accretions of sand and gravel, and through layers of porous rock: the stream never stops. The changing ice makes so much noise that it's possible to surprise the most cautious animals—minks, coyotes, foxes—even watch them at their work for long minutes before scent or some subtler emanation makes them jump.

After a thaw, perhaps a rain, free water overflows the ice in a metastream with its own topography and an icy bed. When the cold returns, the overpools freeze smooth, trapping bubbles and encasing and preserving old footprints and ski trails like dinosaur tracks in lava. Riffles freeze at dozens of incremental levels as the flow diminishes, leaving multistory ice ceilings of varying thicknesses made of the most delicate geometrics—triangles, rhomboids, wands of hoarfrost attached to diaphanous rays of lace by means of crystalline spiderwebs. Your boot falls two inches, breaking through six floors or so with an echoing crunch, no splash at the bottom. You stand there thankful at having not fallen further, then break through the thicker floor below that with a shout and fall six inches more to the old ice. You hesitate—it's like walking on stained glass—the sound is vandal-loud in the streambed silence.

After a snowfall, all goes dark for the beavers. Now they must swim in their pools and canals by scent—and in fact, February is their mating time, when lifelong couples leave the communal warmth of the family lodge for a connubial swim and embrace, coitus under ice and on the move. Above, the streamscape for humans is soft and beautiful as a woodcut, inviting but not always safe for walking or skiing: the snow insulates the ice below, and the warmth of whatever water is flowing beneath that is enough to carve the ceiling away completely in certain spots, leaving only a crust of snow over the current, a trapdoor for bad acts to fall through.

WHEN JULIET AND THE DOGS AND I ARRIVED IN COLUMBUS, the yard in our rented house was still *green*. In fact, late December looked like autumn. The evenings lasted longer too, because we were so far west in the same time zone, and considerably south. It was as if we'd gone back in a time machine to October. I missed the ice.

In Schiller Park, walking the dogs on retractable leashes like garrotes, I spotted a familiar face, a fellow walking his chocolate Lab, said hello as our dogs sniffed at each other and started in with the usual raucous play. And the man—tall, groomed, strong jaw, big grin, booming voice—said hello back, as if he knew me, too.

"I love these uncivilized dogs!" he boomed.

"They do better off-leash," I boomed back.

"Country dogs! Am I right? They just don't translate to town, do they!"

No, they did not.

Very familiar person. Looking for clues, I noted that he was dressed as I was in a mere down vest, while the dog-walking crowd all around us wore heavy parkas and mittens and hats as if the day were cold.

"You're not from here!" he boomed.

And just like that, I placed him: Kyle Karlinski, the K-man, the weather anchor on a prominent Maine TV channel. "You're not either," I said. I started to laugh at the double disjunction of having my favorite Maine weatherman in front of me, and Kyle started to laugh too, a kind of happy thunder. People around us smiled uncertainly, enjoying the good cheer. I told Kyle I was from Farmington, and he roared louder: that's where he'd gone to college!

We talked that morning, and many subsequent mornings, dogs being creatures of habit. I learned that he'd moved "up-market" to an extremely high-paying job at one of the big Columbus stations. He wouldn't say if he was happy or un-happy with the move, had no interest in my complaints about my own change. From our conversations, I'd be hard-pressed to tell you one thing about the man. It was as if, short of the big brown dog, he had no personal life at all. What Kyle Karlinski talked, no matter what subject I broached, was *weather*. I learned, in fact, to ask him weather questions solely, and we became weather friends over our daily meetings with dogs, plastic bags of poop in hand, a mild winter coming down around us. We both missed *winter*-winter, so winter was our weather subject, day in, day out.

From Kyle I learned that snow, like rain, is conceived when adequate water vapor in the atmosphere is cooled enough to condense and form clouds, that snow is born when enough ice particles clump together around a handy piece of dust or ash or sea salt—"The atmosphere is crawling with stuff like that!"—to make flakes heavy enough to fall.

During a mild storm, Kyle told me that Johannes Kepler thought the six-sided snowflake was proof of the existence of God, and suddenly he spread his arms and thrust his head back, a kind of prayer like a kid eating snowflakes. On the eleven o'clock news that night, he did the same, but the flakes were just digital. He was great on the small screen, sunny and cheerful, full of stories (often about his time in Maine), stories that always ended with his viewer knowing another small thing about the weather.

One cold day, he made me guess how many snowflakes

would fill a shovel. By way of a useless clue, he let me in on the fact that each crystal of snow is made up of something on the order of a hundred million water molecules.

I can't remember my guess. Just that he scoffed: too low.

"A million flakes of snow," he said, "will blanket an area about ten inches by twenty to a depth of twelve inches." Roughly a snow-shovel scoop, in other words. "A million flakes, a hundred million-million molecules: you get to big figures quickly, clearing the walks!" He repeated the same information on the TV that night, same phrasing exactly.

To impress him I memorized the names of the seven basic types of falling snow as identified by the International Snow Classification, which I found in one of the science libraries at OSU. I waited for a snowfall during dog hour and recited while the stuff fell on our shoulders: star, plate, needle, column, column with a cap at each end, spatial dentrite, and irregular crystal. Karlinski pulled himself up to his full height, looked down on me, let me know there was a more detailed classification scheme developed by Japanese scientists, which included eighty shapes, all with names, including the seven above in various permutations, and—he knew them all—cups, sheaths, pyramids, bullets, scrolls, ferns, branches, scales, lumps, cones, and skeletons, along with scores of malformations and combinations, which he recited too. "The colder the temperature, the lighter the flake."

That night on the eleven o'clock news, the subject was the seven types of falling snow.

And there were *more* snow words, "As many in English as in Inuit," said Kyle, looking at me as into a camera, one word a day: graupel is ice crystals coated with rime and looking like dusty grains of rice. Firn is packed snow, also called névé. *Firnspiegel,* or firn mirror, is that thin sheet of ice that forms over old snow in certain conditions. Old snow is snow that has been on the ground more than a couple of hours, the flakes starting to meld and metamorphose into different, evolved crystalline forms. Snowpack is the accumulated snow of a given winter. Sastrugi are ridges of drifted snow, as in a field (the singular is sastruga). Frazil is ice crystals formed in turbulent water, as in the sea. Depth hoar is ice that forms under the snowpack, metamorphosed from snowflakes into unstable cups that build a fragile crystalline cavern.

I knew depth hoar: stalwart Wally had suddenly disappeared one afternoon years past during a long ski adventure on the other side of the stream—I had to help him out of what looked to be a nicely decorated igloo basement.

Kyle Karlinski substituted his own dog, old Brownie, and told the exact story on the eleven o'clock news that night, with a special sly smile that I imagined was just for me.

I COLLECT HARD WINTERS. THE ULTIMATE TO DATE HAS TO have been our second on Temple Stream. The daily high temperature was zero degrees for weeks on end, night temperatures as low as thirty below, no wind chill factored in. I'd always been a downhill skier, but that was the winter I finally got comfortable with cross-country skis, since the snow was perfection and I could simply whistle up the dogs, step out the

barn door, and go. Still, one morning in February I got the idea
to ski the millpond—ice you could depend on.

I dressed at home, Labonville snowmobile bib over blue
jeans over laundry-pink long johns, three layers of shirts and
sweaters, hat with earflaps, down vest, silken socks under
woolen socks inside oversized ski shoes under gaiters, heavy
mittens, neck-up, and finally a little rucksack to put clothes in
a piece at a time as I heated up while skiing. I also brought
field guides and safety items like matches, space blanket, and
rope (now I'd bring a cell phone). I added a dry T-shirt and a
pair of socks to change into at the end of the run so as not to
get the chills driving home or lying hurt. The temperature, announced in red on the window thermometer off the porch,
was eleven degrees below zero. No wind, thankfully.

. . . Wallace and Desmond sit up straight in the truck and
watch the road, swaying in perfect synchronization around
every curve as the pavement follows the stream on the way to
the milldam. If I put my arm around Wally he leans into me,
lays his head on my chest. Desi gazes steadfastly out the window. They are young, Desmond just turned three, Wally not
even one, and I am young too, only forty, all muscle and beer
belly and ambition, reading glasses still in the future.

At Walton's Mill Park, I ram the truck into a snowbank,
climb out slowly, bid the dogs wait, survey the ice below the
dam, a crystal palace, kingly curtains of ice, stately columns of
ice, a preternatural pipe organ, all in ruins. I say, "Okay, boys,"
and the dogs leap out, investigate every hump and knob of
snow, piss amply on a pair of spectral snowmen—the ghosts
of millers, no doubt—while I retrieve my skis from the back of

the truck, get them attached to my boots in a rush of bare fingers, painful.

We're off. But not far. The problem is getting on the ice above the dam without going *through* the ice above the dam, which at this temperature would likely be fatal. But the ice looks strong and thick until very close to the lip, where a black curtain of pond urges out from under, spills over. The dogs bound down through cattails and frozen wands of marsh grass to solid pond. I follow their intuition, and we're off. The dogs skitter ahead. I lean into my poles, pushing hard. There's been an overflow, then a freeze, then a light dusting of snow, and the ice is smooth as glass. Wally falls with his hind end, but his front end keeps going. The back end finds its feet again, pushes the front end along. Then his front end falls so his ear is on the ice, speeding. He looks like a theater animal—two people are inside. Desi tippy-tips along on his dependable claws, never falling. My skis threaten to fly out from under me—it's all I can do to make headway straight, pushing with my poles.

Up on the banks of the millpond there are houses to notice—just a few, with columns of smoke moving straight into the sky. I leap past them, my skis squealing now on a layer of drifted snow. My breath freezes my neck-up to my mustache and face. Back to the left, when I look, there's a sudden view of Titcomb Hill, a dozen skiers discernible as black dots weaving down the face of the little mountain. I can't look long, such is my speed. Good-bye lift lines, lift tickets, lift talk. My trail today is called Iceway. It's an emotional double diamond: DANGER—YOU WILL BE ALONE.

Up ahead to the left there's a great hayfield covered a couple of *yards* deep with unblemished, grass-caught snowdrifts, bright in the sun. The air I gaze through is full of glinting crystals, magical. There's the sound of a chain saw somewhere far ahead. And the call of a raven, still at work in the depths of winter. This is a classic impenetrable red-winged blackbird bog, frozen to silence. I think of the breezes in the reeds in summer, the hundred raucous birds dive-bombing my canoe.

I could ski that bog. Winter means easy access to all the secret places. But the stream-shaped pond ahead is a racetrack and I lean into it, pumping legs and arms, picking up speed, flying to a bend, keeping control, making the sweeping turn skating till I'm out of sight of the houses, out of sight of the world, down under high banks and thick alder cover. Warming, I pull my mask off, tuck it into the top of my skier's bib.

There's a split in the stream-pond ahead, what looks like an island, though it could just be blocks of ice stacked. I pick the left fork and *go.* Up on the high bank there's a summer shanty encased in drifts, only the wind chimes free, steel tubes hanging silent in the stillness over a great stack of firewood. Through an occluded window I get a glimpse of gingham curtains. I want to go in, build a fire, bake bread, grill millpond perch, read *Middlemarch* again, read it by candlelight. Well, if ever I did go through the ice, this would be the place to race to, save my life with matches.

Hand-lettered sign on tree:

NO TRESPASSING

The dogs can't read—they're all over the porch. Wally stands to look in the window, whining. Visiting? Are we visiting? Visiting? Whom?

No, we're moving on. Shortly, the pond seems to end—I'm among blown cattails and tumbled reeds. I plow over snow humps and lovely, weird drift patterns, sastrugi and firn. The dogs dolphin-leap through deeper and deeper snow. The wind has packed the stuff hard enough that I can stay on top of it—mostly. Where the bog grass has bent down under the snow there are voids; I lose my balance when a ski sinks and tumble backward into one of them, sit there as in an icy armchair, enjoying the sun. I've got to take my skis off to escape. When I finally stand on them again I realize how warm I've gotten—ten degrees below zero after a mile of all-engines-full and a struggle to stand feels like *summah*. I pull down the suspenders of my bib, take off my vest and sweater and stuff them in my rucksack. I even roll my neck-up down off my chin, roll up the sleeves of the top flannel shirt. It's no day to show skin, however warm I get. My hat stays on, flaps down. There's ice in my eyelashes; my mustache is a winter milldam; the fringe of hair I can't keep under my cap is an ice penumbra at the edges of my vision.

I ski. The dog-dolphins leap through the drifts in bursts of snow. They're panting, well-heated too, bite snow for moisture. Deep in the bog there's a high mound. I ski over to have a look, am mystified by a slight cloud of steam rising as from a street vent in New York, but rising here from a denuded latticework of rimy sticks. Then I know: this is a buried beaver lodge. The steaming is the heat and breath and drying fur of the family of beavers hunkering within. The whole is covered with coyote prints; more than one has been here looking for a warm meal in tough conditions, has dug down through the

snow and torn at the structure—but clearly they haven't gotten far: think of the strength of the frozen mud holding this
whole mess together! My own failed coyotes sniff frantically,
mark the site with parsimonious squirts of yellow. I listen at
the vent and hear mewling, can't get enough of the sound. The
breath of the vent is faintly urinous.

Too cold to linger.

Somewhere up ahead there's the deep roar of a big diesel
engine laboring. It seems in the wrong direction to be on the
road; there's only woods that way. I remember the chain-saw
whine—must be loggers. Always in the silence an engine.

The deep bog is hard and then harder going—it's all grass
humped down by the snow, no more windblown patches of
clear ice. So I turn back, follow my tracks the way I came, back
to the narrow pond. Past the endrifted camp I take a left onto
the fork not taken, and *zoom,* I'm back on clear pond again,
which gradually narrows further and takes more and more the
shape of our familiar stream. The dogs dance ahead.

I slide to a stop at a place where the snow has been blown
off the ice. Inertia countered by no friction keeps me sliding
till I bump the bog edge, where I find a set of animal tracks
poking along the margins in the drifted snow, then find that
thin layer disturbed in such a way as to suggest the animals
had also been sliding. The footprints are round, and come in a
consistent pattern, one-two-three, round-round-oblate. I
throw off my mittens, pull off my rucksack, dig in there for the
tracking guide. Flipping pages with stiff hands, I find the exact
set: these are the prints of a mink patrolling the edge of the
bog for voles and looking among the reeds for any sign of

access to a muskrat house, muskrat being their favorite food. The slide marks have been made by mink at play. I stick a finger in one of the footprints—you can tell fresh tracks by how hard they are. These are old.

I'm glad the dogs have gone on far ahead. They ruin animal tracks and have been known to ruin animals as well. Now I notice the clear, familiar trail of a fox, neat steps at walking speed. And the squat-and-leap trail of a squirrel. Then a meandering line of indistinct round tracks: domestic cat. The fox tracks continue along the pond edge in my direction, then detour up the bank and into the rushes just where multiple hare prints have made a well-trampled highway. I ski slowly, push myself along with poles, searching for more prints, feeling the cold. That diesel engine working up ahead is louder and louder. Somehow, I'm not annoyed—all the exercise I'm getting, perhaps. And maybe some hint of the compassion I'm trying to learn in life: the poor guy has to work in this cold while I play at exercise.

Around the last bend of the pond I'm surprised to see high-voltage lines crossing, bare steel strands on tall double poles, high-voltage lines I've somehow never noticed up where they cross Temple Road. And I'm coming under a familiar dwelling, the Asahel Paine homestead, a Cape Cod house that always has a semitrailer parked out front, the house itself wrapped entirely in plastic this winter, giving a kind of energy-crunch Christo effect. By the stream there's the top of a folding chaise lounge showing through the snow and a worn beach towel hung on a cedar trunk, nicely frosted—somebody's summer swimming hole.

It's a tough old house with a couple of venerable trees in

the dooryard. I rest a moment, looking at it from the rear, a view its owners probably don't expect to offer. I start to think of the shabby backside of my own house, but am interrupted by a hellacious diesel roar ahead, followed by such an enormous re-port—like a cannon fired—that the dogs scoot back to me. Desi cowers and shakes. Even Wally finds my shadow, steps on the backs of my skis as I hurry forward.

Suddenly the empty hills echo a shout: *"Merde!"*

My head fills with moving pictures: A logger's been crushed. I'm yanking the starter cord on the guy's chain saw, cutting a broken body free from tangled branches. First aid—I know what to do, don't I?—and then what? Does he have a radio? Do I cover him and ski up to the Paine homestead for help?

I'm skiing among the large rocks of the stream above the pond—a long riffle in summer, now all ice chocks and wind ridges and surely weakened ice. The dogs follow in my tracks. I have to wave my pole back to remind Wally to stay off the butts of my skis. I climb up onto the bank, ski up into the huge trees there, make my way around two blind bends in the stream.

It's an accident all right: an enormous orange skidder is cocked sideways, two tires of near my height still on the steep bank, two tires down in the stream, broken through the thick ice at the edge of a pool. The tires are encased in huge chains, hand-size links threading great rings of steel. And unmistak-ably, standing out on the ice assessing the problem, hands on hips, an enormous figure, a skidder of a man in outsized insu-lated coveralls, hunting cap, ear protectors: Earl Pomeroy.

Still in rescue mode, I ski down the bank and onto the ice. Too much speed! I skim right behind my man, keep going, ten feet, twenty, till I hit the opposite bank. Earl Pomeroy gets the dogs first; they yelp and jump in the air as they skid around him barking, whining, leaping once more as I come into his vision.

"Goddamn dogs!" he cries as I slide up to him.

"You okay?"

"Goddamn skiers, too! Sneaking up on a man!" Quickly his anger at the skidder gets aimed in my direction.

Preemptively I say, "Earl Pomeroy."

He looks hard under the bill of my hat. "Oh, it's *you*," he growls. "Say a prayer to the Virgin, and what does She send? The Professor!"

"You're stuck?"

"Stuck? *Stuck?* No, Herr Doktor, I am not *stuck*. I am not anything. The skidder is what's in trouble, and the trouble has nothing to do with being *stuck*."

We look at the leviathan a long minute. I can't think what to say. Earl Pomeroy is embarrassed, and embarrassment tends toward attack. As the only available victim for such an assault, I slide back a discreet few feet on my skis. We keep staring at the machine. It's huge, mostly tires and engine, with a black seat up top inside a low steel cage. Rammed into the cage and safely broken off are several fragments of branches big enough to kill someone—the cage seems a sensible idea. At the front of the machine, a grader bar for smoothing twitch roads, moving rocks, pushing logs. At the rear, an enormous eye of steel into which the hook of a heavy tow-chain has been inserted. The chain is tied around what Earl would call a log, but which is the entire trunk of an old white pine, shorn of all encumbering branches, a thick bole of about forty inches diameter, the whole near fifty feet long. The snow behind this concatenation of tree and machine is scraped to earth. Earl, it seems, has been trying to get the skidder aimed back up the hill and onto the rudimentary road he's made. In the woods well above us, I spot his truck, a splash of orange and black like some monstrous oriole. It looks to me as if Earl has driven his skidder too close to the edge, and that the bank—frozen sand, for the most part—has simply given way. There won't be much water underneath at this temperature—but I hear a distinct trickle down there. The machine has fallen into a void. Its angle is extreme, one degree from rolling. The tremendous old white pine chained behind has perhaps acted as a lucky brake.

Earl has settled down some. He mutters, "Not *stuck, gorry!*" and puts a thick hand to his chin. "*Precariously balanced,* that's the term! I been a-driving this bank all week—but it crumbled on me here." Great puffs of steam come with his every breath. His beard is made of frost—his mustache is icicles, like mine.

More troubled silence. The dogs grow bored. Desi picks a refined forepaw up off the ice—too cold for standing around. Wally lays himself down, goes to work pulling ice chunks out from between his furry toes.

Earl says, "It's just tilted s'hard I'm afraid to pull it out. But, hell, you shoulda seen me climbing out of that cage! Another nudge, it could go over." He gives it another long look. "Or, on the other hand, it could just wheel straight out. What I need is another skiddah. You don't have a skiddah, do you?"

No, I do not have a skidder.

More thought and Earl says, "Hell, yes, I'm thinking I could drive it straight out. I'm eighty-five percent on that."

Long pause. I say, "That leaves a kind of tough fifteen percent, don't you think?"

"Yessuh—that's the fifteen that puts you in the flowers. Dead as a can of corned beef!"

I say, "Now, listen. I could ski out and call someone for you."

"Oh, hell, no, Professor. Between my education and your muscle, we can do this."

I laugh. Bad manners, apparently. Earl stares me down. We go back to appraising the skiddah. My feet are aching with cold and I feel the first chill as the sweat from my pond run sublimates through my clothing, which is too light for standing around.

"*Alors.* The problem be that if I try to drive out and the machine goes, my cockpit gets *crushed,* and you'd have a hell of a time extracting my remains for the funeral. But I don't actually think it's going to go over. Still. What we need to do is... I could stand on the box there." Earl points to a gray patch of nonskid paint on the steel bodywork beside the cockpit. "I could reach in and set it going forward. Couldn't steer it quite, but just ease it yup-so onto the ice and drive it right out."

I point at the front of the skidder. "Isn't that a winch there?"

"A *wench,* yes, it is—but that's not gonna work. It's but one hundred feet of cable and there's no suitable anchor that direction, see, not till that hophornbeam tree, which isn't big enough by half, and too far." He points to a squat, lonely, shaggy-barked specimen back up the hill toward his truck, the only tree he's left standing.

So no wench. And I've offended Earl with my suggestions. He stiffens perceptibly, looks in my eye: "If the old girl tumbles, you see, I *jump off.*"

"Jump off?" The next sentence, were I speaking to a friend, would be, *What are you, fucking nuts?* But I hold my tongue.

My tone is sufficient. Earl strokes his beard, breaking icicles. He looks at the sky a long time. "Snow in an hour," he says to himself.

He gets busy suddenly, climbs up the bank, clasps the taut chain connecting the great log to the skidder. With colossal strength, he frees the huge hook from its huge eye. I can only watch, wanting badly to leave. The dogs have taken to poking around in the woods above us, keeping their engines warm, chasing chickadees, the only other moving things in the world.

Once the log is free, Earl rummages around in a toolbox built into the abdomen of the skidder. From my vantage point, I can see what he cannot: small spills of sand dislodging from the stream bank. He rummages with no particular caution, comes up presently with a huge, heavy coil of thick rope. This goes over his shoulder, and he signals me to him. I hesitate, but step out of my skis, stab my poles in the ice, and climb up the bank, slipping in my hard-soled ski shoes.

A little desperately I say, "How about I'll go call somebody for you?"

And he says, "No, no, I got this rope here."

"Oh, man. That's not going to hold anything!"

"It'll hold me, Professor!"

Next thing I know I'm helping him uncoil yards of the heavy rope. When we get a free end he goes back to the skidder and dislodges a heavy stick of popple jammed into the cage. He ties the rope to this stick, gestures at me—stand back!—then he throws repeatedly and mightily up into the branches of the maple tree above us.

I say, "And just what are we doing, monsieur?"

He says, "We, sir, are making a *belay.*"

I know what a goddamn belay is from terrifying rock-climbing experience, and begin to get the picture, a picture I want no role in.

He tries four times, five, six, finally gets the stick to fly over the heaviest, lowest branch, about twelve feet off the ground, twelve more from the skidder, dragging the rope behind it. The dogs see the game in progress, rush down through the trees, pull up yipping and leaping under the branch. "They're right full of it," says Earl ambiguously, not so much as a nod in their direction.

The stick finishes several feet out of Earl's grasp, but no problem, he just yanks another branch off the skidder cage (and the whole skidder shifts a tick), uses it to reach up, and up, kind of dancing on the toes of his rude, thick boots, flanked by the dogs. Rope in hand, he pulls the throwing stick out of its knot, draws up some slack, then quickly ties himself into a nice bowline under his armpits.

"I'll set her rolling from outside the cage," he says. "If she goes over, you'll have me, see? If she stays outta trouble, you feed rope. That's all, Professor."

"Oh, Captain, I don't know."

"Oh, friend, ya gotta. Eliminate the fifteen percent for me."

The frenchified way he says percent catches my ear and stops my caviling. It's fascinating how he doesn't stop, once the game plan is in place. Next thing, I'm standing there holding the rope with him on the other end, only a thick maple branch to help me with the belay.

"Pull her to," he says, and I pull till the rope is tugging at his armpits.

"Pull her tight-to," he says.

And I pull her tight-to, about to keelhaul this near stranger.

Suddenly, to test his arrangement, Earl pulls his legs up, and he's swinging, and I've got him, his weight nicely moderated by the maple branch. The dogs stand back, enthralled. Earl swings a few long seconds, no smile, drops his massive legs. "That's all ya gotta do," he says. "Unless she drives—then you pay out rope, *oui?*"

"Oui," says I. Ten below and I'm perspiring again. I feel it dripping down my sides, freezing on my ribs.

And Earl leaps up on his machine, climbs into the cage further than I would advise if asked, depresses the mighty clutch with one outstretched boot, holds button one, pushes button two to start the thing, lets the clutch out very slowly. The same second the big tires start turning, the skidder lurches sideways and falls, rolling over upside down onto the ice with a tremendous crash. The dogs race away, back toward the millpond, terrified.

I've got pressure on the rope, but the rope simply pulls me off my feet and into the air, slides down the maple branch to the notch at the trunk, where it catches with a snap that makes me let go. I return to earth, find my feet, find the rope, grab hold, only then look: Earl is on his butt on the bank, suspended by the armpits in a high sitting position. I hold that rope, but don't really have to—the tree has got Earl firmly caught, has saved him.

"Merde!" he roars.

The skidder is upside down, still running, all wheels slowly rotating, its cage pushed down through the ice, well crushed. I whip and snap the rope till it disengages, and Earl plumps down on his butt upon the broken stream bank. Wally and Desi rush back to him, lick his face.

He pushes them away, not unkindly. To me, he says, "You done good."

I rush to him. "You okay?"

"Only but lost my shoe."

And it's true—his huge boot is missing, along with whatever sock he had on. His foot looks surprisingly pink and delicate, human, no bigger than my own, nails nicely clipped.

He stands slowly, won't put weight on the foot, as if the problem is only that the ground's too cold, but I can tell he's hurt.

"I've got socks," I say, and tumble down to the frozen stream, where I rifle my rucksack. The Nike swoosh emblazoned upon them looks foolish suddenly, but I rush back to Earl, hand them over. He tugs them on one over the other, wincing.

His skidder starts to smoke, then stalls.

"Diesel in the glow plugs," he mutters.

The silence is sharp.

"Earl," I say. I can't think what else.

"You did that perfect," he murmurs, in the manner of a man who seldom gives or hears praise. "If you hadn't gone gradual like that, you would have torn my foot off. And if you didn't stop me cold when you did, I would have dove into the ice with the cage. And you can see how that woulda been."

We look at the skidder a long, long time. His boot is killed under there somewhere. I'm shivering. Earl is shivering too. The dogs too. It's cold as outer space if you stop, even for a second.

"Well, it was the tree that saved you," I say. "You set it up just right."

He breathes in a rapid "Yuh, yuh, yuh," says, "Would be better if it had worked. I were too anxious." He looks me in the eye for the second time, says, "I'm a little off my stumpage here." It's a surprising confidence, one I know I am not to repeat: stumpage is the right to cut trees on someone else's property, bought and sold like mineral rights. Earl has crossed a boundary line; in effect he's stealing that huge pine.

He stands, clearly hurting. At length, he says, "Back tomorrow with a second machine, get her up and out of here in no time. You, Professor, you better get moving—linger longer, your dogs'll freeze and we'll have to boil 'em in cat grease to get 'em barking again!" No trace of a smile.

He collects his rope and limps up the hill away from me and the dogs on the path his skidder has made. A very fine, dry snow has started to fall. I watch him all the way to his truck, listen for it to start, then hurry to my skis, get them on, and ski myself warm again, then sweaty, sprinting back on the millpond ice in increasingly heavy snowfall (elementary sheaths, dentritic crystals, hollow bullets, bundles of elementary needles, plates with sectorlike extensions), speed to my own truck, then home.

Vernal Equinox

THAT FIRST WEEK BACK IN COLUMBUS, JULIET AND I DUTI-
fully examined ovulation sticks. A blue line on a Monday
morning led to a hasty but vivid conjoining in the minutes before I had to get in the car and drive to the airport for a trip to
Chicago on university business. Juliet, pantsless, waved good-
bye from our dark Ohio porch as I drove off mussed and without my briefcase, suit bag, or reading glasses.

But we'd done it. By March she was two months pregnant,
queasy and cantankerous yet glowing. We didn't know the gender, of course, but both had the strong intuition that it was going to be a boy. We got cute, called the new agglomeration of
cells Dersu Uzala for the hero of the great Kurosawa movie by
that name, which was based on the book by V. K. Arseniev—
Russia's own Meriwether Lewis—and which we'd just seen at
the screening room on campus. Dersu, a Goldi tribesman, had

been Arseniev's guide and savior and beloved friend, an extraordinary woodsman and visionary.

The potential cost of our own Dersu through college and a wedding brought up a small and familiar problem—money. Ms. Bollocks hadn't sent one of her signature postal money orders in February, and none had been forthcoming in the new month. Her rent, modest as it was, was part of the delicate house of cards that was my and Juliet's monthly financial picture.

I detested calling the woman, but did, leaving a pleasant message on my own answering machine in Maine, after her greeting (which no longer gave our Ohio number to stray callers, violating yet another long-standing agreement): "Ms. Bollocks, hello . . . it's Bill and Juliet. We're looking for your rent from February, and now March—and we do need that money to pay our bills. Also, could you please put our Ohio number back on the answering machine?"

At that, she picked up, juggling the phone against something hard.

"Hello, Bill!" she cried. "How is things home there in Ohio!"

She always made a point of calling Ohio our home. I held a long breath, let it out, made small talk: "Good, thanks. All's well. We've got crocuses and even some daffodils here. But it's certainly not home."

"Oh, nothing like that here, Bill. Winter's too hard here! You're in the right place, all right. My house is fine. I had to get up on the porch roof and chip ice, how-some-ever. Put the axe right through the sheet metal! And we have had some snow! But don't you worry—I've been plowing."

"Well, thank you for all that. I'm calling about the rent— you're a little bit late."

"And then there was a *ghost*. I'm dead serious, Bill. I saw a ghost in the hallway just at the bottom of the stairs. Cold chill and a kind of misty-mist, Bill, and she was beckoning to me!"

"And we really need it—we're in danger here of not making our own bills."

"So, naturally, Briana won't go upstairs anymore, so we're sleeping in Juliet's studio, if you don't mind."

Briana? That was the first I'd heard of any Briana. I swallowed my curiosity, stayed firmly with the business at hand: "So, I need to know when you can send some or all of what you owe us. It's getting up there, as you know."

"And Bill, the electric, it's too high. I think your refrigerator is faulty, Bill, I hear it running right now! Listen to this." And suddenly she was knocking the phone against something that did indeed hum.

Evenly, with an effort at a tone of amusement: "Well, the refrigerator is fine. If you don't want your food cold, don't use the refrigerator. The electric bill is the same as it's been every month forever."

"No, it's high. I called the Electric and said I was you and made complaint! They won't talk to me unless I'm you, you know, Bill. So I gave them my low William F. Roorbach voice and told them, 'You can keep your buttfucking bills if they're going to be so cocksucking high.'"

"Ms. Bollocks. Your job is to look after the house, pay the bills, water the plants, mow the lawn in spring, keep the roof clear without putting holes in it, keep the driveway plowed without killing the trees. That's all. That's why you have the reduced rent—you are *housesitting*." How many times had I repeated this? Why did I sound exactly like my father? "The bills are no different from any other year. And we agreed that you wouldn't pile up shutoff notices."

"Now, wait just a minute here, Bill: I'm not the one sends you shutoff notices! You call the Electric if you want to stop getting shutoff notices! I'm just a little strapped right now, Bill. But next week I get paid for the job I'm doing this week; I'm building a sweet little set of bookcases in Fran Bodley's place, just up toward Anson there. But she ain't the cash for the materials, so I had to front that, which was one hundred and fifty-six dollars, Bill. I'm using just number two pine and finish nails, but it's a lot of shelves. And I did borrow your Sawzall to open the wall there for her—you know, the chuck on that thing is no good: you're missing the ferrule, you know?"

The Sawzall was a relic of my days in construction, a powerful bayonet saw, great for demolition and old work. I said, "The ferrule's not missing from my Sawzall! And I asked you not to use it after what happened last year."

The year previous she claimed to have left my Sawzall on a job where it had been stolen. To my face, she had told me this, examining my eyes to see if I believed her—she was such a bad liar. I told her I was shocked that a person could steal that saw, and held her eye and interrogated her with every ounce of my slim reportorial skill, got the name of the job she'd supposedly been on. Right in front of her I dialed the police. She told me, *Wait, wait.* That's all, just, *Wait.* And the Sawzall magically turned up on my porch that very evening.

Still, somehow, perversely, we were fond of her.

She said, "Are you getting mad, Bill? Why would someone with such a good job as you get mad over a Sawzall ferrule—how much could that cost? And a pack of blades? Anyway, as

I've been trying to tell you here for ten minutes, I'm going down to Pennsylvania for a job in a couple of weeks—tons of money, since that's all you ever think about!"

"Ms. Bollocks. You are not to take the cost of the ferrule and pack of blades out of the rent. You lost the ferrule, you used the blades up, using the saw without my permission. And in any case, this isn't the point. The point is, you are behind on your rent, and I can't wait for your chimerical trip."

"Nice language, Bill! Do you talk to your mother with that mouth? So: I'll send two hundred thirty-six next week. Less the ferrule and blades, of course. And less the hundred bucks the Electric wants extra. I'm telling you, it's the refrigerator."

"Please send eight hundred—that's what you owe. And no deductions, you hear me?"

"How do you figure eight hundred?"

"February. March. Four hundred dollars a month, as agreed. Split it with this Briana, why don't you?"

She put on a kind of schoolteacherly condescension, spoke slowly, as if to the class dunce. "Now, Bill. Just wait a minute here. What month are we in?"

"It's March, Ms. Bollocks."

"And how much do I owe you for March, Bill?"

"Four hundred dollars, Ms. Bollocks."

"So it's four hundred bucks, correct?"

"That's correct, Ms. Bollocks, plus four hundred bucks for February."

"No, no, now wait, Bill. This is March. And I owe you four hundred dollars for March, correct?"

"Correct."

"And February is February, correct? And February is *over,*

Bill. It's all done with. So, consequentially, I owe you *four hundred dollars*."

"Ms. Bollocks. You didn't pay rent in February. I should have gotten on you much sooner. I mean, come on, all the breaks we've given you! Your February rent is four hundred dollars. Your March rent is four hundred dollars. The total is eight hundred dollars, which I would like you to remit immediately."

Tenderly, as if holding the hand of a small child: "But, Bill...okay, listen. This is March, correct?"

"Haven't we done this already?"

"And I owe you how much for March?"

"Ms. Bollocks...please. Put eight hundred dollars in the mail, okay? Or do I have to drive back up there and find a tenant I can trust?"

"Four hundred dollars, okay, that's how much for March."

"And four hundred for February."

"But, William F. You are not a good listener. This is *March!*"

FOR SPRING BREAK WE'D PLANNED A TRIP TO SEE JULIET'S PARents in New York and mine in Connecticut, so it was no big deal for me to add seven solo hours to the eleven we'd driven already and go see for myself what was happening in our house, perhaps prevail in person on Ms. Bollocks for some rent before it was April.

I left the Upper West Side at three in the morning, last day of winter 2000, got to Mercer, Maine, at ten, dropped my suitcase at our sweet friends the McNairs and continued on to our place. There'd been a deep, wet snow in the area (while in New York it had rained the previous couple of days), and the new covering made everything look clean and inviting in the bright March sun. Already exhausted, late morning, I drove by our house four times: reconnaissance. It looked the same— scruffy, compact, cute really, and cozy. The driveways were neatly plowed out. On the fifth pass I pulled in, steeled myself, sauntered up the perfectly shoveled walk to the porch door and knocked, looking in: nothing amiss.

A shade answered the door, and it was not Ms. Bollocks's hallway ghost. "Oh," the apparition said when I introduced myself, no surprise in its face. No emotion at all, in fact. She wore an apron covered with flour, but didn't seem to be baking. Her hair hung down to her knees, brushed one hundred strokes. Her hand rose slowly to cover her eyes: I was too much even to gaze upon. "Come in," she said, but stood in the way.

"You're Briana," I said. "I am Bill. I am looking for Ms. Bollocks."

"She's in Pennsylvania," Briana said, still hidden behind her hand.

"I was just in town and thought I'd stop in."

"She didn't leave any money, if that's what you're after." She peeked at me through long fingers.

I shook my head, she shook hers: we both knew what Ms. Bollocks was like. With that small commiseration, Briana moved aside, let me walk in. The house was tidy but unrecognizable, interloper's furniture everywhere among our own, chairs and couches and coffee tables squeezed into the parlor, where the wood stove burned too hot, almost glowing. There was the smell of bacon and maple syrup—nice, but not our own.

Briana gazed at me, neutral. Perhaps she'd been pretty once.

"Mind if I ski out back?" I said.

"Snow's rotten," she said.

"Snowshoe, then?"

In the barn I climbed over half a year of garbage in bags and found my wooden snowshoes, put them on. I missed the dogs—those lucky guys were staying with a slightly wild grad student in Columbus: two A.M. walks, exciting parties, dozens of pretty girls scratching their ears. I missed Juliet, too, but she had it as good as the dogs, warm and well coddled, gazing out over Central Park while she gabbed with her mom and old friends about cribs and changing tables.

The temperature had come up dramatically in a mere hour or so, and all that new snow was melting fast. I was dressed for cold, stomped bigfoot into the woods, tamping the rotting snowpack of our unused trail: you'd flop and founder in normal shoes. The snowpack had started to thin and the world had begun to show, scruffy. The compost heap by the stone wall at the verge of the woods had emerged too, frozen rinds from my and Juliet's sweet autumn, frozen peelings and stalks and cuttings and food scraps from each month since—Briana and Ms. Bollocks—all of it soon to gather ecumenically as proper worm food, food for bacteria, too. By the time Juliet and I returned in June—as quickly as that—it would all be rich black soil. Red knobs showed in the dirt where the rhubarb would rise. Green hands reached up everywhere from tulip and narcissus and crocus and snowdrop and hyacinth bulbs, stuff I'd planted in various bursts of hopefulness, blooms coming soon for the pleasure of ungrateful tenants.

. . . I enter the woods and in minutes begin to sweat. Easy enough to stop and strip out of my jacket, hang it in a tree. Minutes more and I leave my sweater, then my flannel shirt, then my tee, arrive at the stream bare-chested but overheated nevertheless, stand in the sun as on a tropical beach.

The balsams drip, the rocks drip. Everything is a-drip, and not only I. In the naked branches of the black cherry over my head the chickadees sing their plaintive song with evident pleasure, minor key: it-*is*-spring, it-*is*-spring. A savannah sparrow clambers up from the depths of the tangled alders, takes up a perch in hot sun and lets his song go full whistle. Across the stream in a low branch a male cardinal sets himself up on a good high branch and belts it out with a Maine accent (that is, sings a regional song, distinctly different from cardinal song in, say, Columbus, Ohio), still hoping to impress his mate despite being her life partner: *chew, chew, chew, woody, woody, woody, chew.*

I forget about Ms. Bollocks. I forget about ghostly Briana. I forget that in the morning I'm going to have to drive back down to New York. I forget that in a few days, it's back to Ohio. I forget everything. I'm just happy to be in the woods again. And suddenly, it's spring. The sun burns my chest.

Down in the stream, the mysterious beavers have left signs that they are venturing forth: clean-gnawed, waterlogged branchlets in pick-up-sticks piles wherever there's a little free water along the banks. I stomp down the edge on crumbling corn snow and fish a staff out of the shallows, enjoy once again the feel of smooth-peeled wood, examine once again the pointed record of decurved incisors. The hairy woodpecker has left large wood chips on the ground by the big rock—he's chiseling a house from the trunk of a popple half killed by the success of a tinder polypore (which is a common fungus, a conk with fruiting bodies like so many horses' hooves kicking out of the bole of the tree).

The sun on my chest sets oceans flowing under my skin. Trickles form under the snowbanks all around me, meet one another and become rivulets. I hear the burbling and my heart pumps harder: I'm a stream again, and no longer ice. Underneath the birdsong is watersong, everything gurgling with melt. The temperature has passed seventy degrees: I'm still sweating, standing still in snowshoes.

The sun gets hotter. The stream ice gives a loud groan and heave. A skin of clear water flows from a new fracture, eats the snow in front of it, gathers force. The whole surface of the ice lifts slightly, drops. The Temple is under there, impatient. It boils up out of fissures, spouts alongside rocks, flows at the stream edge. Ice breaks free, flips, makes a dam, gathers water, bursts in a wave that melts still more snow. After an hour of suspense—grinding, subtle movements in the ice—there's a roar upstream, then a clapping sound, enormous dominoes, and suddenly around the bend a prodigious wave arrives: a large ice dam has broken. The wave lifts the ice below me three feet in a single heave, breaks it in huge pans that want to move downstream too, lifts whole sections twenty feet square and two feet thick, forms a new dam.

The upstream ice keeps coming—large floes and pans bumping and thumping till they meet the blockade at our bend, where they tilt and flip and add themselves to its mass.

The water rises fast, thrusting new pans on top and adding whole trees. Then higher, raising the dam till abruptly the last piece comes into place, an enormous pan that flips and breaks against all that's already in place just below our bluff and vantage point, blocking the stream utterly to a height of ten feet or more. The water rises fast—a foot a minute, huge pressure building—overflows the lower field. Ice pans like loose diving rafts drift out where cows used to stand, pushing over the forgiving streamside alders till there are no alders in sight, bashing the bark off hardwoods twelve feet up their trunks (those scars will be puzzling in summer—what man or beast or little brook could reach so high?): the lowest field is *flowing*.

Now the stream mounts more slowly, filling a basin of dozens of acres till finally it crests our high bank. I back away reluctantly, not wanting to miss the show, aim my snowshoes toward home, ready to trundle for my life. A pressure bulge grows in the dam, like a balloon inflating, a balloon made out of plates. Upstream, a large new floe gets stuck, flips like a boat capsizing, makes its own dam, one that briefly impounds the stream behind it. Under that force, the great floe explodes into fragments, unleashing a wave. Suddenly, with a sound like close thunder, the dam cracks and opens and climbs up on itself, gargantuan pans of ice pushing up into the lower branches of the streamside trees and onto the banks.

In seconds, all the millions of pounds of backed-up water roar through, extraordinary violence, sticks and logs and rocks and ice floes and bigger pans and muddy water roaring downstream to the next pool, the solid old ice on top of which simply folds up, no match for the onslaught, folds up and forms a slow, roaring accordion pleat in front of an eight-foot-high wall of debris. Within a minute or two the whole mass rounds the bend a couple of hundred yards away, leaving ice chunks in all the fields like bridge sections high and dripping.

Within half an hour the stream is gently flowing in its bed as if the season were autumn, muddy but mild, utterly free of floating ice, its banks strewn as far as I can see, the alders crushed and buried, the sweepers gone, the hard-won beaver dam absent, branches and old leaves and mud and dripping blocks of ice everywhere in the tropical sunshine, enormous marooned ice pans settling like dynamited bunkers, breaking on each other, the whole looking like the doused remains of a tenement after a catastrophic fire, winter washed away in under two hours' time.

I snowshoe-jog back to the house in a heat, anxious to share my experience: the power of nature! There's Briana in the yard, collecting sticks. "The stream!" I cry. "The fields! All the snow! Washed away at once!"

"Ice-out," Briana says, her voice a shrug, and continues her tidying up.

Upstream Four
Twin Bridges to Russell's Mill

SPRING DIDN'T COME TILL APRIL THE YEAR EARL DROPPED HIS skidder on the ice. And Good Friday was good indeed that spring: fifty degrees, comparatively balmy, each breeze carrying a scent that was a memory, every new bit of green an inspiration. I was a bud and opened, too, quit work early, ten A.M. I collected my fly rod and drove just a mile downstream, parked by the Twin Bridges (once two identical covered bridges, now just a single cement span augmented where the old twin had been by an eight-foot-diameter flood-stage pipe, fraternal twin at best). I scrambled down the high bank to the streambed and walked through the tunnel the huge pipe made, whistling to hear the echo.

I made my way downstream, nymphing on the faulty theory that above the millpond in early spring there'd be large trout on the move. (In fly-fishing parlance, nymphing is the use of a specialized lure, or fly, which amounts to a lot of thread and fur and tinsel tightly wound on a hook to resemble the larval stage of several common stream insects. You let the nymph—a woolly bugger, a hare's ear, a stonefly—bounce along the bottom with the hope of attracting the interest of a hungry fish.) The going was tough and the fish weren't biting (or weren't there to begin with), so I turned back exactly where Earl had crashed—no obvious sign of the disaster now, just a quiescent pool with one sandy bank caved in. On the way back upstream I stopped fishing altogether and simply enjoyed the rock hop, concentrating so hard on my footing that I didn't realize I was back at the Twin Bridges, and didn't see the person till she spoke:

"Another little boy with his fishing pole."

Startled, I peered into the dimness of the huge pipe.

"Never fear, I'm just a little wood sprite," she said. Her voice echoed eerily off the corrugations of the galvanized metal, gained volume, but was still the wavering voice of an old woman and no sprite, as sprites are ever young. As my eyes adjusted to the dark in there I saw she was standing at the other end of the tube in dead water to her bare knees, holding up a long skirt. My own feet were cold in boots and I hadn't touched the water.

She said, "You didn't ask, but I'm considering this pipe."

I walked on through to her end on a rim of sand and stones. Standing on a big riprap rock, I loomed over her. She looked up at me with clearest brown eyes, held her skirt, wicked little smile; she could have been ten years old. But she was at the other end of things—very old, it looked. Her hair was a rinse-white puff, her face nicely creased from smiling, her skin dark. She seemed to tilt a little to starboard, wore a neat little gray cardigan over a ruffled blouse, and out of her sleeve stuck a nice wad of tissue, which she pulled out at that moment for a dainty sneeze.

"Pine pollen," she said.

"It gets me, too," I said.

"Just look how this pipe-way is gathering sand," she said. "It's thirty feet long, at a guess, and if you look, you'll see that the latest flow made three turns in that length."

I looked, looked again, saw only slowly that the stream, long receded, had pushed up several sandbars, leaving a sinuous track through the pipe.

"Rather beautiful," she said.

I agreed.

She was encouraged by my interest and continued: "It's just as if the corrugations of the pipe weren't there at all—the water is ignoring the pipe absolutely. You know, they always talk about flood stage clearing the pipe-way, but it doesn't happen in these low-incline installations. The water considers this overflow a back channel and wants to fill it."

She raised a hand for help climbing out of the water and I took it, pulled her up gently so as not to yank the arm right off of her—that's how delicate she seemed, weight of a sparrow, bare feet dripping. She never let go of the hem of her skirt, which was a lovely thick drape of blue cloth I couldn't name— I thought wool, that light sort of wool cloth you find in good pants, with a weave to it. I looked up by my truck and spied her car: an older-model Mercedes, very sporty, polished and gleaming, the same blue as her skirt.

"You are a lovely man," she said in thanks.

"The pleasure is all mine," I said, giving the words a courtly flourish for her sake; clearly, she came from a more formal time.

"I would like to go sit on that log." She pointed upstream to a large beech tree lying stripped on a sandbar in the bright sun. We climbed slowly up the bank and made our way holding hands along a sand ledge that formed a shelf over the stream, a hundred yards or so. At the root end of the old tree a suitable throne had formed, and there my little stream queen alighted, her bare feet in the warm sand. I sat on the log next to her, pushed my heavy hiking boots into the sand to form mounds, kicked them down, formed new mounds, over and over.

"Tell me your name, winter bird," she said.

I did.

"Tell me what you do," she said.

I said English professor, since that was the quickest thing to say and was true at the time, true enough.

"How unpleasant," she said pleasantly.

And I tried to make it sound actually quite wonderful, which you could see was what she'd hoped in a way, that such a job could be wonderful.

"Do you bring your classes here?" she said.

Well, no, I hadn't, but often brought them outside in spring. "But the outdoors, you know, it's distracting."

She grimaced at that observation, said, "It's the proper distraction. You must bring them here."

In the next hour I learned her name, Connie Nosalli, and lots more: that she was from Mississippi originally, that she considered herself "colored" though she was very "light-skinned" in her terms, that she seldom thought about race anymore, except to get out in the sun as much as possible to be as dark as possible in honor of her heritage. Her hometown was called Roxie, near McComb, Mississippi, "not too terribly far" from New Orleans, Louisiana, which she pronounced carefully for me, as if it were possible I might never have heard of it. All this sitting on a log in a stream of talk—clearly she hadn't had anyone to regale in quite a while.

She said things like "Tell me about you, and I'll tell you about what a fool I've been, including that I voted for Richard Nixon *twice*."

I told her lots about me, starting with a quick version of my views on Ronald Reagan (loving him, she gasped at my calumny). I told her about my whole life, really. I loved the way she smiled and nodded and frowned and sputtered and laughed and groaned alternately at my revelations. She had a way of keeping eye contact, keeping it most comfortably. I stopped my mounding of the sand, stopped eyeing my escape truck there on the steep bank far on the other side of the stream.

She'd been born in May of 1908: her eighty-sixth birthday was coming in two weeks. She had a clear, almost British, accent, no trace of the South whatsoever. She had met her husband late—she'd been an "old maid" (she said) of thirty-four, a high school teacher of science who'd never been further north than Jackson till older than *that*, but who had "started down" to Texas to get a master's degree in biology, which was just one unspecialized science at the time.

Later, she would tell me about some difficulties of race she'd suffered: particularly, that she had been "passing" as "white" from college into middle age—staying out of the sun (as she said lightly), treating and bleaching her hair, and simply never raising the subject of her heritage with anyone ever, and no one asked. She was quite proud of herself, not for "passing" but for fooling racists and getting what she wanted, which wasn't the degree, as it turned out, but a husband. She'd been "injured" as a teen in a way that left her "barren" and "scarred" (I didn't pry further) and had simply never thought of herself as marriageable.

After college, which she'd attended across the border at Louisiana State, in Monroe (accent on the first syllable), she'd started teaching high school biology, "passing" once again—never had a date, not once—spending her afternoons in the field making observations, studying at night, amassing a natural sciences library for the woebegone school. Soon she'd tired of that life, wanting more, but stayed with it ten years until she despaired and applied with little hope to graduate schools, using only a first initial and her maiden name. She was the sole woman in her graduate program at the University of Texas, Austin, which covered multiple sciences, just showed up to begin the program without letting them know her gender because no one had asked, and none of the application forms had inquired. "I was so ugly they never balked." She must have had some stories about the South at that time, but she never told them, never spoke of the South unless I asked impertinent questions, which she answered shortly or not at all.

She achieved her master's in two years, but had to leave school in her third, which would have started her on the road to a Ph.D., forced out not by what she'd always feared—racial or gender issues—but by a romantic scandal. She'd fallen in love with one of her professors, an "Italian from the snowy

Alps," as she put it, a charming, tiny man with a thick accent. He was a hydrologist of little note, a sparkling, funny teacher in his sixties, beloved of students but not so much by colleagues at the university, a deeply troubled soul who had lost his family—all but his beloved baby brother—in the First World War. He taught future engineers practical science but saw his own area as purest field science, a kind of formalized love of rivers.

Dr. Nosalli and Connie had begun their romance (apparently quite torrid for the era—one of Connie's charms was the constant, coruscating juxtaposition of frankness and modesty), begun it at the end of her first year in school and kept it secret till they were wed, at which time they left for Massachusetts—the professor had applied for and won a fine job with the federal government as a civilian hydrologist for the Army Corps of Engineers. In 1950, flush times, he and Connie bought a secluded cottage on Long Pond, down in the Belgrade Lakes of Maine (about twenty miles from Farmington), and from there they'd explored widely, doing his brand of science, which was also hers, and forming an impenetrably tight alliance, a kind of dual solitude. His pet interest was sandbars, gravel bars, sand carry, and just plain sand, and his late lifework—a hobby, really, since he never managed to write his papers or even abstracts—was the Kennebec River, the Sandy River, and two of the Sandy's tributaries.

Memorably, she said, "The trouble with marrying a much older man is that much older men die." And, indeed, Dr. Nosalli had died in 1961, at eighty-five, which was Connie's age when we met on Temple Stream.

She said, "You could always find us right here on Sundays.

In fact, if you want to be in touch, come looking for us. I'm not in the book. I haven't an address, at least not one I'll give you! I'm a summer bird!"

Later, I would learn that Connie came to Temple Stream nearly every Sunday when she was in Maine, which was about six months of the year, from midspring to midautumn (the rest of the year she was somewhere she wouldn't disclose in Massachusetts, one of the Boston suburbs). And later still, she would give me her P.O. box in Belgrade Lakes, to which I might send an invitation to a summer potluck (these she never took up) or a Christmas card for forwarding. Temple Stream was just a stop on the Sunday tour of her husband's study locations. And in this weekly tour she not only remembered him and their life together but continued his research, in a way, which in honesty had been all observation. Looking closely at streams was her work and her calling. She seemed a Buddhist nun to me, engaged in this seemingly pointless and purposefully endless task.

She said, "I think of him every day."

THAT WAS MY BIRD SPRING. I'D HAD AN INTEREST FROM CHILD-hood (birding was my only easy merit badge in Boy Scouts), but that was the year I really began to revel in the dawn chorus, to walk around with binoculars, to keep lists and notes and dates, to acquire more and more sophisticated bird guides. Birding, in fact, quickly supplanted my old love of fishing.

Most of the winter birds were around, of course, what

Connie called the year-rounders: the chickadees, three kinds of woodpeckers, the stalwart blue jay, tree sparrows, song sparrows, the occasional pair of pine grosbeaks, the occasional flock of yellow grosbeaks, juncos in slate flocks, one pair of cardinals dependably, several rock doves (i.e., city pigeons) from my neighbor's 1820 dairy barn, a large flock of mourning doves, huge ravens, noisier crows, nuthatches white- and red-breasted, pine siskins, redpolls in large flocks, tufted titmice on no discernible schedule, starlings in great flocks, robins, golden-crowned kinglets (a chipper, busy little flock of tiny birds back in the balsams of our woods intermittently), goldfinches. The male goldfinches turned bright yellow from a tarnishy green in late March, just as the summer birds began to turn up.

Around solstice, a pair of hooded mergansers arrived on the stream, he with his great retractable hat of black feathers, garish parabolas of white behind the eyes, hooked black beak, she with her bouffant feather-do slicked way back—punk-rock babe with Carnaby Street dude, sporting around, paddling upstream and out of sight, floating back on the current and into view.[1] They seemed to be looking for nest sites, paddling to the edges of the stream, looking up under snags, inspecting the muskrat den that I'd thought was in use still. Did that winter mink get our local muskrat? He must have, as the birds took over the den, diving to its underwater entrance, appearing anytime I stomped on the opposite bank, popping up out of the water one at a time, male first, paddling fast at sight of me,

---

1. Mergansers are in the same family as geese and ducks, but occupy their own subfamily. I've heard old-timers around here (and Earl) call them sheldrakes, sawbills, and even goosanders.

taking to the sky in squeaky protest, a long loop I followed with binoculars. If I sat out of sight they'd return within ten minutes. By late April, no amount of stomping would get the female to show herself. Only the male would appear, and attempt to lead me away. Of course, I let him. (Later, when the female was out and about with her brood of nine merganserlings, the male went missing.)

And Wally flushed a common snipe out of the boggy edges of the first hayfield, the bird flying over my head showing that comically long bill and landing not far from my feet, playing statue. The bill weighted the head earthward—the bird looked downcast even though he was a nice, plump, leaf-colored soul, looked abashed, perhaps about that long nose. But he was not abashed, he was a bird, and that beak found food for him nicely, shaped to its use as a mud probe and forceps to search out then pinch and extract worms from soft soils.

A brown creeper—that small busy bird with decurved bill and self-absorbed air—appeared on the dead young elm where I'd hung a ball of suet in a net bag left over from onions. He started at the bottom of the tree, crept busily up to the suet, pecked out a sample, flew down to the base of the next tree.

And dream-gazing out the kitchen window while putting dishes away, I spotted a huge wingspan soaring high over the stream, subtle turns to follow the watercourse, an air of dominance, deep calm. It took a minute to let myself see that white head—a bald eagle, of course, on a reconnaissance flight. I watched it a full three or four minutes till it disappeared over the trees upstream, and then I watched the sky where it'd been, dishes forgotten. When I snapped to, I called my friend Bob Kimber, who lives three miles up the Temple. "Eagle coming your way," I said. A few minutes later my phone rang, and it was Bob: "Here he comes."

Later that week I walked down to the water early in the morning to see who might turn up, found the usual chickadees and blue jays. With my binoculars I spotted some juncos, too: winter birds all. Then, just across the stream, a fluttering caught my eye, resolved into a large flock of cedar waxwings busily eating something off the remains of snow. I looked at the granular snowpack around my feet: snow fleas, tiny black bugs hatching everywhere. The waxwings dove and ascended, perched and leapt, noisily snapping up the bounty. I got the briefest glimpses of pointed crests and dark masks, red wax-seals stamped on wings.

I spotted a sharp-shinned hawk only because it had insinu-ated itself among the mourning doves in the dog yard, and one of them in fright flew into the big screen on the laundry room window. I turned from loading the dryer in time to see the baf-fled dove leap to flight from the lawn, only to be snatched from the air by the waiting sharpie: flash of wing, silent death. Later I'd find the feathers fanned neatly on a stump in our woods, all else gone.

I knew the advent of summer was irreversible when the first grackle of the year appeared, swaggering among the lesser birds under the feeders, collecting the cracked corn I'd strewn. More so when I heard the first red-winged blackbirds calling: that's a swamp song, the first selection on summer's sound track.

An April Fool sleet storm left five inches of the tiniest of ice balls, colorful sun prisms that the mourning doves crunched in their bills one at a time for hours.

Past dusk on a warmer day, I heard the familiar croak of the

American woodcock in my neighbor's barnyard. Initially, I
thought it was a misplaced frog, but then came the twittering
tones of the male's ascent, that weird whistling of air through
wings that announced a very fine specimen was here in the
world and owned that territory. The female of the pair simply
waited on the ground for her lover's antics to cease, for the advent of the stiff-legged approach he'd make in the end for her
favors. I looked to the dusky sky in time to see his spiral
progress up and up and up till I lost sight. Then I listened
harder. Soon the bird's invisible plummet to earth was complete, and I heard a brief song and scrabbling, then the croaking again, then the whole process repeated, a cock for each
field in the neighborhood, solo croaking, solo flights till midnight, while the females, less excitable, stayed put. I felt so
fond, each male like some bumbling friend with a crazy plan to
attract women that in the end, and against all logic, *works*.

As April grew, my sightings increased: vulture, mallard pair,
fox sparrow. On the fifth, I moved the birdhouses on their
posts away from the garden into newly dug holes near the apple tree. That very afternoon a bluebird flew in and perched on
the roof of the middle house. In the sun the next morning I
spotted darker blue flashes, forked tails in the sky, and the tree
swallows were back, birds born in the boxes I'd built: fine by
me, even if the result was the displacement of the bluebird.

Maligned cowbirds joined the other blackbirds: which of
the many nesters around would they choose to host their eggs?

On a walk down to the stream I saw our kestrel—that small
falcon—harassing starlings, saw him perched imperious on
the popple top he'd always preferred, emperor's square head.
He perched twenty minutes without a movement, surveyed

the great world. I left him to it, walked to the water, used my binoculars to scan the trees alongside the Temple, spotted a kingbird. This new arrival took the highest bare branch around, skydived rhythmically for insects. A raucous cry made me wheel to see a kingfisher hunkered on the lowest branches, watching the water for fish: the Temple is a world of kings. And along the sandbars, rusty blackbirds, Lincoln's sparrows, spotted sandpipers. A savannah sparrow piped on a top-twig perch in the alders, throwing its head back with passion. Vireo, veery, yellow-bellied flycatcher, phoebe, thrush.

Suddenly, a pair of common mergansers swooped in over my head like aircraft (I could hear their wings whistling), landed fast on the water, skied in on their feet leaving wakes, bright orange bills, the male purest white with a mallard-green head, wingspan of almost three feet (by contrast, the hooded merganser's span is about two feet).

On the answering machine at home I found a message from Juliet: driving into town she'd seen wild turkeys in the cleared land across from the Kings' house. Thinking about that, absently surveying the sky, I spotted the first heron of the year, flying the eagle's route, but effortfully. In the woods I heard the first warbler song: *witchety, witchety, witchety:* common yellowthroat. A partridge drummed, a hermit thrush whistled.

Chorus in the evenings: spring peepers.

Then it was May, and merry, merry. In the yard, purple and house finches sang. In the woods, a hermit thrush called from a regular perch on a low branch under balsams. On the stream, a wood-duck pair mingled with a large flock of black ducks. In the sky, a red-tailed hawk took evasive action, harassed by crows. In the brush, new warblers sang, warblers everywhere, some on migration, some to stay the summer: black-and-white, chestnut-sided, yellow, Canada, Wilson's. In the neighboring fields, bobolinks tootled, back from a winter's sojourn in Brazil. *Carnaval!* Under the hemlocks, white-crowned sparrows appeared, six pair. In the night sky at the edges of the forest the first fireflies blinked. In the neighbor's high sugar tree that same night, the whip-poor-will sang its first plaint of the season.

In the heirloom apple trees, a catbird mewled. At the kitchen window, the first ruby-throated hummingbird materialized, pure motion looking for the feeder that had been there the summer previous. In the beaver bog I spotted a sora, a green heron, a night-heron, and, of course, a great blue. Up in the elm tree, our northern orioles were back, working on a nest. From the neighbor's barn on the first of June, chimney swifts emerged at dawn. Down in the morning stream after, I saw a dragonfly dipping her long tail, methodically laying eggs.

ABOUT THEN, WARBLER TIME, CAME THE FIRST TRULY WARM morning that spring—an irresistible stream day. I pedaled my old bike half a mile down to Russell's Mill Road, admiring the tulips and narcissuses of the six neighbors along the way, coasted to the perfunctory concrete bridge over the Temple, a favorite spot to watch the water, just above the spot where Russell had built his dam. Once, a covered bridge stood there, I knew, but the town burned it in 1967 after a truck went through—unsentimental solution. Stubby granite obelisks from the old bridge lay on their sides at both ends: once even the most minor stream crossing could be a thing of studied grandeur.

I balanced on the bike by holding the battered, inadequate bridge railing and stared down into the clarity of the pool below, the mud of the spring floods having settled out. The sun was so nice on my back that I contemplated leaving the bike and rock-hopping in the stream down to the Twin Bridges—always a good stretch, but better aboard a canoe in flood time: shoot under the Russell's Mill Road bridge, rage through a quick rocky rapids, pause in the long pond that bends hairpin around the tip of a nicely mowed peninsula (someone's pointy yard), finally take a breath and dive into an extended chute of wild water. The same chute that once in a fit of bad judgment I rode with Desi and Wally onboard; we blasted past a porcupine having a drink at the banks while, as it happened, the dogs were looking the other way: close call.

And many times in low water I'd walked and swum the stretch—deep woods down there, good birding, curious fungi. But it was a bike day, and maybe not a day for perfect solitude, and so I puffed and pedaled back up the hill to our road, took a right and coasted downhill. Not far, just at the place the stream returns to the road, I saw my downstream neighbor Erick Apland standing in his dooryard. He was gazing upward, contemplating a large broken branch in one of the old maples at the front of his property. Erick is my age, tall, large-boned, a kind of Farmington Viking, a builder by trade and a member of the town planning board. You often see his picture in the paper, Erick planting trees on Arbor Day or organizing volunteer projects at the nursing home. His wife is a doctor in town. I'd done a little backcountry skiing with him, drunk a beer or two streamside. His house—one of the originals around here—is beautifully restored, with a magnificent post-and-beam barn of his own design and construction.

I pulled up and hailed him, and he hailed me: company. "Nice bike," he said—my bike was a wreck.

"Nice tree," I said.

Mild white water coursed and pounded not a hundred feet away.

Erick was wearing a green T-shirt printed discreetly over the pocket with the following brief poem:

> TEMPLE STREAM
> POST AND BEAM

He offered me a light beer. We drank and traded amiable insults, came too quickly to that point in neighborly conversation when the small talk is used up. There was just the sound of the stream knocking gently past. In high water, the knocking would turn to roaring, I knew. In flood, it'd be like locomotives racing all night. We finished our beers. We gazed past the trunks of small trees to the stream. We were two people who knew the water well, standing like mutual friends of the bride at a sudden wedding.

So I asked about the clover mill, which I'd read was nearby.

"Ah, the clover mill," Erick said, and explained: settlers had had to import clover seed, a pricey Eurasian native. To save the expense, thrifty farmers would let a crop go to seed. But hulling clover was difficult, tedious work. Temple Stream power—the height of technology—changed all that, allowed seed to be cleaned in large quantities quickly by transferring motion to a system of notched troughs and hulling boards.

"Not much of it left," Erick said. Down at the stream, he showed me the remains: a bulwark of large rocks, flat sides showing, some as big as the oxen that must have helped move them there. The miller was one Moses Craig, who lived with his father. "After the dam and the mill, they built my house."

I asked how it was living so close to the Temple.

"It's fucking loud," Erick said, "but don't quote me."

Back on my bike, I continued downstream, past the neighborhood swimming hole, past a fallen house (there's a bed frame in there still, and a hand pump), and to the Twin Bridges.

And there was Connie Nosalli's Mercedes parked in its spot over the water. I found the woman herself perched on a rock in an impossible spot partway across the stream, just gazing into the current with her head cocked, dressed in a fish-print pinafore and big straw sun hat. "Oh, you're here," she said when I called, as if it had been me she'd been listening for. "Good, good. You'll help me to my log."

I struggled out to her spot, rock by rock, and rock by rock helped her out of the stream and up the steep bank to the path that took us to her fallen beech tree. There on the smooth wood I helped her sit. She patted the bole beside her and I sat too. The stream tumbled past forcefully, but nothing like in flood. Hidden, a red-eyed vireo sang its strong song: *hey-you-two, on-your-log, look-up, look-at-me.* The trees, newly leafed-out in palest green, waved and sighed in the breeze.

At length, continuing some thought to which I hadn't been privy, Connie spoke: "Fortunately, I make friends easily. In fact, I'm seldom alone. Although, come to think of it, when I'm alone is when I'm most together."

More silence, which grew a little uncomfortable. I wasn't quite sure of my welcome. Connie seemed wrapped in herself.

Conversationally I said, "So, what are you up to today?"

"Hydrology."

I laughed, but Connie took visible offense, so I gulped it back. And we sat. Then sat more. The stream rose and fell slightly, a rhythm of bubbling then quiet, a swelling and recession of volume. I began to think of exit lines, and once again the sand began to mound beneath my boots. Connie's bare feet and ankles were tucked into the sand, which she wore like socks. It could not have been very warm, though the sun shone on us still.

"Hydrology," I said, trying for a tone of reverence.

And at length, still aggrieved, Connie spoke: "Water, dear, is what connects heaven and earth. Do you understand? There is a constant exchange, earth to atmosphere. It's the breathing of the planet." Then she sighed, deciding to give me the full discussion: Water, she explained, evaporates under the influence of wind and sun wherever it's exposed, "whether in puddles or ponds or lakes or oceans or streams," or sublimates from the surface of snow and ice in cold weather. She said the other source of water in the atmosphere is transpiration, water drawn up as sap by plants and trees through capillary action, all the way from the roots through vascular systems to the thousands of microscopic perforations of each leaf, from which the plant exhales it as vapor—constantly, in huge amounts.

Connie put on her quiz face: "How much do you think ten

acres of corn, such as will be grown down the way, might tran-
spire, for example?"

"In a year?"

"How about just in a day?"

"Hundreds of gallons in a day," I said, thinking immediately
that I'd guessed too high.

"No, hundreds of gallons in a minute! They will exchange
to the air *thirty thousand, forty thousand* gallons of water a day.
And remember that a big deciduous tree can give off that
much, too, in just a year. Look at all the trees around us here!"

I pictured millions of gallons flying up from them in aggre-
gate each growing season. Instead of a downpour, an up-pour,
more on sunny days. Plants, she told me, are second only to
oceans as sources of water vapor. And as vapor, water defies
gravity, is heated by the sun and rises like the steam from an
iron. "Not that you have seen an iron lately."

She was the acerbic high-school teacher she hadn't been
for half a century, explaining the hydrological cycle to a recal-
citrant student, winning him with every wile. The stream
soughed past; my head filled with scientific questions; I quit
my squirming.

"And, as you have seen in your shower bath, water vapor
condenses on cool surfaces. So in nature, from gas to liquid.
Which is rain, most often. Your next question: why does vapor
condense into rain?" She explained: warm air rises to areas of
lower pressure that allows it to expand. The expansion cools
the air and thus the water vapor, which forms droplets around
motes of dust, and if heavy enough, they fall as rain.

My teacher looked at me closely to see if she was getting
through. "What is a stream?" she asked.

I had one right in front of me for inspiration. Slowly I came up with this: "A stream is a crowd of attractive water molecules heading downhill."

"That's good. Good. How does the water get to the stream?"

"Rain."

"By what process?"

"Runoff? It flows off the mountains and the hills and every inclined plane and to the stream."

"No," Connie said. "Though sometimes when the land is saturated or frozen that is true. What actually happens is that nearly all rain soaks into the ground." And rain fills the crevices between every rock and grain of sand. It fills the holes in permeable rocks; it sinks in at various rates until it finds something impermeable, like a layer of bedrock or dense clay. It then begins to collect, filling all the spaces it can until the land is full, so to speak, at which point the water spills into the streams. Water in a stream and water in the ground are both just rain—the same water, only at different places. And all water is pulled downhill by gravity. Movement through permeable rock is relatively slow. Movement in an open streambed is fast.

"And to the sea," I said.

"And to the sky, as well."

"And to the sky."

Most of the water on earth is in the oceans, she told me, ninety-six percent or more. Most of the fresh water is in the ice caps, most of that in Antarctica, something on the order of seven million cubic miles, enough to feed all the rivers in the United States for twenty thousand years. A lot of water is in the ground at any one time too. No one knows exactly how much, Connie said, but less than in the ice caps. Yearly, some one hundred thousand cubic miles of water leap into the atmosphere. Most of that falls back into the ocean, but enough falls back on land to feed the streams and rivers and fill the pores of the earth. Lakes get a lot—but all the lakes of the world do not hold as much water as the atmosphere holds in a year, perhaps half as much. And all the rivers in the world at any given moment hold only about three hundred cubic miles of water. The Mississippi might be a mile wide, but it's not a mile deep. It's but a ribbon of water and can't hold a bucket to the sky. Still, it carries something like forty percent of all the water brought to the sea in the United States each year.

"And here is Temple Stream," Connie said.

"Pretty," I said, pleased when she laughed.

The sun fell back behind the hill, and we grew chilly fast. Connie rose without my aid, held her arms out to the stream, said, "What gifts you bring us," and put her elbow up to be taken. My pickup was only ten years old then, but looked a junker next to her swanky Mercedes. Into which she easily climbed, closed her door, rolled her window down quickly.

She said, "Another Sunday, then?"

I said, "Another Sunday, yes."

"Hydrology," she said.

"Hydrology," I repeated.

"It's no laughing matter," she said, and burbled out an extended giggle of such merriment that I couldn't help but laugh too.

I said, "I'm happy I found you."

"Well," said Connie Nosalli, composing herself, pulling her wad of tissue from her sleeve, daubing her eyes, "that's what's so important about spending time where you want to be: you meet people of like mind, or at least you meet yourself."

FLASH FORWARD TO THE SPRING OF 2000. ONE EARLY APRIL morning, sleepless with her pregnancy, Juliet woke me, said: "We have to leave Ohio."

"Yes," I said.

"Promise me," she said.

I promised, just couldn't say when. I knew at least that we'd spend the summer in Maine—her last trimester—and that I'd be on leave from Ohio State again in the fall: the baby would be born in Farmington.

In the high stack of forwarded mail that had accumulated during our New York trip (and my solo mission to Maine) came a small padded envelope from Ms. Bollocks, the sort you buy at the post office: inside was a squashed Animal Crackers box containing three hundred forty extremely wrinkled, pawed, and greasy one-dollar bills along with two crumpled receipts, one for a Sawzall ferrule and blades (she'd shopped for these in Pennsylvania), one for the padded envelope. There was also a dim photocopy of a months-old electric bill, copiously marked in red pen, various amounts underlined, crossed out, added, and readded. A triple circle surrounded just the number thirty-four in the bottom line (at least two months unpaid), which in full was one hundred thirty-four. *Refrigerator!!!* was the only notation. The four dollars unaccounted for after that, I knew, was for the postage, rounded up. In the stack of mail, too, in a red-bordered envelope, lurked a shutoff notice from Central Maine Power. The cutoff date—which was not only Ms. Bollock's problem—had been March 20, first day of spring, the very day I'd prowled my own property on snow-shoes and watched the ice go out.

In the same pile of mail there was a postcard—image of a sand dune—no return address, Massachusetts postmark, de-teriorated handwriting: Connie Nosalli was ill. She didn't say what was wrong, or how serious (just like her, of course), and despite best intentions I didn't manage to write back: I'd get to it eventually.

In mid-May there was another letter from Farmington. I braced myself for more bad news. But no. The handwriting was backslanted, large, a child's. The paper was heavily wrin-kled, with a deep fold down the center, and the typing upon it was my own:

TO: BILL . . . FROM: COLLEEN CALLAHAN
FARMINGTON ME

1. As exactly as you can: where did you find your bottle?

   I FOUND THE BOTTLE 200 YARDS NORTH OF THE TWIN BRIDGES IN FARMINGTON.

2. On what date?

   MAY 7, 2000

3. In what circumstances? That is, what were you doing when you happened on your bottle?

   ME AND MY FAMILY WERE FIDDLEHEADING. AND I TOBBLED ACROSS THE BOTTLE.

4. Who are you?

I AM A STUDENT AT CASCADE BROOK SCHOOL,
FOURTH GRADE. MR. HARDY'S CLASS. I LIVE ON
PORTER HILL. I'M TEN YEARS OLD TOO!

5. Add any notes or information or anything at
   all you'd like.

WHERE DID YOU TOSS THE BOTTLE? WHO ARE
YOU? IS THIS THE ONLY BOTTLE? HOW MANY
HAVE YOU GOTTEN BACK? WILL YOU WRITE ME
BACK PLEASE? I WOULD LIKE YOU TO WRITE
BACK!

   THANKS! COLLEEN CALLAHAN

My first bottle to return hadn't gotten far: two hundred yards
north of the Twin Bridges, or something less than a mile from
home, not far from Connie Nosalli's log. Colleen Callahan's
address on Porter Hill made her a near neighbor—she lived in
one of the unprepossessing new houses recently built on lots
cut out of the extensive woods there. Sweet luck! Someone
had found a bottle. I wrote her back immediately, greetings
and thanks, answers to her questions (who am I?—good question), and said I'd see her in the summer.

Upstream Five
Russell's Mill to Our Place

THE FLAT STRETCH OF TEMPLE STREAM BETWEEN THE REM-
nants of the covered bridge at Russell's Mill Road and our
place is my home water. It's intervale land, and the stream is
mostly sluggish, forms several long pools between high mud
banks. The juncture of woods and stream and clearing makes
good habitat for wild things: in every corner there's a world.
My neighbor the dairy farmer owns the fields down there. First
haying is generally in late June—cutting, drying, baling—all of
it a one-man, one-tractor operation. The huge cylindrical bales
are beautiful to look at, upward of thirty per field per cutting in
good years, four fields of perhaps ten acres each, carved out of
the rich intervale a very long time ago, first by the stream,
which tends through ice and flood to keep such land open,
then by the Abenakis, then by the settlers of the Sandy River
Plantation. The bales on a misty morning are mirages, fugitives
from some soft-lit Monet.

Farmers and beavers have had a disagreement about this land for two centuries. Where the farmers see fields, the beavers see ponds. The farmers have long practiced something that's now called beaver management. But the beavers practice farmer management, a subtler game. All along the banks of the intervale stream are ramps and slides and bitten stumps and whole sections of cleared woods: beaver work. Bank lodges are the preferred construction in our stretch—harder to see than the familiar mound lodge, more secure, entrance tunnels dug into the mud underwater and leading back to underground rooms lined with sticks and patted with mud, watertight and weather tight except for clandestine air vents opening in among the roots and flowers of the forest floor.

On a midnight beaver expedition in the moderately high water of May 1995—placid full moon—I floated my canoe quietly downstream, paddling just enough to steer. Watching, listening, breathing quietly, I got the idea to spin the boat and sneak through the meanders ass-backward so as to show as little hull as possible until I could spy around the bend. At twelve-thirty A.M., paddling thus in reverse, I caught a raccoon washing a large egg (several of my neighbors keep chickens). At sight of me, the marauder calmly stuffed the prize in his mouth without breaking it, waddled up into the moonlit trees.

But I'd hung around enough evenings and early mornings without the dogs for at least the beavers to tolerate my presence; the days of tail-slapping insults were over. Still, I seldom got a long look. I'd devised this middle-of-the-night foray as a way to get more observation time. Even if it didn't work, I thought, there would be the consolation of bright moonlight on water. After the last bend downstream, in the pond just above the bedrock waterfall under the Russell's Mill bridge, I nosed the boat onto a gravel bar and sat there waiting. Not long—seconds—and a silent beaver swam by, then another. A third quietly dove and swam under the boat, surfaced quietly beyond with a brief backward look in my direction, sound of bubbles.

And in the bright moonlight, four or five or perhaps more animals (hard to differentiate individuals of the same size, therefore hard to count) went about their chores. The littlest one turned out to be two little ones, identical yearlings that I finally saw together. The biggest beaver (Wally's size) surfaced late and sat on the next gravel bar—not too close, thirty feet— and worked on a stick, peeling the bark methodically and noisily chewing it. Not entirely trusting, but tolerant, the animal stopped after each strip had been swallowed down and sniffed in my direction. The stick must have come from the remains of the winter cache—I hadn't heard any popple harvesting going on. The gentle animal dropped the stick in the water when the bark was gone, then spent a luxurious twenty minutes grooming. It sat up straight, patted itself aggressively around the belly, carefully wiped at its head with its little front paws like hands, patted its belly again, wiped its neck, and so on, patting and wiping till it had attended to every inch of fur.

Almost all beavers are born in late May or June (there are rare examples of fall litters), meaning that almost all beavers are Geminis (as is Juliet, and as are some five hundred million humans besides her), which must count for something. The litter size is one to five creatures—tiny, complete beavers, already showing their buck teeth. These kits nurse for up to two months. The female of the couple is the primary caregiver, mostly stays in the lodge to nurse and warm her babies. Before one month of age, they try the water and before long have learned to swim through the tunnels and out of the lodge. On the night of my canoe trip the colony's matriarch was most likely nursing kits back in the lodge.

The big beaver on the gravel bar—Papa? some bachelor uncle?—finished barking his stick and slipped into the water with it firmly in his teeth, headed upstream to the dam: more lumber. The yearlings swam by in tandem, up and down, back and forth, paying me no mind, disappearing underwater for minutes at a time. Then, in a particularly quiet moment, one of them startled me by leaping loony out of the water and onto the bank full speed, as if chased by a shark. The shark in the skit turned out to be his sibling, who appeared as suddenly with a hiss like laughter, leaping onto the gravel. The first character parried and leapt and bowled the second over, scurried into the water. The shark tumbled and hissed and leapt into the current after his prey, and the two of them sped at me, dove under the boat effortlessly, surfaced in the shallow water beyond, wrestled there a full minute in splashing abandon loud as a city fountain, dove suddenly and were gone, leaving moonlit ripples and plain silence.

THE TROUT LILY IS NAMED FOR ITS LEAF, A BROWN-MOTTLED, fishy shape that leaps from leaf-litter rapids in large schools throughout our woods, often through a layer of late snow. The flower—a limply epicene hand bedizened with sweet spots of red—appears later, fades quickly, dries, falls. The leaf loses its mottling as summer comes in, grows tattered, settles back into the forest floor. Later in summer, adventuring white roots show aboveground like so much strewn spaghetti as the essential plant below works to increase its domain.

I'd known the trout lily from childhood, though not by name. Inspired by Connie Nosalli's sense of precision, I went to look it up but found that the Peterson *Wildflowers* my mother had given me when I was in college had gone missing. At Twice Sold Tales (an inviting forest of used books in a beautiful old storefront in downtown Farmington), Peterson was between visits. But I found a stern little handbook dated 1910: hardcover, faded lettering, nice paintings of specimens, old-fashioned handwriting in brown fountain-pen ink on the flyleaf—*This book belongs to Muriel Winter.*

Right in the store I looked up my plant, discovered its name and, further (rightly or wrongly—there's still plenty of lively disagreement even in botany, the settled science), that it was a spring ephemeral. Spring ephemerals, the encyclopedic voice of the handbook explained, are plants that arise and bloom and fade in earliest spring, all before the leaf canopy above comes to rob light.

The trout lily led me to a closer inspection of the forest floor. I was pleased to find that nearly every odd leaf was familiar to me—not always by name, but by the simple expertise of boyhood, which was the last time I'd spent so much of each day just looking hard at everything. I'd had my own names for the little plants of the woods: "thumb things," for example, which fuzzy leaf I still recognize wherever I see it (field or sheep sorrel, according to Muriel's handbook—if you are a kid they are good to eat, if adult, quite sour); "frog belly" (or live-forever, a sedum—I used to put the thick leaves in my mouth to loosen the skin, then blow them up—thus the name); "eye-balls" (deep-purple berries, dusty bluish leaves, not in Muriel's book). I know more about these plants now, but keep the old names anyway. And as a boy I knew actual names, too, and the generic names of many things. My mother taught me a great deal informally on walks, and I'd been a Boy Scout, too, and been to summer camp, aced contest quizzes for prizes like lanyard kits: trillium, Indian pipe, club mosses, poison ivy, Jack-in-the-pulpit, wild violets (in yellow, white, purple, or blue), wild cucumber (those spiny fruits great for practical jokes), bluets (darling little light-facing stars, blue, white, or blue and white), coltsfoot (flower something like a dandelion, but no leaves around it, and for that reason called son-without-father in England, where it's from, a pharmacy escapee, once used as a cough remedy).

Later in life I wanted to know more, and book learning—even with Muriel over my shoulder—was slow and often inconclusive, so: I invited an old acquaintance named Nancy Prentiss to have a look at spring plants with me. She lives in Industry, the next town north of Farmington, on a settler farm set amid lots of good forestland that backs up Norton Mountain and the True Mountain Ridge. Her husband, Mark, is a cabinetmaker who's evolved into a log specialist—he searches out, cuts, dries, and sells only the most musical wood from Maine trees to makers of violins and guitars (few trees, even within a given species, are instrument quality, he told me: in the heyday of Maine logging, all work would stop when a melodious log came gonging down the flume, and it would be saved for the fiddle shop), also baseball bats (some of the heaviest hitters in the major leagues are using Mark's flawless maple now: it's hard as George Steinbrenner's heart).

Nancy is a field botanist. She earned her master's in marine invertebrates from the University of Maine at Orono, but her first love (and the subject of her B.A.) is botany. At seven she had a flower book like Emily Dickinson's, in which she pressed flowers from the abandoned fields around her family's house, each with the Latin names penned in her "little scrawny handwriting." She's tall and athletic, strong, walks with confidence—hard to imagine anything about her being little and scrawny. Driving, she watches the road verges. In fact, she's full of stories of rare and remarkable plant species encountered just down an inviting path during a lull in a Little League baseball game (she and her husband have three boys, who, the first time I met them, were dressed up as beavers for Halloween) or, by way of contrast, above the tree line in alpine arctic-tundra zones with one or another dean of area botany. I knew that Nancy was besieged by friends and fans and newspapers looking for identifications of odd plants, and indeed she sounded ambivalent on the phone when I called.

But she agreed to help me. And on a Friday morning, just before the start of her popular May-term field botany class at UMF, she rearranged her schedule to come identify Temple Stream ephemerals. Ephemerals, she had explained to me, grow fast from extensive root systems, throw leaves up, make all the photosynthetic nutrients they need for root growth and sustained life in a month or so, and then disappear from the upper world entirely. The rest of the year, that long period of leaf senescence, ephemerals spend in improving the root and slowly spreading. During the short leaf-and-flower season the plants are operating in cold temperatures, diverting nutrients to the brief green growth at a high rate that requires rich soil, the kind found in healthy forests.

Nancy arrived on that cool, bright May morning and pulled her sweater over her head immediately, dropped it back in her car, tucked her turtleneck into her blue jeans, fixed her shining auburn hair, put a special little necklace magnifier around her neck, all business, and finally gave me her cocked smile. She's got a good nose, solid chin, wore a look of harried confidence, but with something a little suspicious in her gaze (like a mom whose child is being awfully nice to her and taking an interest at last: What's this kid really want?).

She said, "I'm pretty busy this week. We'll have to be efficient!"

So I trotted to the barn for canoe paddles, and then we were off. Right behind the break in the stone wall that is the entrance to our little woods, she spotted a nodding, somewhat limp plant with pleasingly blue-green leaves standing all by itself: "Blue cohosh," she said. And, delicately, she showed me the unassuming flowers, which were mostly green, with a hint of yellow. "They have blue berries later," she said, and flipped expertly through her *Newcomb's Wildflower Guide* to show me dramatic blue beads that stand on upright stalks, each with its own stem, six or so in a group, delicious-looking but inedible, even mildly poisonous: the eyeballs of my youth!

"It's not an ephemeral," Nancy said, meaning *Let's stay focused.*

We moved on, eyes to the ground, me following, absently using my canoe paddles as walking sticks. A certain pretty-leafed plant caught her attention. "Three-lobed leaflets," she said, crouching to caress it fondly. "Tall meadow rue, which won't flower until midsummer. *Thalictrum pubescens*. Bursts of white stamens, no petals. Buttercup family. Not an ephemeral."

She pointed offhandedly to a very familiar arched stem of alternate ribbed leaves. She shook the stem for me. "Do you know this?"

Not intimately—but I recognized it.

"False Solomon's seal. And this one is false hellebore." Another familiar plant, large leaves on a thick stalk growing in a wet spot. "Could be called false skunk cabbage, too. People around here do call it skunk cabbage, but it's not. Skunk cabbage simply doesn't grow here."

I got a superior feeling because I'm from Connecticut and I know from skunk cabbage. Nancy is from Connecticut too. She built her wry smile efficiently—she'd found someone who liked a skunk cabbage story. "And people around here *know* I'm looking for skunk cabbage, in order to establish its range in Maine, and they call me all the time, and sometimes I go out to look, and it is always, always, false hellebore. But there *is* skunk cabbage down along the coast. I've seen it there."

False Solomon's seal and false hellebore are not ephemerals—they would be around all summer, the leaves getting more and more torn and frayed and broken, but hanging on. The false Solomon's seal flower is a tall white spray. The false hellebore flower is a greeny-yellow, star-shaped thing, and the plants get very tall, over my head in places. Why "false"?

"That just means they were once mistaken for something. There's no judgment implied."

The ferns aren't ephemerals, either, but there they were,

curling up from the ground, most at the fiddlehead stage. The first one we saw was a sensitive fern, which did look rather moody with its naked red stalk. Nancy pointed out the previous year's fertile fronds, which stood up dryly, tall brown sticks with long clusters of brown beads at their tops. I knew these fronds from Juliet's late-fall bouquets—they'd been in our blue vase all winter. To tell the truth, they looked like seventies-vintage Thai sticks, buds of serious marijuana tied to satay skewers that soldiers stuffed into their green underpants and brought back in prodigious quantities from Vietnam.

I moved toward the stream, could smell the stream, but Nancy walked only a few yards before she was squatting again. "Now, this is running dewberry," she said. "Or dwarf raspberry," a pretty, viny thing growing along the ground. When you stopped to look at it, it did have a sense of speed. I ventured the opinion that the flowers looked like strawberry blooms.

"Good, good," Nancy said. "Rose family. Raspberries, blackberries, strawberries, too. Dewberries are like underweight blackberries, very seedy and sour." She moved on, looking at everything. A vision of my mother came unbidden, my younger mom, that wavy dark hair crossing her eye, cigarette at her lips, 1959, saying the names of plants so tenderly. I basked in her warm presence, those rare chances to be with her alone: gentian, mustard, horse-balm, rose. Wild sweet william, she'd say, and that was a flower, and me.

Nancy said, "Club moss. Star moss. Nice mat of it there. These lichens are pretty. I find them interesting, but I'm waiting until I can invest some time in learning them. This is more blue cohosh. There's that false Solomon's seal again. Good rich soil. And, oh . . . a silvery spleenwort. And *this*." She kneeled, pointed out a small leaf pushing its way up through a hole in a large pad of moss. "This is Canada mayflower."

Nancy was visiting with old friends now, visibly relaxing. Almost dreamily: "See, it's just a leaf at this point, but it'll end up with two or three leaves on a stalk that will culminate in a white raceme, which is small individual flowers each attached to the main stalk by a little stem. Some people call it wild lily of the valley, and it grows like that, spreading, forming large patches if the habitat is any good. It'll bloom by late May."[1]

While she inspected the foliage, I poked around and found a hidden little white flower of my own, pointed it out tentatively.

"Good, good," Nancy said. "Oh, that *is* interesting."

I beamed.

She said, "Goldthread. *Coptis trifolia.*" She squatted down and dug quickly, carefully pulled a tangle of bright yellow rhizomes and roots up out of the leaf mold without detaching them from the soil: threads of gold indeed. She said, "I taught an elder hostel once and these great older folks knew all these important things we're forgetting. When I showed them goldthread, an elderly man—he'd been very bored—got all excited and said he remembered digging goldthread for a penny a pound for the pharmacist. These were all medicines then. Can you imagine what it would take to get a pound of this stuff?"

We passed through an old loggers' clearing filled in with

---

1. "May-Flower," by Emily Dickinson: "Pink, small, and punctual / Aromatic, low, / Covert in April, / Candid in May, // Dear to the moss, / Known by the knoll, / Next to the robin / In every human soul, // Bold little beauty, / Bedecked with thee, / Nature forswears / Antiquity."

bracken, a tall fern with strong stems, very upright. I said the name, proud of myself. Nancy merely nodded. "You know English novels? When they say they're off in the bracken? And Peter Rabbit? He was always lost in the bracken. It forms these dense colonies and gets waist-high. Good place to hide."

We moved on, but not far. I pointed out a nice patch of bluets, white flowers the size of blouse buttons standing on lank stalks no thicker than pine needles.

"The settlers called them Quaker-ladies," Nancy said. "Also innocence." And the flowers did seem to nod modestly, intent on the good.

We made a brief effort at hurrying, made some progress toward the stream, but Nancy stopped again: "Oh, you know this stuff," and bent to pluck a single leaf, which she popped in her mouth. "One of my very favorites. And good in salad."

"Trout lily!" I said triumphantly. I hadn't known they were edible.

The hundred or so feet to the stream was slow going—plant after plant, name by name. When we finally got there, Nancy gazed briefly at the high water. The sun reached us there and it was hot. A common yellowthroat, newly arrived, sang somewhere among the ice-flattened alders. The buds on all the trees were ripe to bursting, tinting the naked branches of the forest canopy across the way fresh green, a distinct softening of the sharp contrasts of winter. "Nice," Nancy said. But seconds later her head was down again and she was pointing out a single leaf with the size and shape and bend of a goose-quill pen. "*Clintonia borealis,* named after Governor Clinton of New York."

I had gone to college in Upstate New York, so knew something about the governor and ventured it, sounding like a schoolboy: "He was mayor of New York City for ten years at the beginning of the nineteenth century, then a U.S. senator and a failed presidential candidate, then sponsor and commissioner of the Erie Canal project, and author of the Twelfth Amendment to the Constitution."

Nancy dismissed all that with a wave of her hand: "He was an amateur botanist, too."

We ducked through the tangle of alders and red osier dogwood, eyes on the ground. A stick poked my ear. I said, "Here is some more Canada mayflower."

"Canada mayflower," Nancy said, straightening. She kept her voice efficient even while the muscles of her face relaxed in fondness for the plant, said, "Exactly right." And then she told me the next thing, the inefficient thing: "You know, I'll never ever forget where I was when I first saw it. Canoe trip with my family. And I had my little field guide and looked it up and there it was. I pressed it in my collection. Wrote the scientific name, *Maianthemum canadense*. Never forgot it."

She straightened, pushed along the stream into thicker undergrowth yet, said, "Hobblebush." She opened a passage through blackberry branches and alder shoots with her hands, stood intimate with the blooming shrub, pointed out the large clusters of white flowers. "Now, look at these—the big, showy flowers around the outside are just that, just for show—the real flowers are in the middle here." They were tiny indeed. "Honeysuckle relative, a Viburnum. A shrub. There's another Viburnum you probably have around here, northern wild raisin, it's called—has an edible fruit the settlers collected."

She crouched obliviously down through the scratching

branches of the hobblebush to show me further treasures, the first a tiny thing with drooping leaves: "Windflower. *Anemone quinquefolia*. Also known as wood anemone." Next, a slightly bigger plant, more upright: "Sessile-leaved bellwort, *Uvularia sessilifolia*. See how the leaves wrap the stalk? That's what *sessile* means. *Uvularia* means bell-like, referring to the flowers. Not an ephemeral. Also known as wild oats."

We broke out of the verdure and onto the old beaver path to the water, where my canoe waited. Aware of how much of her time I'd already taken, I suggested we cross the stream.

Nancy grinned. "So *that's* what the paddles are for."

"What'd you think?"

"Oh, I don't know. People are so eccentric. I just thought you carried paddles around."

New Englanders are always sure someone else is doing something stupid for show!

The stream is never terribly wide there, but had been quite high after rain. We dragged the boat down the beaver ramp through a small forest of false hellebore, big ribbed leaves on tall stalks, just the height to soak our thighs with dew. "Also called Indian poke," Nancy said, reaching into the hawthorn brambles and parting the thorny branches without a care to reveal nodding leaves. "More wood anemone," she said, then pulled gently at a tangle of vines: "And here's a wild cucumber." That brought her face-to-face with a prickly, spiky plant still sporting last year's red berries: "Yuck, barberry. Invasive!" She backed out, looked up, took a serrated heart-shaped leaf in hand. I might have guessed dogwood, but she didn't give me the chance: "See this? That's your wild raisin."

I slid the canoe into the water, tossed the paddles in, the one life jacket, and Nancy climbed aboard. I hopped in the stern and pushed off such that the current caught the bow, and we were quickly dragged downstream. Nancy paddled expertly, draw stroke, cross-draw, brought the bow into the current, and we headed up.

"I didn't expect a canoe ride," Nancy said happily. "I grew up canoeing—I was the kid who would go with my father most often. We'd go white-water canoeing with some die-hard canoeists from the Appalachian Mountain Club—caught the spring runoff on some *wild* rivers."

We pulled into a cow ramp. The day had grown balmy, nice breeze from the west. The banks are high there, where the stream has cut through the bottomland. We climbed up to the hayfield. "Buttercup," Nancy said. "Yuck. An alien from Europe." Long pause. "Well, now we're being encouraged to call them 'naturalized.' And I guess you can't ignore aliens in Maine. They make up a third of the plants around here. And I'm basically an alien here, too, being from Connecticut, so I shouldn't be so snobbish. I'm going to have to shift, not make them out to be such bad guys."

"Coltsfoot," I said, pointing to the familiar naked stalk and yellow flower growing in the middle of the path.

Nancy tried to hide it, but she distinctly made that face— coltsfoot an alien—a snobby grimace that went against her natural cheerful lineaments. We crossed the field on muddy tractor ruts. "Oak ferns," Nancy said as we reached the forest edge. "These are my favorite little ferns." They were small, like miniature bracken, delicately branched, stood erect on their dark stalks, leaves horizontal to the ground, a handsome little group.

We continued up the hill, left the tractor path halfway up, ducked into a long-uncut section of my dairying neighbor's forest: mixed hardwoods, tall and stately, a few white pines. We crunched through the dry leaf mold, eyes cast downward. "Well-drained habitat," Nancy said. "Depauperate, meaning: kind of *barren*. Let's move." She pointed down through the wood to the edge of the hayfield, a large boggy area, greener. As we made our way, she said, "This whole ridge was probably in cultivation up to fifty years ago or so, seventy years. So you're not going to find unbroken speciation, undisturbed forest soils—none of that."

The second we reached the edge of the wet area she crouched to caress a small plant with triple-lobed, egg-shaped, serrated leaves hiding amid spring-pale poison ivy, which we both ignored: "This one is toothwort, a toothache medicine, *Cardamine diphylla*. It'll bloom soon. It's not an ephemeral. Also called crinkleroot, guess why. Worts were medicines. The word stems from the Old English for *root*."

The ground beneath our feet grew wet, then wetter, and we slogged into a thick stand of balsams and hemlocks rising from rocky soil, ferns coiling up from every hump and crevice, every rock a moss garden. Several balsam firs had fallen over and their root masses stood in arcs like dark crèches. Nancy said, "This is a nice rich spot here. And oh! Oh, look." She hurried to where the ground rose into a dry hump not twenty feet from the field's bright edge. The hump was covered thickly by tall leaf-pairs newly emerged, pale green, not so much goose quills as angel wings. Nancy knelt among them: "Remind you of

Clintonia? I've made that mistake before. But do you know what these are? Let me try that knife of yours."

I handed it over. Quickly she dug down along the white, deep stem of one of the plants. She rooted with the knife blade and with her expert fingers a long, careful time, eventually came up with a slender white bulb. "Wild leek." She cut it and held it to my nose and it was good—smelled of garlic and onion both. "Oh, delicious," she said. "These are really rare. Very special. They speak of a habitat long undisturbed. And they're true ephemerals, Bill."

A mosquito buzzed in my ear, landed on my neck—the first of spring. The sun bore through the budded branches above us and warmed my shoulders, seemed indeed to warm my soul. The field was bright with sunlight, just ten paces distant, but a universe away. Far across those brilliant grasses lay the bed of the stream. The sky was bluer for the juxtaposition with the high branches of the firs around us. The fragrance of the leek lingered and I felt myself urging toward the light, toward the open, even as Nancy bent lower, moved deeper into the bog and darkness—the leeks had won her over. She muttered, "See how green the floor of the forest is here? I knew it. From the ridge this just looked *bold.*"

We mucked along through vernal puddles and rotted leaves, in and out of the warmth of the sun, over an old stone wall, around fallen firs, under a broken popple trunk, finding specimens of nearly all the plants we'd seen so far, ignoring the aliens more and less vehemently (I am one to quickly adopt the prejudices of a teacher). Then a new one, just getting started, two different kinds of leaves, one heart-shaped, one with sharply elongated toes: "Small-flowered crowfoot. Now, that's a native. It's a buttercup, but not the European that you see everywhere in the fields here—it'll bloom in June."

Another deeply lobed leaf lurked a little further along, and I would have missed it without my guide, mistaken it for crow-foot. Nancy said, "Wild geranium."

I said I had some in my garden.

"Oh, no. People think so around here, but what you've got is actually just a garden variety—that purply stuff that makes great mounds of vegetation? That was cultivated long ago. But this is truly wild. It's called spotted cranesbill. *Geranium maculatum*. The flower has a bit of a beak, thus the common name. Very special."

I felt again the sunny pull of the field, so near, but Nancy crept yet deeper into the bog. "Foamflower," she called. I trotted to catch up to her. "I'm looking for one in bloom for you. . . . And here we *are*." Tall fuzzy stem, flowers on a raceme, only one open. "It will make a show," she said. Then, with her grin: "Not a true ephemeral."

We climbed over the remains of a tremendous yellow birch trunk, skirted a pool by hopping rock to mossy rock to stump to hummock. Everywhere I stepped I was suddenly aware of the forest floor, of what I was trampling, could suddenly name the victims of my boot, could not always avoid stepping on some lovely flower, tender plant.

Abruptly, my guide was splashing off across the rocks in the direction of a certain wide hummock. I followed, Watson after Sherlock Holmes, under the branches of a small beech still rattling with last fall's dried leaves. At the hummock—an old stump buried in moss—Nancy crouched, sighed, gently

tipped up a tiny palmate leaf for me to admire: "Dwarf ginseng. The prettiest thing you've ever seen. So fragile. One of
my favorites. *Cutest* little thing! So *fleeting,*" she said, meaning
that in their fleetingness all plants are ephemerals, despite
whatever official classification. I found myself wondering
if Earth itself is but something in bloom for a billion-year
moment.

That grin. The plants were indeed cute, each leaf whorled
around a slight stem and divided into three leaflets like charms
on a bracelet, two plants on each side of the hummock, which
was a fairy-ground. We searched the immediate vicinity then,
but found no further examples of the dwarf ginseng. Those
few, those four, about to bloom, showed precious beads like
pearls, buds for the flowers to come. "Any day now," Nancy
said. "Oh, the flower is so delicate." She opened her Newcomb's
guide to show me the bloom as it would soon be, a tiny explosion of white flowers. "It's in its own family. Araliaceae. This
is *Panax—P. trifolium,* for the three leaves. Very rare around
here. Oh, you are lucky to have this habitat nearby."

Without Nancy, I would have trampled the uncommon little plants without notice. We lingered over the ginseng awhile,
stood up from it only reluctantly, climbed back over the stone
wall, back under the broken popple, back around the vernal
pool on stepping-stones and stumps, under the reaching
branches of a white birch, and into the field and bright sunlight. Three hours had passed since we'd crossed the stream,
three hours like no time at all. We struck out through timothy
grass to the water, trying to love the naturalized buttercups as
we went, the settlers' clovers. At streamside we walked the

wrong way to get to the canoe—I was following Nancy; she was following me. But the diversion brought us to another rich plant patch, up in an uncultivated area on the high bank of the stream, wild leek abounding, that new friend.

"Ah," Nancy said, "and this is bloodroot." This one I knew well from a patch deep in our backyard. It was in bloom, the single wide leaf of each plant folded around the single stem as if presenting to the world of sky the single white flower. Nancy pulled up a specimen, broke the root, dabbed a little of the pale blood on the back of my hand by way of etymology.

"Okay, and here." Just at the crumbling edge of the bank, the stream flowing fast below us, my guide squatted once again and cupped a tiny plant, showed me the tender flowers— white, five petals, lovely striations of pink on each. "Spring beauties—that's the common name. *Claytonia virginica*.

"These are true ephemerals."

Happy too, I stopped to inspect the beaver stump I'd seen chickadees attending—and found a nice cavity and a few shreds of nesting material, but not the actual nest. Nancy, no bird head, called me over to something more important: "Here we go," she said. "Dutchman's breeches. Another true ephemeral. You look all day, and finally here they are." This one had a nice, well-divided leaf, looked tender indeed. "There will be no sign of these guys in a few weeks." She splayed the foliage over her hand, unfolded her necklace magnifier for the first time that morning, squatted down to look closer. "So fleeting," she murmured.

I squatted with her, head to head, shared the eyepiece back and forth, found the next plant, shifted on our popping knees to look. The flowers were puffed, pretty, creamy yellow, shaped something like their relative the bleeding heart, two distinct horns making the legs of a little pair of short pants. We looked and looked more.

I was a boy, a boy with his mother, and Mom knew the world.

Summer Solstice

FINALLY IT WAS JUNE. WE PACKED UP THE OHIO HOUSE, stuffed the dogs into the car, waved good-bye to our acceptably bizarre subletter, drove home a thousand miles via two motels: Juliet was six months along and couldn't ride forever. Wally whined as we pulled into the mouth of our road. Desi joined him, having caught the scent of Temple Stream. And here was the house, smaller than in memory, in more desperate need of paint, more ramshackle, hardscrabble, isolated, forlorn. White planks from the long horse fence I'd built along the road with such effort and expense lay broken in the grass—snowplow damage. Ms. Bollocks hadn't done the usual repairs, always in favor of leaving signs of our foolishness in returning to this godforsaken place. We pulled into the empty driveway, sat there awhile staring at the sobering tableau, then let the dogs free. They exploded into the yard, dog delirium, dog joy.

On the kitchen table, a crayoned note blamed me for the

fence and explained that as the electric bill was clearly in my
name, no money was owed by her, this on top of a numbered
sheet of four botched phone messages in a huge, childish hand:

1. SIXTY MINUTES PRODUCER BUT I DIDN'T HAVE
   A PENCIL
2. JULIET'S MOTHER OR FATHER WANT A
3. SOMEONE WHO HAVE A CONTRACT OUT ON
   YOU
4. A MAN CALLED

In the freezer compartment of our fridge we found candle
butts melted into our best little dishes (this in response, I
guessed, to my complaint about the gobs of candle wax on bare
tables the previous year, which in turn had been a response to
my own lackluster apology for getting candle wax on the picnic
table Ms. Bollocks had left in our yard the year before that).
In my top dresser drawer I found a fancy, unopened penis-
enlargement kit that must have cost plenty, message unclear. In
the wood stove we found a season's worth of densely packed paper trash, primarily pizza boxes. In the woodshed, a thoughtful-
seeming pile of firewood turned out to be an old telephone pole
preserved in chimney-clogging, seam-dripping creosote, carefully cut, split, and stacked. In the bread box, still in the plastic
bag I'd zipped closed with my own hands six months before . . .
the corn muffins we'd left her in welcome, encased in green
mold so dark it was black. In the oil tank: nothing.

SOLSTICE, ROUGHLY TRANSLATED, MEANS SUN STANDS STILL. And the sun stood still at the notch of Spruce Mountain. Slowly, under its influence, we opened like flowers. I stopped at the diner for blueberry pie, asked Zimbabwe to tell Earl we were back if she saw him: time to get our firewood in—we'd be staying all fall. I felt myself breathe again, began to see past the scruffier elements of our surroundings to the sublime. We swam in the local ponds, we waded in the stream, we brought lobstahs and steamahs home from Dunham's Lobster Pot and ate them on the deck at sunset. Sitting back-to-back on the couch, we read terrifying pregnancy and parenting books, compared notes in hushed tones. I was going to have to vacate my studio upstairs, make room for a crib and rocker, changing table, toys. Time and space were no longer ours.

On the twenty-second of June, first day of summer, I made the enjoyable walk out to the mailbox, stood in the sun sorting the stack, came to a spotted envelope addressed with my own rubber stamp, and stamped again, in red: RECEIVED IN BAD CONDITION. I started when I realized what it was: one of my bottle notes, this one mailed back to me by one John Atwood, of Fairfield, Maine.

1. As exactly as you can: where did you find your bottle?

   APPROX: 1 MI JUST BELOW THE SHAWMUT DAM

2. On what date?

   JUNE 19, 2000

3. In what circumstances? That is, what were you doing when you happened on your bottle?

BASS FISHING
P.S. YOUR BOTTLE LEAKS.

The Shawmut Dam is on the Kennebec River just above Waterville and more than sixty river miles from our place, an hour by car on good roads: I've fished down there. My bottle had made it over the Davis Mill dam in roaring water, taken the harrowing gravel-pit turn into the Sandy, bobbed past Pierpole's camp in Farmington Falls, surfed the rocky white water of New Sharon, negotiated the series of wide meanders where the Sandy meets the Kennebec, raged eight or more miles through the Bombazee Rips, spun through the Central Maine Power turbines housed in the huge dam at Skowhegan, spun again in the Great Eddy of the Kennebec, spurted thence fourteen miles to Shawmut Dam and its complement of fearsome turbines, finally pulling up in some reeds after the riffles near Goodwin Corner, nine months of travel to reach its fateful meeting with John Atwood, who'd only come for bass.

JULIET AND I BURN ABOUT SIX CORDS OF FIREWOOD A YEAR, releasing quickly the carbon that nature would have released through the slower fires of death, rot, or ingestion. The first year in the house, I bought our wood what is called tree-length, sixteen-foot logs of rock maple, beech, a little oak, a little ash, one stick birch, all dropped on the grass of my side yard from a log truck with a boom and claw in a neat, imposing pyramid that would promise months of morning work, but only twenty-five dollars a cord. You balance on the pile in ear protectors and chain-saw eighteen-inchers by the hour, slowly diminishing the mountain. And then comes the splitting. I like the heft of my splitting maul, the crack of the wood, the rhythm that develops, the sore muscles. My friend Bob Kimber uses nothing but an axe, expertise I don't have, and came to help me keep pace with the season that first year. But mostly I was on my own, an hour each summer morning of hard labor: free workout, no gym. Finally, there's the stacking, a log-by-log process of bringing the wood into the shed and piling it such that air can circulate between the splits. Last comes the burning, an armload at a time, the summer's seemingly unassailable pile slowly succumbing, all the way through to the last fire on a rainy day in June, just before the next load of wood arrives.

The year we bought the woods next door, I took all our fuel from it, thinning and culling about as much as I thought the small acreage could sustain. That, of course, was much more work than tree-length, very difficult on my own with only a chain saw and peavey pole, wheelbarrow for a skidder. I learned how dangerous the work is, and what poor firewood popple makes, and how much carpenter ants like black cherry.

After a year of tree-length and a year on the woodlot, I was quite ready for what's called "cut, split, and delivered," for which the going rate was ninety dollars a cord, leaving only the stacking and a little recreational splitting for me. I began buying from Earl, who delivered my wood for the couple of years before I took the Ohio State job, excellent loads of well-cut and uniformly split hardwoods. (When his first delivery was complete, I started to write him a check. He said, "Now, what am I supposed to do with that?" He didn't believe, he said, in "banking relationships," had never had a bank account of any kind.) But when he learned we were headed for Ohio, that was the end of it. He let it be known he could no longer supply us, not even a small amount. Among flatlanders, in Earl's estimation, there were two types: summer yups, and year-round summer yups. Year-rounders you might tolerate. But Earl wasn't in the business of summer yups, no-suh. By then the firewood was mostly Ms. Bollocks's problem in any case, and she had her own ways of obtaining it.

I had the idea that Earl would reconsider with the baby coming, and our staying through the fall. And, having put word out at the diner, I waited, reasonably sure he'd turn up to talk turkey. So I knew exactly who was calling at five-thirty on a Monday morning in July when Juliet and I were awakened by the savage blast of an air horn not thirty feet from our bedroom window.

Earl made use of an enormous borrowed dump truck for his firewood deliveries, had to make his rounds before the trucker's day started. I leapt into pants and a T-shirt, raced out into the yard, confirmed my hunch: there was Earl, up high in the cab of the truck, his size undiminished by its dimensions; only Earl could make a dump-truck cab looked cramped. "Got your three-cord," he said, his only greeting, though we hadn't seen one another for nearly a year.

Well, good man, he'd figured out on his own that he should halve my order. I said, "Good morning, Earl." I was genuinely happy to see him, felt a surge of friendship, a sense that we'd come some distance together despite our differences. The sky lightened by the minute, deep blue to azure then pink, great streaks of light rising in the east ahead of the sun, the rosy fingers of dawn, as Homer had it.

Earl said, "Must be nice sleeping in while the rest of us work!"

I patted my hair down, squeezed it into a rough ponytail, gave him a welcoming smile. "How've you been?" I said.

"Now, that's an intellectual's query!" No sense of comradeship, even after nearly a decade of interaction.

"You've been fine. Now, Earl. Listen to this. Two of our bottles have come back."

Quick: "You could have got ten cents for those."

"One from the Twin Bridges—not too impressive, I admit—the other from all the way down at Shawmut Dam. Now, how about that?"

He looked at me a long time. His eyes were distant-mountain blue in the pink light, and I could not see into them. He said, "Could you move these cars?"

"Let me get my keys," I said.

"Make hay," he said. "I've only got the truck an hour more. No time for gollynosters." The sun broke the ridge to the east, lit him as if he were a player arriving onstage.

Upstairs in our bedroom, Juliet was already back asleep in her nest of pillows. I pat-searched my dresser, found my keys, looked out the window at the load of wood, pleased it had gotten here in whatever fashion. But something looked funny. The load was nearly glowing in the dawn light, none of the familiar hard gray of maple bark. Wait a minute—most of the visible wood was *white birch*. Birch smells good and burns hot, but it burns quickly. And what else was in that load? Strips of bark seemed to hang on some of the darker logs. Was that *cedar?* Cedar won't season timely, burns like a torch once it does: truly horrible firewood. And from the view above I thought I saw an awful lot of small sticks.

Back outside, I said, "Earl, let me get a look at this load before you dump it, okay?"

"Not okay," said Earl. "I've got another load to do up the hill here. You move those cars for me."

"I smell pine," I said.

"Maybe a stick or two," said Earl, squinting into the new sunlight.

"I see birch," I said.

"Good autumn firewood, Professor, and you won't be around further, from what I gather, so not to moan."

A decorative chrome ladder was bolted to the side of the truck's cab and I climbed it so I could look at the load. This put Earl and me nearly face-to-face. He scowled as I craned to see the firewood, which was an even worse load than I'd thought, generously shot through with cut pine branches and hunks of slab wood.

I said, "Earl, it's all birch and softwood. There's still needles on some of those branches!"

"You get down off there and move those caz, Professor." His face, already pink with the dawn, surged red.

I said, "I won't pay for this, Earl."

He spun such that I thought he was reaching for something to hit me with, but he only put the truck in gear. It leapt backward with a sigh of hydraulics, then forward up the street with a lurch and roar. I fell down the ladder a couple of rungs and bailed out, hopping off into the roadside ditch as the truck gathered speed. Earl pulled it up short, the brakes hissing and squealing, threw it in reverse, and squeezed the truck expertly into the narrow opening of our second little driveway. I heard his door slam, prepared myself for a loud negotiation. But then there was another great sigh of hydraulics. Suddenly, the dump body was tilting. Before I could shout, before I could gather my thoughts, and with a sound like a herd of panicked hooves, my load of wood plummeted out of the dumper, right in the face of my pickup. Earl, not a word, got back in his cab and pulled it forward, jolting the brakes a couple of times to get the last portion of the cordage to fall, and then just kept going, dump body raised, roared up the road and over the rise toward Temple Village.

Upstream Six
Our Place to Temple Village

YOU CAN'T TALK ABOUT THE TEMPLE WITHOUT TALKING ABOUT rock. Our stream is eons younger than its bed, which was once mud on the ocean floor. The scoops and whorls and screws and potholes carved into the slumped, folded, compressed, and lifted mudstone—our local bedrock—are the handiwork not of the stream, but of a down-spiraling, corrosive slurry of meltwater and rock flour pouring under pressure from crevices in the receding glacier, the same rough beast that left us our landscape a mere twelve to fourteen thousand years ago. Soil filled in the scraped rock only slowly as lichens and erosive rains did their work. When there was enough, plants took hold, creating yet more soil from carbon in the air and from plain sunlight, and eventually the forests took hold. Hard to imagine, but the glacial ocean made its most inland incursion right at our doorstep. If we'd been living here twenty thousand years ago, the top of the glacier would have been a mile over

our heads. And a mere twelve thousand years ago, not long before the arrival of the first humans, our land would have been
beachfront property.

In the Temple section upstream from our house the forest
is dense, the bedrock—exposed by the stream—well carved.
Juliet and I had walked or skied that stretch often, and on a
hot morning in early August 2000, eight months pregnant and
full of new energy, she got a notion to take a dip up there in
one of our favorite potholes. The stream was low after a period
of rainless weather and I wondered if there'd be enough water
for more than a foot bath, but was happy for the walk with my
girl. We crossed our neighbor's first field in roasting sun, found
the stream a mere brook, walked through it like nothing where
just that past spring it would have carried us away and
drowned us, then swished sweatily in tall grass through the
second field and along the stream on that side till we reached
the forest. At the margin, beavers had toppled two large black
cherries (the bigger one twenty-two inches in diameter at the
bole) and abandoned them, perhaps because they hadn't
fallen in the water, perhaps because black cherry wood is bitter. The stumps had been so overworked that they were sculptures, busts with blank, chewed faces and points on their
heads. The dogs sniffed them abundantly as we caught up.

And into the woods, where an unkempt snowmobile trail
follows the stream, climbing incrementally through hillocks
and ridges and humps left by the glaciers: cool and dark and
open understory, mossy glades, tiny brooks and rivulets heading to the stream from springs. That morning there was much
birdsong, hermit thrush foremost. Juliet plodded along steadily,

all-terrain momma, belly first, a pair of my jeans slung low on her butt. The sunlight fell crashing into the cut the stream made, underlit the heavy canopy of beech and red oak, basswood and sugar maple, bigtooth aspen and wizened yellow birch, canopy specimens that climbed the hill there, shading bracken and New York ferns, Jack-in-the-pulpit, tall meadow rue, false Solomon's seal, all of it rising from the thick leaf litter amid a few scraggly, sun-starved saplings, interspersed balsam nurseries, an occasional hophornbeam tree, and boulders, boulders strewn everywhere, covered in mosses and lichens, glacier-broken and glacier-tumbled examples of the local metamorphic rock: schist and mudstone. Every tenth boulder or so looked different, yellow and round. These were erratics, rocks that the glaciers carried in from distant places that geologists can determine with minute accuracy.[1]

The stream flows through a tumble of rocks, the same mixture of large and small and infinitesimal that I recognized from the layer under the topsoil in my gardens, a near-sterile matrix called glacial till.

Juliet and I passed great old trees that had fallen and become host to bright fungi. Along the trail, streamside, shadeside, all was humid, damp, bursting, even in the midst of drought. The

---

1. Tom Weddle, a geologist from the Maine State Geological Survey who happened to be in the midst of making a surficial materials map of Temple Stream, told me on a hike that the yellow erratics are from significantly west (and a little south). "Quite a trip under a mile of ice." He was interested in the light-gray clay at the end of our road, too: "Here's the ocean bed. Glacial Marine mud. Presumscot Pleistocene!" Upstream, he pointed out a house under construction: "When they were digging the foundation a few months ago I happened to be driving by and stopped and told 'em what I was doing and I got to look in the excavation. A basement hole is like a window on the history of the planet."

switch across our neighbor's property line into a dense pine forest was from light to dark, from broadleaf to needle, the result of an old cut and purposeful tree-farm planting.

We made our way to a small, man-made clearing filled with bracken, then into a dense hemlock glade over the stream, dark, atmospheric old trees clinging untouched to a large rock formation above a diminutive gorge. Among the drooping branches someone had set up a living room *en plein air*—nice wicker furniture, bright white, two chairs and a couch, smart little tea table, the lot rescued, no doubt, from consignment to the dump. The effect was uncanny, as if elves had visited the place since our last trip. We made like it was no big surprise, just in case the little people were watching—best not to let them see us puzzled. Juliet, in fact, sat in one of the chairs, put her feet up on the table.

I wanted to keep going, though I knew the path would leave the stream soon, wanted to bushwhack along the water and show Juliet the old field where once I'd come upon a marijuana patch among high weeds—I'd scrammed, scared of a sudden meeting with either cops or grower. And past that, almost to Temple Village, the dogs and I had crossed the stream on a pretty little dam, climbed a steep bank that crunched underfoot with what turned out to be tin cans, most of them mere webs of rust. But then there was a Pabst Blue Ribbon can with church-key holes. And an enameled pot, spotted by rust, but still a pleasing blue. Below the metal layer were the heavier items: wine bottles, old dishes, car windshields, broken crockery, broken china, parts of bottles, the deeper the older, no doubt the source of all the potsherds the stream coughs up down by my place, all the beach glass, all the rusty fragments and leather shoe soles, porcelain doll arms, billiard balls, and bottles (Johnson's American Anodyne Liniment, Kerry's Balsam, Dr. Miles Remedy for the Heart).

You can't push someone who's about to give birth. I took the elfin couch, stretched out.

"I feel this kid waking up," Juliet said. She bent with some difficulty to untie her hiking boots, pulled them off, stripped her socks off too. I did the same. The moss there was deep and thick and preternaturally cool, sprouted pixie rings of brown boletes like catchers' mitts propped on stems. Juliet dropped her pants, her underwear, pulled her shirt and bra over her head, stepped out of the pile of clothes as from a chrysalis, lumbered calmly to the rocks, climbed down to the stream, waded in, her skin fairly glowing in the sun. When had her hair gotten so thick and lustrous?

I followed, stripping as fast as I could manage. Together, we waded upstream to our tub, a double pothole, something of a figure-eight open on the upstream end, the Temple current slow but still overflowing a dam of trapped rocks on the downstream end, room for two, serendipitous glacial sculpting, the product of merely tens of years—not hundreds or thousands, as I had once thought. These tubs would have been the bottom of a particularly fierce vortex spiraling down through nearly a mile of ice. The ripples on the bedrock all around were like marks on a beach at low tide, and, in fact, that's what they were: beach ripples frozen in time four hundred million years back. The glaciers of several ice ages had worked on that blank page, leaving long gouges made by dragged pebbles.

Plenty of history, all written on a Seboomook pavement above Temple Stream, four hundred million years of rock, two million years of ice, then the ocean receding, polar bears and walruses moving along north, then the first people arriving from continents far away, then more from other continents, then wars and disasters and love and peace, now us.

Juliet took my hand and stepped into her tub ladylike, if ponderously, lay back in the water in hard sunlight. I sank in, too, and we let the cool current wash over us, our goodly twin bellies looming out of the water like islands, our toes meeting at the waist of the pothole eight.

EARL'S LOAD OF FIREWOOD LOOMED IN OUR SECOND DRIVE-way, blocking my truck. It wasn't as bad as I'd thought, but it wasn't wonderful, either. Still, what was there would see us through the fall. I began to feel bad about my part in this latest *pas de deux* with Earl. To get it off my mind, I put the full cash price of three cords in an envelope (no bills bigger than a ten, as was his rule) and left it for him at the diner without a note.

So opening our dented mailbox to post some outgoing letters one morning just a week later I was surprised to find a package in there, neatly wrapped in grocery-bag kraft paper and old-fashioned string, no stamp (Earl refused tape and other plastic products and all government relationships, so he said). On the face of it was my name in teacher's-pet handwriting that I recognized as Earl's. I turned my face away as I unwrapped the Grape-Nuts box inside, just in case it might explode (such was the state of my feelings about Earl). In the Grape-Nuts box was no bomb but a balled pair of socks, Nike swoosh showing, the

very pair I'd loaned Earl some years before to warm his foot after his accident. The socks had been well worn but were freshly
cleaned, Laundromat fragrant, and inside was a surprise: cash,
exactly half the amount I'd left for him.

THE AMERICAN STORY FROM THE NINETEENTH CENTURY FOR-
ward is one of abandoned farmsteads. The life of the small
farm is so precarious, so vulnerable to accidents of weather or
economies, so conducive to illness, injury, or madness, so sus-
ceptible to cold hearts and greed, that it's amazing we have
ever had food to eat. Where the farming was easy—Ohio, for
example, and further west and south—every falter was met
with foreclosure, every foreclosure by a sale, every sale by con-
solidators and developers, finally reaching the corporate fellow
who sees no profit in sentiment and burns down the old house
and barns to make room for the center-pivot irrigation. The
town dies next, asphyxiated. Where the farming was difficult,
as in most of New England (you don't often see large-scale
rolling irrigation equipment here—the land's too lumpy), the
end of individual farms came more slowly, because no one was
waiting in line to prey on the desperate.

Early photos around Temple Village show a nearly treeless
place. The intervale is in crops straight to the alder-lined
stream, with a single grand old elm presiding. Temple Stream
cuts and fills and meanders its way through two nearly un-
shaded miles of bottomland. The village is bare too, except
for big maples in the dooryards of well-kept houses. The

surrounding hills have been cleared of forest and cultivated, too; the fields rise to the steeps, mostly hay, a little corn. Enormous stray erratics stand exposed. Smaller rocks are piled everywhere, or built into handsome walls at property lines. In the distance, farm fields and farmhouses and large barns and even storage silos appear in neat relation to one another, all of them gone now, detectable on side-hill bushwhacking missions through thick forest as rock-lined holes in the woods, as phantom apple groves in the midst of maple and oak, as lonely blooms of lilac or roses or lilies where once a front door opened onto gardens: gone, gone. The photos show Temple life and Temple culture: cider press, sawmill, icehouse, church and store, busy adults and eager children.

Temple, Maine, was first settled by Europeans in 1796, after life in Farmington was well under way. The town was named Abbottsville, after its founder, Jacob Abbott, and the stream that ran through it, Abbott's Stream. As quickly as 1803, the settlement had grown to thirty-eight families. The town was incorporated at that time as Temple, named after the town of Temple, New Hampshire, where many of the settlers had come from.

From the start, Temple Stream powered mills, and in fact Temple Village was often referred to as Temple Mills. Eventually there were at least four grist and sawmills, with at least one operating continuously for 130 years, most in the village. Also along the stream was a clay pit, a brick kiln, a tannery, a bark mill (which produced tannin for the tannery), a potash house, a shingle mill, a spool-stock factory, a stave maker's shop, a cider press, and a slate quarry.

Oxen were indispensable, and skiing or orienteering in the

hills around the village, one still encounters amazing feats of down-home engineering, a great double stone wall, for one example, that today runs a mysterious mile through plain forest.

The first exodus from Maine and from Temple Village was in 1816, the year without a summer. Late in 1815, the Indonesian volcano Tambora exploded, expelling fifty cubic miles of material and creating an enormous column of fine ash (the noise of the explosion was reportedly heard nine hundred miles distant, which would be like hearing something in Maine that had happened in Ohio). The ash spread around the globe and shaded the sun over North America for months. Some fifteen thousand farming people left Maine for the Western Reserve under the influence of Ohio Fever: flat, rich farmland, no rocks.

Maine had been the New England frontier, and the belief in the future of that frontier kept people tied to their farms. But by the mid-nineteenth century, faith had faltered. In a second great exodus, people left in droves, the young particularly, this time for the burgeoning cities, a movement coincident with the rise of industry, and, for better or worse, a phenomenon one can observe today in "developing" countries around the world.

By the end of World War II, there was really little left in Temple to call a town. The dwindling population was aging—was, in fact and on average, elderly. Enter Richard Donald Pierce, newly graduated from the Andover Theological Seminary down in Massachusetts, who took on the job as pastor to the two surviving churches of Temple, churches that could afford him for summers only, and occasional autumn weekends. One, the Congregational Church, had erected its meetinghouse on the banks of Temple Stream in 1832. While in Temple, Pierce worked assiduously on the Boston College doctorate that would get him out of there. His dissertation, "A History of Temple, Maine: Its Rise and Decline," is an uneven, ponderous work, but thorough and impressive in its research and notable for its prickly opinions of Temple people and prospects. The chapter titles from the second half of the manuscript give a sense of the tone: "Economic Decline," "Population Decline," "Agricultural and Industrial Failure," "Institutional Failure," "Sociological Decline." In the last chapter, "Future Prospect," he uses the word *disaster* to sum things up.

Pierce is trenchant on the subject, harsh on his neighbors:

> When it becomes the established trend decade after decade for the more alert, more intelligent, and more ambitious young men and women to abandon their home town and move westward or cityward, the resultant effect upon the local community becomes obvious. Evolution is predicated on the survival of the fittest; the survival of the unfittest explains in large measure the appalling decadence evident in so many of the back towns of New England.
>
> The rural towns of New England over an extended period lost their radical aggressive blood to the west and to the urban centers and they have become so preponderantly conservative and fearful of change that the result has encouraged cultural and social stagnation.

Who can resist a bitter historian?

The population of Temple peaked around 1840, never quite reaching a thousand. The decline from there is swift. The 1850 census records seven hundred eighty-five, the 1860 census, seven hundred twenty-six. The Civil War was a factor, of course. In Temple, as everywhere in the North, there was much public discussion of the issues of that conflict: slavery, oppression, patriotism. President Lincoln called for one thousand Maine men to volunteer. Pierce observes that the pressures in such a small town were tremendous: "Slackers were scorned and volunteers were cheered." And more important, the army was "an open door to the outside world." In the end, forty-five men who might otherwise never have left Maine in their lives marched from Temple to muster in Farmington for the trip south. Thirteen were killed.

Temple's population in 1870 was six hundred forty.

Soon after that, farm machinery arrived—expensive behemoths that would have worked much better on flat fields. Farmers took loans they couldn't hope to pay, bought tractors to work on land that simply couldn't compete with that freely available in Ohio.

By 1880, the population of Temple is recorded as five hundred eighty.

Those who stayed bought farms on the cheap from those who left, consolidating fields and buildings into huge, ungainly holdings. Clearing land was no longer an issue, and in any case, all that building in the treeless prairies out west had made the price of lumber peak. Suddenly a woodlot was of more value than a hayfield. So the fields were let go, one by one, acre by acre (a process that is still going on, as local farmers give up on haying or even farming and homeowners give up on hobby fields), became untended pasture, then scrub, then forest once again. The old homesteads—clapboard capes and federals fitted out with hard-won windows, field-stone basements, granite sills, large barns, hand-dug wells, stables, corrals, stone walls, orchards—went unoccupied, col-lapsed to rot in mere decades, or burned. Old barns were torn down and used to repair and enlarge the few remaining.

By 1890, the population was four hundred seventy. By 1900, a mere three hundred ninety-four. Then there was a spurt of growth, fueled by the resurgence of the mills in the village. The 1910 census shows four-hundred-five souls. The 1920 census shows twenty more than that. According to Pierce, the growth was the result of the vision of one man: Charles T. Hodgkins, who bought the Thurston Mill in the village and with borrowed money built it up. Soon, everyone in Temple was connected to the mill in one way or another—farmers sold their trees, em-ployed their oxen and horses. Miller Hodgkins purchased the local store, and was "paymaster to most of town," eventually, in fact, owning many if not most of the dwellings in the village, us-ing them for worker housing.

But, of course, the stock market crash of 1929 brought the price of lumber down so dismally far that Hodgkins couldn't meet his debt. He crept downstream and out of town in 1930, leaving Temple devastated—his taxes unpaid, his workers des-titute. There was a brief breath of hope when a local named Mark Mosher bought the mill, but by then the internal com-bustion engine had arrived. Roving loggers using portable mills loaded lumber onto the new diesel trucks and drove all the jobs right out of town on Hodgkins's heels.

In 1930, the population was three hundred fifteen.

In 1940, it was a disheartening two hundred fifty-two.

Grumpy Pierce felt he knew them all: "A shifting population which has learned the habit of living on in one place just so long as the rental can be evaded has taken over. Probably one third of the population in 1940 was of this class." Another one third, in his estimation, was the hopelessly aging old stock, the last third, woodsmen (always a disreputable bunch, warns Pierce) and benighted newcomers trying to make a go of farming.

"The future of towns like Temple, situated far back in the hills without resources and with a depleted population, seem to have no immediate prospect of a revival of prosperity or restoration of cultural integrity."

Upstream Seven
Temple Village to the End of the Pavement

DERSU WAS A GIRL, THE LATEST SONOGRAM HAD REVEALED. The time had come for me to clear out of her room. My plan was to build a studio in the sugar shack, which was the smallest of our outbuildings, a junky old place with a short door and a deep sag in the roof. I made a few flyers and posted them at the university: "Summer Work, Good Pay, Jolly Demeanor Required." I got just a single call, from one Cherry Edwards, whose boyfriend needed work. The thing was, she said, he wasn't very jolly. No choice: I hired Pit Marcus.

Mr. Marcus came to work the following Monday, tall and grim, bursting with muscles, amateurish tattoos on every extremity. His face was set gloomy, his eyes dark, his chin a little weak. He focused on a spot just above my eyes as I outlined our work.

The first job I'd planned was a dump run. Ms. Bollocks had used the sugar shack to store rubbish: a couch, seven bags of cement gone hard, four broken chain saws, a defunct mini-refrigerator complete with mysterious biotic mass in the freezer compartment. I, too, had stored some things: drafting table, several windows, all my fishing gear, boxes of nails, scavenged baseboard heaters. You couldn't get in there. I stood at the entrance with my new helper five full minutes. He smelled like strong soap. Eventually I came up with an opening move. Pit watched me take the door off its hinges, watched me carry it to the truck.

Then he watched me start pulling out junk. I suggested that he help, perhaps by transporting what I pulled out of the shack to the truck. The suggestion didn't seem to suit him, but even so, as there was nothing better to do, he went ahead and took it, gradually warming to the work, finding an unspoken competition to make it interesting—could he get back in place at the door before I was there with the next load? That sped things up for both of us. As we worked, I tried questions, like "Why the Merchant Marine Academy?"

And got answers like, "No idea, chief."

Or, "How does a guy named Pit find a woman named Cherry?"

"Tits, boss."

Quickly I stopped trying for conversation, and we just unloaded the shack into my pickup. The couch, when we pulled the cushions, jumped in our faces and skittered across the floor and into a dozen holes and gone. I gave a shout, cried "Mice!" But Pit was unimpressed: more silence. We piled the pickup high, climbed in, creaked off together toward the dump, not a word to say. After lunch, we ripped the old siding off the emptied shack. Along with the miniature door and mis-

cellaneous detritus, that made another load, not ten words between Pit and me as we drove.

He said, "Windows go?"

I said, "No, we're going to keep those."

He said, "Stupid."

But the windows were from the Millinocket High School
(built in the 1850s, demolished in the 1970s), which I knew because our dairying neighbor, who had a number of the same on
his barn, had told me so. I pointed across the way so Pit could
see. And I showed him how the windows were in remarkable
shape, four sashes simply nailed across the stained old studs
side-by-side to make a sixteen-foot-long vista. And I scratched
off some paint to show him the wood: American chestnut (I
knew this from having worked old beams as a college kid laboring for a contractor, knew the grain and fragrance the way I
knew the grain and fragrance of white pine, for example, or red
oak, or cedar). American chestnut may be almost extinct in life,
but it's common to find it in old windows and barn beams,
where it was used for its toughness and resistance to rot.

Pit: "I'd get new."

Late in the afternoon we put the crowbar carefully to the
window sashes, hefted them into the shop, laid them out on a
dusty worktable I'd set up on sawhorses. Back in the sugar
shack, we stood looking at our work: bare sheathing planks,
bare studs, adequate tin roof nailed to more sheathing on
adequate rafters, ridge pole to be replaced, no windows, no
door. Pit cocked his head, seemed to hear something. He took
a step, cocked his head again, leapt suddenly to knock on
the pair of thick old studs that made the corner post of the
building.

"Listen," he said, and knocked again.

I thought he was teasing me at first, but I did listen. The post distinctly buzzed.

"Ants," he said, delighted.

I was nonplussed, tapped at the post, heard the buzz again, shuffle of ten thousand sets of legs, I knocked the lip of the wrecking bar under some of the sheathing and pulled a board free. Carpenter ants poked their heads out of each nail hole.

"Deep shit," quoth Pit.

I got the big crowbar and several hammers and together we wailed on the corner of the building, pulled that chunk of wood free just as quickly as we could work, five feet of old farm lumber bristling with nails. Pit gave it the last yank, hugged it to his chest heroically, ran all the way across the yard, far from any of my buildings, flung the post and the ant colony into the forest. I brushed enraged ants by the hundreds off the floor. The sheathing planks hung loose—the corner of the building was air. And then came Pit Marcus, walking slowly, impassively brushing ants from his neck.

"You best hope we got the queen," he said.

"Where else would she be?" I said.

"In the ground," said Pit, pointing.

We dug awhile, taking turns, but found no further ants, swept up the mess we'd made, and that was it for the day, except ten minutes of staring at the skeleton of my future office.

After that, Pit came three days a week, and if I insulted him in just the right measure, he worked hard. This, apparently, was how his dad treated him, and certainly how he was treated as a student swabbie on the scows the Merchant Marine Academy used for training. My impulse is to be kind, but the swaggering culture of boys mistakes kindness for weakness every time, and Pit was a man of his culture. He smashed his finger with the wrecking bar one morning and I stopped everything to have a look, took his hand in mine, brushed off the bloody crumbs of sawdust, suggested he go wash it off, get a bandage.

He tugged his hand away from me. "Homo," he said, with only the barest trace of humor.

Later that afternoon I planned to go write for a while, which meant finding a self-contained task for my man. When it was time, I said, "I've got to go to my Man-Boy Love Society Meeting."

Pit didn't seem sure I was kidding.

I took my tool belt off, brushed the dust out of my hair, and said, "I know you said you were anxious to learn some electrician skills."

"I didn't say 'anxious,'" he said, again with that bare glimmer of humor.

"Well, whatever—I've got a job fit for a man of your intelligence."

Outside, between the shack and the shed, I set him up with our garden spade and showed him where the trench for the underground feeder cable would go.

"A ditch," said Pit.

"A ditch," said I.

And at that he gave me a big, warm smile.

Thereafter, we maintained a laconic banter. He developed and refined the homosexual theme in his references to me; I developed the troglodyte theme in mine to him. I was a fem, he was an ox. To our mail carrier, Pam Dodge, I introduced him cheerfully as my "submental helper," and never saw him laugh so hard. Pam laughed too.

Pit introduced me to busty Cherry Edwards as his "transgender boss."

"I think he's cute," she said, twitting us both.

We thought we were pretty funny, and the joke about our not getting along helped us get along pretty well.

One afternoon I went off to work in my soon-to-be decommissioned study, leaving him to scrape windows—a horrible job, dragging the hardened old putty out of thirty-two small panes in the ungainly old Millinocket School sashes. "High-precision work," I said. "You can handle it."

When I came out a couple of hours later he'd barely started in, had scraped one pane, and poorly. I pondered my response. I could yell at him, which is what he was courting, clearly. I could make fun of him, which would have gotten him moving at least. But instead I just shook my head and started scraping. He watched me a minute, started in on the other end of the sash.

"You're so fucking slow," he said, and we were off, scraping and bantering, in hot competition. An hour later it was quitting time and we'd finished all thirty-two lights.

The next morning we roughed out the electric, which both of us liked—it was pleasing, rapid work, and I was good at it from having worked in the trade back during college summers. I taught him as much as I could, given the limited application we were working on, and felt his respect grow. I called him stupid and lunkhead when he made mistakes, to get him to smile, but praised him too, and the pleasure of the praise went much deeper inside him, came out at the very corners of his studied frown.

That afternoon we worked back at the windows, the less pleasant job, starting in with the careful puttying, at which he was terrible. I got to call him more names and we had a good time even with the radio, switching back and forth in mock battle between the twang of his so-called country station and what he saw as the blah-blah of Maine Public Radio.

I knocked off to go write and left him at it. In the house, I was daydreaming over the keyboard when I heard a horrendous squealing of tires up the road—not so unusual, but this one ended with a thump so loud I felt it in my gut. I trotted out front, looked up the road, and saw there had been an accident—a car off to one side, a dazed man milling around. Still, I wasn't in a hurry. I went back in the house, called the police station. The clerk said she'd already had calls from several of my neighbors, who'd heard the crash too.

Outside, I thought I'd better go see if I could help, walked toward the scene, then ran, then sprinted: there was a mangled bicycle under the stop sign on the old traffic island. The new neighbors from the corner house—he with a biker's beard, she with long braids—held the unrecognizable boy who'd been hit across their two laps. They looked up at me thinking I was the father. The boy was bent, his legs twisted four ways, his back arched, his head cocked weirdly, his face smashed, every nerve firing, causing jerking and jactitation of his whole frame. His T-shirt had been torn off such that just the collar stayed on him like a necklace. You could see the harmed places, you could see his heart beat up out of his chest. This was the awful thump I'd heard: a *boy*. My estimate was that he was not going to make it. "He's hanging on," the man holding him said. "Guy there brought a blanket." Pointing breathlessly to the neighbor's house up the hill. Suddenly I recognized the child: he lived down around the corner. He was a lively thirteen. I felt furious: there was a kid gone unprotected here. In front of me I saw how *fragile*.

Pit stormed up the hill. In the past I'd made fun of the local ambulance for running its siren on empty country roads, but never again: I could hear it coming the entire way and the noise was deeply reassuring. The police arrived, and I moved away, stood by my helper, watched the EMTs go about their work.

Pit said, "He's toast."

I began to weep, at first just tears in my eyes, but then hard. Pit stepped away, poked along the side of the road, retrieved the bicycle seat and handle bars—he was close enough to a kid to have noticed them—put them on the stone wall there, anything but look at me.

THOSE LATE DAYS OF AUGUST WERE THE DAYS THAT A BABY might come at any time. She wasn't due until September twenty-first, but whenever I left the house I found myself hurrying at my tasks, wanting to get back home. Marnie, our midwife, gave me a long look as I explained my worries, said, "You take a break, buster."

She even offered to spend a morning with Juliet. So on the Monday after Pit had to leave to go back to the Merchant

Marine Academy, I left the two of them sitting on couch cushions on the living room floor facing each other counting breaths, and drove to the Temple Intervale in my truck—a little more than a mile up the road—parked in a turnout past the village at an oxbow in the stream, dumped the canoe unceremoniously in the water, turned in time to wave to a full logging truck roaring past, got an air-horn toot back. In the boat I floated downstream a little to have a look—nice bedrock, deeply sculpted, dramatic corkscrew vortex halves, assorted potholes, "nail head" striations, ripples. In the bend there were boulders, one of them sporting a huge naked maple stump, heavy roots broken off in every direction and flood-decorated with round rocks jammed in crevices, the whole balanced upside down like a sculpture on a pedestal.

Just at that spot, the beavers had dug a ramp into the bank. The old clay mine across the road, brook fed, would make an appropriate site for a beaver lodge. But there wasn't the slightest spot of dried mud on the road and there would have to be if beavers were crossing regularly. I climbed out of the boat and laid myself in the weeds under the lip of the pavement, reached down into the water, and felt out an upward-rising tunnel. Beavers know how to prevent roadkill: go underground.

Amazed, bemused, I fell back into the boat and chopped my way stiffly upstream, my head surrounded by gnats that arrived one by one till I was hosting a cloud, bugs landing five by five on my face and walking unswervingly to my eyes—I could actually kill them with hard blinks—hundreds of them taking flight with every swat of my hand, landing again, crawling into my collar, my ears, my armpits, intimate creatures. A clap in front of my face caused a dozen deaths, black spots on my palms to mark them. Then, as suddenly as they had appeared, the gnats were gone. The resulting peace was a portal: suddenly I was right there on the water, and the water was under me.

I made it to the beaver dam I'd seen so often from the road, pulled the boat over it. Upstream, sands and silt and gravel had built up against the dam over the years, forming a gentle incline that slowed the stream as surely as the sticks and logs of the blunter dam face, but which would last through ice and flood and resist the implacable farmer and the wantonness of little boys. So: part of the function of the wooden portion of the beaver dam is to collect alluvium and form a more permanent streambed structure.

Minnows and darters scooted away from my shadow as I paddled. At last I lost sight of the road. Every few yards on both sides of the stream a beaver ramp was cut into the muddy banks, and every third ramp looked to be a major route, well and freshly used. I paddled as noiselessly as I could, backed around each bend as it came, hoping for a daytime glimpse, a beaver sunning on his dam or carrying sticks. A phoebe perching on a dead branch twitched its tail, dove after an insect, returned. A robin lurked streamside, head cocked, looking for some other little life to end. The alders were so thick on both sides that I felt I was entering a tunnel. I was in a beaver place, made accessible to me by beaver work. A catbird mewled in the alders, a breeze rattled through all those heart-shaped leaves, a Lincoln's sparrow hopped noisily through the branches.

I whistled a *ship-ship-ship*, something my mother had taught me when I was very little, almost no sound, and waited, then whistled again. Suddenly, out of the deep thick of the alders, twig to twig, hopped a male yellowthroat, a tiny banana of a bird, black mask, black beak, bright yellow throat. He finished at a perch not two feet from my nose, not even arm's length. In his own good time he broke off the meeting, hopped branch to branch back into the brush and disappeared. I paddled on, hearing his insistent call all the way to the next beaver dam, which I gave a name: Dam Three.

Dam Three was completely submerged. In fact, I was able to paddle right over it, bumping my long green keel only slightly. This was a robust dam in deep water, heavy branches tangled together. The new work on Dam Two, below, must have drowned it. I peered down, trying to see bottom, dunked my paddle to its full length, dunked my arm too, some seven feet of paddle and arm without touching bottom. The banks were different here, made of rock in sheer walls like a swimming pool, cut too square for nature. I realized only slowly that this was the slate quarry of settler days. The beavers had built their dam on the very upstream edge of the quarrymen's pit.

Further along, I paddled past an enormous stump tilted into the water off the high bank, sawn through in tiers with a two-man crosscut saw, hard work across the (easily) six-foot diameter. This was the lone elm of the old intervale photos, cut down long since. The beavers had all but drowned the grand stump and built a bank lodge entrance in among its roots.

Dam Four, Dam Five, Dam Six. Pools, meanders and bogs, drowned logs, no riffles. In one deep hole I spied a ghostly tractor tire, air pocket keeping it upright under water. Potato Hill (anthill shaped) came into view, then Day Mountain (a tapered loaf). Seeing the mountains come one by one like that, stuck as I was in the stream bottom, was like our seeing the major planets come by in succession, stuck as we are in our spot in the universe.

Hurrying a little—I couldn't seem to help hurrying—I reached the first riffle in the intervale, the first place in that stretch the beavers had let water flow. On both sides of the stream were old fields and several rotting round bales of hay. I realized with a start that I was just behind a house I'd visited often—Bob and Rita Kimber's place—but hadn't even known it, had lost track utterly of road sense, of distance covered. I stood in the canoe, saw my friends' roof, let the canoe ground itself on the gravel there, leapt out amid tall Joe Pye weed, climbed the high bank. Well: it was an odd way to come visiting, an odd feeling of trespass, too, informal arrival being as antiquated as straw hats in summer.

I stood looking fondly at the house—I love the Kimbers— when suddenly the porch door opened and out popped Bob. Fit and youthful at nearly seventy, he'd spent the early part of the summer on a canoe expedition in northern Labrador. He held the door for Rita, and she came out carrying something— a salad bowl—and they were talking, and then laughing, Bob guffawing hard and audibly, throwing his head back, and Rita stepping carefully down the stairs with a smile, and the two of them climbing into their car and pulling out. I could hear the laugh and hear the car doors shut (a small delay as the sound caught up with the image), hear the engine and hear the driveway gravel crunch; these good friends would not know till later that I'd been on their stretch of stream watching them.

The Kimbers exemplify the saner corner of the so-called

back-to-the-land movement that would repopulate and rede-
fine dying rural towns all over the United States in the 1960s
and 1970s. And as an integral part of the new history of
Temple, Bob and Rita could pick up where Richard Donald
Pierce had had to leave off in despair, with a tale of the town's
(at least partial) resurrection.

They bought this farm in the early 1970s, grew their own
meat and vegetables, raised chickens, churned their own butter. No phone, of course. The first two years, they lived in the
one finished room. Their son, Greg, now grown, was born the
next spring, and spent his first years living in the kitchen, baths
in a big washtub till the stream got warm in summer.

Bob himself had grown up in New Jersey but spent summers and hunting seasons in remote Eustis Township, Maine,
working at his father's hunting and fishing camp. He attended
Princeton University. Drafted in December 1957, he was suddenly a soldier in Berlin. After his honorable discharge, he applied to the graduate German program at Princeton.

Rita Kimber grew up in Thalwil, Switzerland, spent summers on the extended family's farm. She came to the U.S. in
1955 as an *au pair*, took a degree at the University of Massachusetts at Amherst, won an academic scholarship for graduate work at Harvard, taught a year at Smith, then went back
to Harvard, where she completed her Ph.D. in comparative
literature. Her dissertation was on Alfred Döblin and Feodor
Dostoyevsky. Her first job out of Harvard was a three-year position at Wellesley College.

At Princeton, Bob did his course work, then went back to
Berlin to work on his dissertation: "Alfred Döblin's Godless

Mysticism." He came home in 1968, roamed the woods of Maine until he landed a one-year replacement stint as an assistant professor of German at Wellesley College.

Where, of course, he met Rita (one imagines the first conversations: two mutually attractive Döblin scholars in the suburbs of Boston, Massachusetts). Their courtship was brief, and they married in the fall of 1970. They didn't want to teach, didn't want to be part of what was called "the System." They weren't hippies—they were too old for that—but together they dreamed of homesteading in Maine. To earn what little money they needed, they could translate books.

And now here it was, thirty years later.

I pulled the boat through their riffle, climbed in, and continued upstream. A kind of Kimber sense pervaded the next several hundred yards—their kindness, their intelligence, their appealing orneriness, their backward-looking ambition, all of that seemed to imbue the land. I crossed Bob's tractor ford, dragging the boat. Under a pine tree just there I spotted the most beautiful odd mushroom, a fairy trumpet standing four inches high, ridged yellow outside, bright orange inside, with flecks of white like sparse scales. Later I'd look in the book and find that it was called a scaly vase chanterelle.

Always something new in the world.

Ahead, there was a commotion. I looked up and in an instant saw the eye, the rack, the tail, the legs from the side, the legs from the rear, as if all at once, cubist form—that's how fast the buck was moving in fear of me. I watched where he had been as if his shape were still discernible in the atmosphere there, as if the space he had occupied were him, watched it a long time, stream time, paddled on.

Dam Seven looked new. I flopped the canoe up and over it. The stream immediately behind the dam was very nearly as deep as the dam—no ramp of alluvium, no generations of the accumulation of stream-borne solids, just stick butts and fresh mud and a few rocks here and there to anchor things. The mud had come from the stream bottom, and recently: further from the dam, the water was still murky, the streambed considerably deeper than natural—my paddle dipped clear to the handle before hitting a firm bottom, the beavers having made a channel in anticipation of low water, and after that, winter ice. The hillside through the scrub to starboard was all popple—beaver food, beaver paradise. And the new project was no doubt the work of a new pair striking out on its own, beavers in their second year pushed out of the home place by the presence of two litters' worth of younger siblings.

They'd incidentally given me about a hundred fifty deep yards of paddling, up toward a white-pine wood. The new inundation clarified as I proceeded, and I paddled over swaying grasses, drowned anthills, vole holes, squirrel stashes. A log had been floated, and on it squatted a formidable, oblivious bullfrog taking advantage of the new surroundings, a fat little Buddha sitting in meditation, content, serene, green on top, pale below, eyeballs shining. The prow of the boat eased right past him, one foot away, then the whole side of the canoe. I couldn't help the impulse, reached out my hand. The frog didn't flinch, not even when I tapped his head lightly with a forefinger, counting coup. He was so deep in frog world, fly world, stream world, and I so foreign, that he didn't know I was there. I floated past him, feeling he had touched me, too. A muscle in my neck unknotted. A blue butterfly glided carelessly overhead. My heart rate slowed to match the pulse of the breeze, the surge of the water, the indolent beat of that butterfly's wings.

Abruptly I had the sense of being watched. I told myself not to have that feeling, but it was so sure and dense that I couldn't shake it. I thought, Bear. I stopped paddling, stopped breathing really, hoping for a bear (it would be a black, and not particularly dangerous to me if I didn't surprise it), peered into the dense weeds there in the hot sun—blooming asters, tattered false hellebore, stalky goldenrod, bees hard at work, spider strands shining in the light. The canoe glided upstream against the current, slowing and veering starboard. And there on the bank was a broken-stem trail into the weeds, plain as could be, still wet from something leaving the stream. I sniffed, found a strong animal scent, pointed the canoe into the bank right there, listened.

How full the silent world is with noises! I heard a chain saw somewhere far away, heard a dragonfly's wings click close by, heard a screen door slam in between. Downstream, there was the sound of water filtering through Dam Seven. Upstream, a pine-needle breeze in high trees. Near me in the weeds, a snapping, creaking unfolding, as recently trampled vegetation rose back as best it could. Birdcalls all around: kingfisher, distant crows, enamored song sparrow, scolding chickadee, all at once, all the time. But all that noise was silence, too, in a way, and in it I thought I could hear hard breathing.

Stupidly—I knew it was stupid, but I wanted to see—carefully, I threw the bow line up into the weeds and climbed out of the boat. The trail was very clear, threading into the high stand of Joe Pye weed. I took cautious, slow-motion steps. The track turned once, turned again quickly, and suddenly, right there on the ground in front of me, were two dead beavers. I froze, stared. They were the same size, not large, belly up, one dark brown, one a little lighter, the fur sleek and glistening, almost combed. The beavers didn't look bitten or chewed, no blood. I stood over them. Those tails! Scaly, paddlelike. The little front paws were charming and doll-like yet wicked-looking—leathery and dark with long black claws drawn up to the still chests. The hind feet were disproportionately large, webbed, as if borrowed from oversize geese. The weeds ahead rustled. I backed away. The weeds ahead shook. I leapt backward with a shout as the beast appeared:

Earl Pomeroy, holding loops of what looked to be stainless-steel wire, the sourest expression on his face. "These yours?" he cried, shaking the traps over the dead animals.

"No, no!" I tried to calm my breathing, surprised and somehow heartened to note that Earl was affected by our meeting too, puffing mightily. He looked bigger than ever, more used up, his face sunburned beyond belief, the usual overalls bibbed taut across his massive chest, the usual flannel shirt thick under there, long johns showing at the collar under the ends of his beard: daily wear, summer or winter. I never forgot how big he was, but always forgot how tall until he was there in front of me, looming. The traps were snares, heavy wire loops, blank metal tabs where an honest trapper writes his name.

He barked, "Well, I should hope not, out of season!"

I said, "I'm in my boat," as if that explained anything.

"Hell if I didn't see you coming o'er the dam! All those badges!"...The tourist stickers on my boat. "I thought you were Fish and Game!" He shook the traps.

"Fish and Game?"

"Woulda been the first time I ever saw 'em, too!" And he laughed, a big chuckle entirely for himself, since the joke would have to be translated for the likes of me. In the gray space where our separate worlds met, we stood over the beavers and studied them intently, which surely beat trying to talk or maintain eye contact, two guys who'd been in parallel but probably not-very-similar states of deep privacy, thinking their private thoughts in what amounted to two languages, suddenly finding themselves in awkward company.

I settled down. "Hi, Earl."

Earl settled down too. "Professor."

"I got the socks. Thanks." I knew the money best go un-mentioned. The beavers were between us. I decided to take an interest. Anything else might seem an accusation, and I was not in a position to accuse Earl of anything. I said, "These two look pretty small."

He said, "Well, yes, sure, *oui*, but now that's a pair of house shoes, right there."

"House shoes?"

"How do you call 'em? Slippers. The early plew is softer leather, see, if you treat it correct." He dropped onto a massive knee among the weeds, drew a finger down one of the dead beaver bellies. "Boy or girl?"

I looked in the obvious place, saw nothing, reluctantly guessed: "Girl?"

"Possibly, *voyageur*, but you cannot tell without looking inside."

"Great," I said, with the growing sense that I was at a murder scene. Not that I hadn't seen plenty of dead animals. I'd even trapped muskrats and sometimes raccoons for spare cash during that sojourn out west when I worked for room and board on my uncle's farm after college, had vivid memories of the fur shed, the squalid little operation that bought my animals and skinned, stretched, scraped, and dried them, sold them to tanners.

Earl flipped the first beaver over, clearly proud of it. The coat was nice, but not what it would be in winter, which was trapping season. That much I knew.

I made my accusation into a disingenuous question: "Someone poaching?"

Earl flipped the second beaver over, stretched out the tail, stretched out the legs. The animal hadn't stiffened yet, smelled richly of what we'd called beaver butter, a scent I knew from the fur shed too. So much for the young beaver couple starting out.

"Well, *merde*," he said thoughtfully. "Poaching is in the eye of the beholder." He checked my eye very briefly, looking up from kneeling. I turned away. He had sawn his beard off square under his chin, trimmed his mustache so I could see his mouth. He smiled and I saw his straight, perfect teeth. He said, "The castor is just a big rat with a nice coat on—look at the mess they're making here. They'll have the log yard back there under water quick like that." He snapped his fingers, flipped his thumb over his shoulder. I had no idea what log yard he was talking about, though months later I'd ski back up in there and see that there was a scraggly logging road that ended in a rough clearing where logs would have been put up on trucks. Peering through the brush and weeds, I could just make out Earl's orange pickup parked there.

I turned my gaze back on the beavers. I wanted to be safe in my boat, but I wanted to look, too. I said, "I think they're so . . . interesting." I was going to say *beautiful,* or something stronger like *exalted,* but didn't want to be teased.

"They are big rats."

"When is the beaver-trapping season?"

"When is the canoe-sinking season?"

"Look at those tails!"

He flipped one of the beavers again, pulled at one of the webbed rear feet, showed me the claws. He said, "See this! Little logger has a set of combs here." The claws of two toes were split, in a way, a nail opposed to a thick pad of skin. "They groom up with these." He drew his finger to an opening in the lower belly. "And this is the *anus,*" *ay-noose.* "I don't know the English for it."

"Anus," I said. "But I think in the beaver it's called a cloaca."

"So you say." He put thick fingers to the lower part of the furry belly, opened a pouch of loose skin, turned the insides out in one skilled motion. Two large sacs protruded, two smaller. I remembered the fur shed, the smell of the oil. I began to recall some of this anatomy.

Earl said, "Tell me the sex of this one."

I thought I was seeing testicles. "Male."

"No, see, that's a female. These organs you see aren't the nuts but the wax castors." He gave a small squeeze, and a yellowish cream emerged. "Beaver wax. That's what makes 'em waterproof, stroked all over their fur."[1]

He flipped the other animal, turned its cloaca inside out. He said, "How about this one?"

It was exactly the same as the other.

"Female."

"No, Professor, that is the male." He pulled at something I'd missed, pointed: "Penis bone," he said.

He finished the tour with the anal glands. I wasn't sickened, just fascinated. But I found myself getting angrier with him, and angry that there was nothing safe to say, no room for criticism.

And because I was quiet, Earl grew prouder. "In the old days, you would leg-hold them. But it's so horrible, that. You come to shoot them, you know, and they *cry.* They cry real tears, right down their cheeks. Then they cover their faces— you see the little hands, yes? They cover their faces with their little hands when the billy falls. I hate to find a live beaver— much rather to drown 'em."

"How did you kill these?"

Short pause. "I thought it was you who killed 'em," he said.

"How do those traps work?"

He held them in his hand, loops of wire. "They are *your* traps, Professor!" His tone was mocking, but suddenly threatening,

---

1. Beaver wax is also called castoreum. Castoreum is used in the scent marking of territory as well as for grooming. The source is indeed the castors, two leathery pouches, which are enlarged perineal scent glands, each the size of a small fist, located on either side of the genital openings in both males and females. The stuff is thick, unctuous, redolent. The Indian tribes and settlers alike used castoreum for waterproofing and as medicine for every possible ailment, including insanity (bad cases were actually brought to beaver ponds to absorb the peace—this of all treatments back then probably worked).

too. And suddenly, belatedly, I understood. He thought I was going to rat him out. My anger softened. He was the tiniest bit
afraid of me, for the first time. But of course I couldn't rat him
out. He'd know exactly who'd done it, in the event anyone took
me seriously, and I'd pay for my crime indefinitely, long after his
fines were paid. We looked the animals over at length, like looking at a chessboard deep into the game. I had the impression
that he wanted to head to his truck, that we were both lingering
for diplomatic reasons only. The old bind: I didn't want to be the
person Earl expected me to be, the queasy yuppie animal lover,
the shrill suburban rule-lover, but I didn't want to be complicit
in this assassination of these gentle builders either.

My move. I adopted his tone, slightly mocking, said, "Can a
person sell these, this time of year?"

Another long silence as we studied the animals. He said,
"Well, whoever got 'em must not have been thinking about
selling 'em, sir. Whoever got 'em must have been thinking of
something to *eat,* and a pair of house shoes for wintah, and a
little ball of beaver wax for baiting later on."

I said, "So really, there's no crime here to speak of. More
like just subsistence foraging of the indigenous people."

Earl softened too: "Maybe just a little civil disobedience,
Professor."

I didn't smile. Earl didn't smile. We looked at the animals.

At length, I said, "You would really *eat* these?"

Earl lit up. "Oh, but Professor, it's delicious meat. As sweet!
The Indians used to roast them in their skins on the open fire.
The settlers craved beaver meat! And beaver, it was the base
meat of real pemmican, yessuh! You're looking at a week of

good chow here. The tail, you slice it this a-ways," across the paddle, chop-chop with his hand, "and it's firm, and awful good. And it keeps like nothing."

"A meal is a meal, yuh, yuh," I said, losing track of myself, starting to sound like him.

He heard it as mocking, looked at me sharply, gripped the two beavers by their tails in one huge fist, rose slowly to his feet, the traps in his other hand, stepped at me, stood too close, leaned into my face, pushed the beavers against my chest, said, "So you'll sell these to me?"

I didn't want to smile, but that's what my mouth did. I didn't get the game. Was he offering a bribe?

Cryptically, he said, "Ain't worth much, these little ones."

"They're all yours," I said, backing a step away from him.

Earl grinned too, stepped back into me, leaned over me. He shook the traps. He pressed the beavers into my chest, a soggy thud. He was enormous. He said, "I'll drop by an appreciation."

I said, "No, Earl, I'm kidding."

He grinned bigger, like having a wolf smile at you, gave me a wet little push with the beavers, swung them by their tails, then turned abruptly and stomped off through the tall weeds the way he'd come.

REVEREND PIERCE COULDN'T ANTICIPATE THE BACK-TO-LAND movement (such as it was, and is), couldn't anticipate the new wave of people it would bring to Temple. And the grandsons and granddaughters of his parishioners didn't all leave town. Many have found ways to prosper. A community still thrives. But Pierce wasn't wrong, either: the Temple he eulogized really is dead.

He called it: today's Temple is a suburb of Farmington. Temple kids go to school in Farmington, K–12. The last schoolhouse the Reverend would recognize is the one at the foot of Day Mountain Road, now the Temple Historical Society library, at the edge of a small hayfield that borders Temple Stream. Which is all but a brook at that point, pebbled and clear, flowing straight-line from the schoolhouse to the end of the intervale, bounded on one bank by dense hillside forest, on the other by a succession of homesteads, what had been the intervale settlement, the settler houses interspersed now with mobile homes and ranch houses at divergent levels of upkeep.

Reverend Pierce's Congregational Church along the way is still a handsome building, well kept and surrounded by tall pines, with the stream bubbling through the backyard. The place has been bought by children of the back-to-the-land generation, an impressive, progressive couple who happen to be nationally known puppeteers, and has evolved from their generosity into a sort of people's theater. Sunday country-music jams replace Reverend Pierce, and kids learn to walk on stilts: so much for the death of culture. The bell remains in the steeple, and the pews are still in place, but there's a stage inside now, and over the handsome old doors there's a nicely lettered sign:

TEMPLE STREAM THEATRE

Upstream from the old church, the Temple flows through crowded boulders over the remains of some of the smaller mills of history, little left to see. I've stopped to visit with several older people in houses along the way, people who remember the reverend. Not too fondly, I'm afraid. None of them used the word *disaster* about the fate of the town, which they have lived to see, though some seemed a little sad about the place, disinclined to talk.

A fellow in his eighties, standing out in the very dooryard he'd played in as a boy, claimed he knew Reverend Pierce well, used my questions as the occasion to tall-tale me in the classic Yankee manner, said he'd been raised on a coyote farm till his father was eaten, said in those days a family kept the cow in the kitchen and drank from her teats, said it used to get so cold in his house that they'd had to melt their mother's words over the fire "just to see if we was in trouble." He went on for an hour in that vein, had me laughing, but wouldn't answer any question directly, offered exactly nothing of his real memory of the place. But, oh, yes, he remembered Pierce. He said the reverend would come by on Sunday nights to have his way with the sheep and take the Lord's name in vain out in the barn. Later, I'm sure, he told his friends about me: nosy rube he'd fooled with his stories.

Other older folks I visited said they'd rather not, but then went ahead and talked, used the word *suburb* with a certain kind of distaste. Still, *suburb* is accurate enough, even though there's nothing even faintly suburban about the town, or what we've come to see as suburban: neat lawns and paved driveways are not a high priority in Temple. It's simply that most

people in Temple arise in the morning and go to work elsewhere. Some work at home via the Internet. And a few small
businesses operate sporadically from the garages and sheds
along the stream. But there are no more active farms, none,
just a cow here and there, a team of hobby oxen, a goat. The
loggers the reverend disdained are still in the woods. Probably
there are fewer renters than in his day, and the town meeting is
still a lively affair. Temple people go to school elsewhere, and
to the grocery store elsewhere, and to the doctor, and to
church, and finally to the funeral home: elsewhere. But I'll bet
Reverend Pierce, whatever circle of Hell or precinct of
Heaven he ended up in, would be especially happy to see all
the children that marched in the bicentennial parade of 2003,
some of them on stilts, and pleased to count all the proud
adults: the population is growing again.

Up at the end of the intervale, there's still a diversion canal
evident where Pierce tells us that Temple's first sawmill stood.
Across the road, up on a nice hill at the top of an angled driveway, is the old Oakes house, that tall federal the reverend men-
tions with admiration. It's been lovingly restored. The old fields
close around it are still in use, filled with . . . Christmas trees,
cut your own. John Hodgkins is the current owner. We buy a
nicely trimmed balsam fir from him every year. He was born at
home in Temple, 1935. His grand-uncle was the Hodgkins who
purchased Thurston Mills, his cousin Bill runs the general
store in town—third generation—so that hasn't died.

Meanwhile, the stream emerges same as ever from deep
woods where the pavement stops.

Autumnal Equinox

OUR GIRL WAS BORN AFTER LONG LABOR ON THE FIRST DAY OF fall, a girl of the equal night. We had meant to call her Daphne, but when we saw her both Juliet and I knew, independently, that Daphne was not her name. The maternity nurse warned us to name her quickly—even suggested a long, impatient list—but we couldn't, didn't know who the girl was. We left Franklin Memorial with Baby Girl Roorbach safely in her car seat, brought her home to the dogs and her own little room where my office had been.

That was the fall of the Supreme Court election. I listened to the radio obsessively as Al Gore went down, held the baby in the darkening kitchen every afternoon while mother Juliet napped, took her out in the yard in her blanket when the alpenglow rose and Jupiter came visible in the eastern sky, followed closely by Saturn and night.

One morning after no sleep, I put the dogs out in my as yet

unused (but ready) studio, slunk back to the house, lay myself down on the couch in the living room to work, and promptly fell asleep, an open master's thesis (some five hundred pages of good prose from a favorite student) dropping straight onto my face and staying there. Upstairs, Juliet and the baby girl slept too. Perhaps we'd sleep all morning and all the way till two in the afternoon, just as we had the day before.

Not fifteen minutes later I leapt to my feet at the sound of heavy footsteps on the porch, and then the front door opening, that familiar creak of old hinges. My head swam. And someone huge was standing by the wood stove bellowing at me: "The new fah-tha!"

"Earl, quiet!"

"I've just a-come to see the baby!" *Bay-bay,* he said it. And at that he stepped toward me, ducking his head under the parlor beam, this behemoth in overalls, homemade shoes rocking the house with each heavy step. He smiled through his layers of beard grown back and proffered a pink-wrapped present in one of his battered hands. "Saw the *Franklin Journal!*"

"Don't you knock?"

Fondly, and at volume: "Now, ain't you ferocious!"

Upstairs I heard the baby's cry, that tiniest, most wrenching sound, pulled my face into the sternest shape I'm able, hissed, "Get out!"

Earl fell back, shocked, wounded. His face fell too; he was genuinely hurt. He composed his face sober, ducked his way back to the kitchen, board-creaking steps in the otherwise silent house. "I'll put this right here," he said, still too loud, and put the pink package (cigars, as it turned out) delicately on our sideboard. "And I'll be on my way, unwelcome!"

"Earl, I'm sorry," I said, still angry despite myself. The baby's wail came again, spiraling louder. I tried to soften, said, "The baby. She's not sleeping."

Earl peered over my shoulder back into the parlor and past that into the living room—empty chairs and couches, silent stereo, silent radio. Pityingly, earnestly, he said, "Where are your people?"

I begged: "Earl, please, we're not getting any sleep. Please call before you come. Okay? Thank you for coming. But please call. And please don't barge in here. Knock on the door."

"Where are your *people*?" he said again, genuinely puzzled. Where are your parents, he meant, where are Juliet's parents, where are your brothers and sisters, your aunts and uncles, your cousins, your grandparents, and of course your neighbors, and all your many friends and the hundred casseroles and the cheese platter and the bottles of sparkling cider and the rabbis and mullahs and ministers and priests: where are they?

I took to doing my schoolwork outdoors in the hammock, where I could intercept the UPS man, or the Jehovah's Witness gang, or Earl. One afternoon, wrapped in my thick old sleeping bag and swaying in the breeze, I opened my eyes to a shout of hello only to spy a bustling young woman bearing down, tall, purple tank top, bra straps falling off strong shoulders, dark long hair, good jeans, good posture.

Meghan Bitterauf, our neighbor, come to babysit. I felt a warm surge of affection, thought of her dad: I was a man with a daughter now too. Meghan had been eleven when we first met, her family generous with the new neighbors. They lived a couple of doors up the hill in the handsome old James Butterfield house. I'd heard she'd dropped out of college, the University of Montana.

There I was, unshaven, sleepy, disheveled.

Meghan, nonjudgmental, gave me a minute to disentangle myself from the hammock's old sleeping bag, mark my place in the thesis at hand, get my feet on the ground. She said, "You name the baby yet?"

No, we had not.

And in fact, the baby and Juliet were asleep, golden hour for all of us, no need for a babysitter quite yet, so I suggested a walk. Meghan shrugged, gave me a hand out of the hammock, and we marched down across the fields and to the stream, sat on a nice rock under oak trees over fast water. She had a clean new tattoo needled partway around her wrist, showed it to me first thing: "If it goes all the way around, you know, your soul can't leave your body when you die, and you're stuck." And apropos of that, she said, "Did you hear about the boy who got hit?"

I felt again the lurch in my stomach, saw that twitching form. I'd sent money to the fund I'd read about in the paper— empty response—felt guilty I hadn't stopped in to visit his parents, not that I knew them, not that I could offer anything useful.

I told Meghan what I'd seen, already two months past.

She said, "They flew him down to Portland in the medevac helicopter. He's still in a coma."

I didn't understand how he had lived at all, so in a way, the coma was good news. We sat and watched the water. My thoughts went back to the unnamed baby. Meghan's thoughts had paddled on ahead upstream. She said, "Isn't it good down here? Abby and Carrie and I would just tell people: 'Party on Temple Stream!' And we'd go up past where the pavement ends? In the afternoon? And we'd set up tents and by nighttime sixty people would be there. We'd have a huge fire in the rocks, put music on someone's car stereo, and *shake*. Your daughter will do the same thing!"

We watched the stream some more. I said, "So, what happened to Montana?"

Meghan tried not to grin: "I kinda flunked a couple of courses? But I had fun! I played folf. That's Frisbee golf. I loved it there. But I couldn't stay. Don't worry—I'm enrolled at UMF. What happened to Ohio?"

"I'm 'Not Teaching, on Duty.' N-TOD, it's called. I'm reading theses and doing e-mail and stuff. We go back in January."

"*What?* Bizzle! You go back?"

"We go back."

"You shouldn't go back."

"Well, we have to go back."

"Just quit."

"Meghan, I'm a tenured professor."

"But I thought you loved Maine so much."

"I do."

"I don't know, Bill. You'd better think about this."

Upstream Eight
End of Pavement to the Poet's House

BEFORE JOHN HODGKINS BOUGHT AND RESTORED THE OAKES house at the end of the Temple intervale, the poet Theodore Enslin lived there fourteen years. Bob Kimber had spent winter evenings with Enslin in memorable conversation, and told me the house had been an icebox. But the Oakes place (also known as the Albert Mitchell place, for an earlier owner) had been a step out of the woods for Enslin, who'd been living in isolation a few miles upstream, alone in one of the last of the hill farms. Denise Levertov had lived up that way too, with her husband, the writer Mitch Goodman, whom I knew a little after their divorce and before his death of cancer.

I'd loved Levertov's poetry and was pleased to learn she'd lived nearby and written some poems about the area: Levertov was a big fish. And the great, later-to-win-the-National-Book-Award-poet Hayden Carruth had lived in Temple for a while too. But Theodore Enslin was my own big poet, important to me because he'd been a particular obsession of a beloved English professor of mine at Ithaca College—Darlene Mills—and because somehow his work had spoken to me. Until I read Enslin, I didn't know you were allowed to break lines like that, that words could fall like leaves, that the broken pieces of a poem were as important as the whole, that sense might come in collaboration with a reader, with me. He'd been trained as a musician, and Professor Mills said his poems were a *musication* of language, and I (a musician too!) felt myself a player in his band.[1] Best of all, the man had dropped out of society, gone off to live in the woods, had eschewed the fast streets of New York, left the academic and careerist and sellout poets behind.

Professor Mills was a nut, at least to my adolescent sensibility, but was passionate about the beat poets and the confessional poets and the language poets, anyone more or less contemporary, anyone who hadn't died and been interred in the big Norton anthology. Her hair was a fright wig; she had orange lipstick on her teeth almost always; she wore the same dress daily; she sat too close to you in conference. I loved her. She could dig into a single bebop or die-Daddy poem for a whole period, left us seeing the very bricks of the classroom differently, left us staggering around campus with new visionary brains, declaiming. The poem I memorized per assignment was by Theodore Enslin, a long one called "The Town That Ends the Road," which I've only recently realized was about Temple, Maine. I had to stand in front of the whole class and say it, stumbling right to the last stanza: *You have found the town / that ends the road, / but it finds you / as surely. / In your*

---

1. During those college years and for a few years after in New York City, I played keyboards with no great distinction in a number of raging bar bands.

love of it, / you come close to its horror, / and cling there. / It will murder / you in the end." [2]

Dr. Mills okayed my term paper, too, a long treatise trying to fit Theodore Enslin into a tradition. I was unaware that she didn't believe in the concept of tradition and expected me to *subvert* the notion. In an authoritative voice, I declared Enslin's work even more obscure than the poet, thinking obscurity a compliment, and tried to compare him to Longfellow, who was the only other poet I really knew back then, callow lad. In her note back, fierce handwriting, Professor Mills declared that *I* was the one who was obscure, and how about that? I went to her office to complain, came out with marching orders: show that Ted Enslin exists outside tradition. She loved Ted, as it turned out, had known him in Cape Cod. She handed me a pile of his books and sent me home to write a proper paper, which, of course, knowing nothing, I couldn't do (and that C minus still stings).

Still, Theodore Enslin, along with Ludwig Wittgenstein and the wine-dark sea and the second law of thermodynamics and the painter Maurice de Vlaminck and Margaret Mead's marriages and the "Two Worlds" of C. P. Snow, joined the long list of arcanities I learned in college that would become part of my mind forever, useful in understanding the world, and also over drinks with smart dates. And to learn when I came to Farmington that Theodore Enslin—my Theodore Enslin— had lived nearby, why, that was as wonderful as if I'd learned that Vlaminck had lived in my house and painted the gardens.

But Enslin had moved away years before I came, out to the

2. You will find the whole poem reproduced in Appendix A, page 275.

Maine coast, where the moderating effect of the ocean made for easier winters. I asked after him, found he'd left a lot of admiring friends. When he came to UMF to give a reading, it was like meeting Homer. Newly a prof, I stammered and gazed on him (he already seemed old to me), and felt his wise calm, something earned. He signed a book for me—*From Near the Great Pine*—and I kept it on my desk as a talisman.

AFTER A FEW WEEKS OF INFANT-ENFORCED DOMESTIC solitude—intoxicating stuff, but trouble in large doses—I needed to get out. I don't mean out to the wild bars of Farmington, or even out to a movie or some concert at UMF, just outside the *house*. I swaddled the small creature in blankets and cautiously propped her in a product called a BabyBjörn, a kind of pack worn on the chest, and carried her down to the stream morning and night cradling her head, showing her the changing leaves, all the color floating to the ground, whispering to her always. Once I slipped in icy mud and fell over backward, just let myself hit the ground—*oof*—never took my hands off her, the instinct to break my fall subsumed by the instinct to protect my child.

The walks in our woods got me thinking about bigger projects, more freedom, treks a three-week-old couldn't manage: I wanted to find Ted Enslin's mountain house, for example, which Bob Kimber had shown me offhandedly once on a ski loop. The place had been buried in snow at twilight, and we'd had to hurry past, but the vision had lingered. So, when my mother-in-law arrived to help out for a week, I called my friend Drew Barton, who was always keen for a hike.

Drew parked his car at the little turnout below John Hodgkins's house, the old Oakes house, and we piled out into the bright October afternoon, long shadows. "Wood ferns," he said, quickly taking in the history of the forest around us. "Popples, birches, black cherry—this was cut in the last twenty years or so. That stuff is older back there. Hard to imagine that this was all fields just a hundred years ago."

"Enslin lived in that house right there," I said. "But not till he came out of the woods."

"Whoever built it planted those sugar maples out front. Look at those circumferences now!"

"Oakes," I said.

"*Maples*," said Drew. He's a forest ecologist, and a poet of forests, to my mind. His interest is in the relationship between all the elements of the forest—the big picture—and he doesn't exclude beauty from the list. His dream day is wandering in the woods, compass in hand, knapsack on back, scientist-vest stuffed with gadgets, fanny pack nerdily frontward, maps and field guides and charts inside. He's slight, meets you with an open face (scraggly beard notwithstanding), warm dark eyes bespectacled and thus magnified, something shy back in there, something supremely cocky, too, an appealing combination. He speaks fondly and tenderly of almost everything, always frank and forthcoming, funny too, often ribald.

Drew's idea of a perfect friend goes together with his idea of the perfect day. A friend is someone you can walk with through the woods inspecting for however long absolutely anything that catches the collective eye. My idea of the perfect friend is someone who gets excited about the notion of, say, finding a poet's lost house in the woods.

Drew sees his scientific job as making sense of the ecological landscape in space and time. He's trained to think in terms of deep time, always looking for evidence of disturbances, events in the past—flood, fire, farming, logging, wayward poet—to explain what's here now, what kind of forests past events favor (or don't). "It's all about vegetation," and "Vegetation is the flesh on the skeleton of the natural world."

We hiked at speed up the dirt road side by side, pausing to inspect the multiplicity: mysterious seed pod, unexplained depression in the forest floor, mountain maple, Christmas fern, Japanese knotweed's upper limit, abandoned apple orchard, spiderweb in dew, elaborate sedge flower dried and preserved and still springing from bristling leaves. "*Sedges have edges, and rushes are round*," said Drew, singsong, quoting an old botanist's mnemonic ditty. "*But grasses, like asses, have holes.*"

I quoted Walt Whitman: "*I loafe and invite my soul / I lean and loafe at my ease observing a spear of summer grass.*"

The mild drought of the summer had ended emphatically with a week of rain in early October, and the stream was flowing strongly. For a mile or so it runs hard by the road there, quite diminished from its size at my house, not a quarter as wide, something just a little bigger than a brook, even full. I said so.

Drew said, "What's the difference between a brook and a stream?"

I spoke my old line: "A stream is something you have to think about how to cross."

"Too anthropocentric. I've always thought of it in terms of trees: they touch over a brook, but not a stream."

"So a road is a stream."

"Of sorts."

We passed Meghan Bitterauf's party rock, several unoccupied camps, one dilapidated old house covered with a huge sheet of mill cloth, a thick material the paper mills use to protect their gargantuan rolls of new paper, commonly liberated and used around here as a mud-season driveway or a garden cover in winter. Draped over the collapsing rafters of the shack, it made a nice roof till Repairs Could Be Made, that particular form of never.

The stream fell deeper into the forest, further from the road. We passed three or four modest new cabins, hand-built, metal chimneys pleasantly puffing wood smoke on the cool day. Bright orange signs let hunters and firefighters know a dwelling was hidden up in there. On one sign we noticed that someone had drawn three little stick figures, a family. At the last house, four flags flew: Stars and Stripes, Stars and Bars, MIA/POW, Don't Tread on Me. And as a pair of large canines sprang unchained out of a shed we noted the hand-painted poem posted on a wooden sign:

BEWARE OF DOGS:

WE BITE

Well, they didn't bite us, only followed at a respectful (but authoritative) distance, barking ferociously: *Move along!* Drew and I hurried without wanting to seem to hurry, till the dogs fell away and turned for home and we reached a faint track that was the old settler way to Potato Hill, marked clearly JEEP on our map, but too grown in for vehicles. A hundred yards in

was the stream and a sweet swimming hole that had been polished into the bedrock by a goodly glacial vortex, sinuous bare
stone forming chute and tub down a sharp incline. The air
there was loud and charged by the falling water. Our acquaintance Henry Braun, a poet living in Weld on the other side of
Mount Blue, had told us that this was the swimming hole
Denise Levertov had loved.

"'Eros at Temple Stream,'" said Drew, showing off.

I'd e-mailed him the Levertov poem of that name some
weeks earlier (Henry had supplied it) and was pleased he remembered it at all, said so.

"Anything with sex," Drew said.

We climbed out of the streambed and back to the old road.
I'd been this way dozens of times, particularly admired the
farmhouse that I knew was coming, one of the last standing
relics of the farming past buried so deeply in this forest. (The
road itself was another relic, and of course the stone walls
crumbling off into the forest everywhere.) I'd described the
homestead to Drew with some excitement—goats, chickens,
classic Cape Cod house, tall barn, shy occupant good for a
wave but no talk, his big poem of a sign, a highlight of the trip:

DOGS

BOTHERING

GOATS

WILL BE SHOT

But the sign was gone, and then, around the corner, just as
the house should have come into view, a pyramid of waste
came into view instead, piles of old lathe and bigger boards

and hand-hewn beams and broken plaster and mangled sheets of metal roofing, an exploded orange easy chair high atop, blue milk crates punctuating, waterlogged books, a smashed bureau, an entire existence bulldozed carefully into its own basement and then into a shocking mound. By whom? The barn, same thing, all those old pegged beams a-tumble, partly burned, the odd tire, chicken wire. I was so taken aback by the sight that tears started to my eyes. Drew felt it too—put a hand on my back. Where was the shy man who always waved, and where were his goats and chickens? I'd admired him for holding out. He'd carved a homestead from the ruins of old Temple. The violence looked methodical. We could arrive at no hypothesis.

We stared. A blue jay piped. That was the only sound, and it was mournful. I told Drew about the goats, how they'd stood in the road and blocked our path when Juliet and I had ventured up here long since, how the chickens had rushed to get around us and back to their pecking, about the little steer on a staked rope chewing his cud standing in his own mud circle in the rudimentary, goat-tended lawn. How the shy man had waved over his head at me as if from a great distance, as if from leagues away, when in fact his door was only fifty feet from the road. Now we could almost feel the forest growing in on the suddenly abandoned place, this final failure of civilization after two hundred years. Soon again, there'd be no obvious trace.

The settlers' farms had come and gone. And, as Drew reminded me, two or more harvests of large amounts of lumber had come and gone subsequently. The forest had persisted with barely a blink. Temple wasn't tender desert habitat, in which scars are permanent. Temple wasn't rain forest over delicate soils, where clear-cuts never grow back. Still, I thought, huge canopy trees in open glades would look awfully nice around there, an undisturbed, plant-rich forest floor: mosses, ephemerals, rich humus, the million living creatures. I said all that.

"Just the thing the settlers came upon," Drew said. "And they *hated* it."

The road after that was two mere tracks. A hundred years back it would have been three, one for the horse. The stream at that place is at its most lovely, a strong brook tumbling through bedrock and boulders in a slight gorge through deep woods, elegiac. Out of nowhere, Drew said, "My father was a nature person too. He died three years ago. His favorite thing was to rock-hop streams."

Quietly we came to a log yard, a widened place in the road where someone with a skidder had brought logs for loading onto his truck. Drew looked up into the woods, pointing out the boundaries of the cut, which were property lines. He said, "This is not too bad. Not like down the road, where they've cut it right down to the limit, which is thirty basal feet per acre, which could be thirty misshapen trees. But here, see all the good stuff that's been left? Yellow birch, sugar maple, balsam fir, oak up top. And here we have some beech coming up, some red maple, popple for sure and black cherry, which will both get shaded out, eventually. Much more happening here than back there, already, and this is the newer harvest by years. Not a bad cut. And you know I'm not speaking of aesthetics, but the future of the forest."

We walked, Drew talked: "Aldo Leopold has this quote about how an ecologist's training dooms him to always see the ecological damage in the landscape.[3] But I'm an optimist, and even though I do see all the damage, I see the resilience in these forests too, and that makes me feel better about chances for recovery in the long run, or as long as the forests are here, even if they're very different because of global warming. I mean, I always feel good being in the woods. Especially thinking five hundred years in the future, five hundred years in the past. When I first got to Maine the high levels and poor quality of the cutting bothered me, but now I'm less upset by it— it's all forest, cut or not, and we're out here in the forest, and all this could be developed or paved as it has been in so many places, and that's much worse than any kind of cut. In fifty years, this could be Connecticut, houses everywhere on two- and three-acre lots, or it could be even further regenerated from the farming days, and cut over yet again. Which one would we want?"

We passed a new beaver dam that pooled the Temple in a thicket of alders and new popple: venerable beaver habitat reclaimed. Staring at a new stump, Drew said, "Beaver are a keystone species." And he explained: the pond builders alter the environment and make new habitat, create their own ecology, make opportunities for a host of other species. Further examples of keystone species are oaks, elephants, and people.

We hiked onward, slowed as we heard a truck coming, stood at the verge to let it pass: not just a truck, but a familiar orange GMC pickup. Earl Pomeroy. With a *passenger.* A passenger

3. Aldo Leopold was a forester and college professor who roamed the country doing various kinds of science during the first half of the twentieth century. He is the author of *A Sand County Almanac* (1949), a collection of poetical yet incisive essays and journal entries about his life in the wild, about the importance of nature, about the imminence and sadness of its loss.

seated right up close to him, close as a high-school girlfriend. He slowed, had a disdainful look at me, pulled to a stop past me, made me walk to him twenty yards. The person at his side was a woman with long, dark hair, attractive features, dark eyes amused. She was tiny, even compensating for the impression of tininess caused by proximity to Earl squashed in the driver's seat. My face—it must have betrayed everything. He grinned over her head, grinned through his beard, those dainty teeth. I had never seen him grin like that. He grinned, and grinned wider, seeing my grin. We didn't have to say a word.

But I spoke: "Earl! Jesus! What the hell are *you* doing way back here?"

"None of your beeswax, Professor."

The tiny, sturdy woman seemed willing to meet new people. Earl's massive biceps pressed her shoulder, his big forearm hung down her side, his big freckled hairy mitt over her little pale hand. She said, "I am Dunya."

Earl said, "And who's *your* little friend?"

Drew stepped up, meaning to introduce himself, but Earl jammed the old truck in gear and it leapt, throwing gravel and dust, roared around the corner, and was gone. We watched after them. I was speechless. Dunya? So much for good logging versus bad logging and basal feet per acre; Earl had found himself a woman! Further, I'd had a revelation: the two of them lived up there somewhere. Drew and I hiked on in their dust. I did my best to fill him in on the Earl phenomenon. We shook our heads and laughed and marched, a couple of professors in fancy hiking shoes, passing judgment. Was she a mail-order bride? Or had Earl conjured her from so much pine tar and birch bark, night fantasies? I told Drew about the poached beavers, found I still hadn't forgiven Earl, not just for killing them young, or for killing them out of season, but also for exposing my own hypocrisy: I'd always been a fan of civil disobedience. Drew pointed out that there were any number of brutal places that civil disobedience might lead. We wondered if Thoreau had thought of that.

Quickly, Drew and I came to an old crossing, now nothing more than a snowmobile bridge, three tall spruce logs dropped over the cut and paved with planks but spanning two formidable, ox-built, granite-block buttresses over two hundred years old, built by settlers in payment of taxes. Once, according to town records, there had been a covered bridge here. This was the road to Theodore Enslin's house, nothing that day but a grassy trail kept open by the occasional hike, hunt, or snowmobile ride.

Potato Hill grew before us as we walked, seemed a mountain. Bronzed oak leaves showered us in a breeze, the big trees letting go sooner than those down in the intervale. Even the portion of the road that the skidder men had used was growing back to grasses, healing.

A new-looking camp road leading off to the left was posted in free verse:

> TRAIL CLOSED
>
> CABLED OFF
> AT OTHER END
> DUE TO THEFT

Those hunting camps are vulnerable—but many are still left unlocked and open: safety for winter roamers, enough canned food cached for a meal, enough kindling to save your life after a snowmobile accident, say, or a broken ankle skiing, or any of the softer ways hypothermia can kill when the temperature falls below zero. The vandals take more than the odd orange jacket or camp chair or shotgun—they take trust itself. Only the very strong can rescue it then, refuse to submit, leave things unlocked despite all. Or so Drew and I said as we walked.

At the top of a long incline in strong sun, before I was quite ready for it (my memory of its whereabouts having been somewhat faulty), we came upon Enslin's house, a ruin. As I had when Bob Kimber first pointed the place out to me, I caught my breath: the place was the very essence of the poem I'd memorized so long before, verse come to life somehow, the essence of decrepitude, too, of entropy. What was left of the house looked like a hermit's cottage, tilted, exposed. Young trees leaned into the airspace over the violated roof. One whole outside wall—lathe and plaster—was papered in flower baskets, had been the interior of a nice room once, moldy now. The other side was simply a collapse, beams and lathe piled on rocks and bricks.

The section that remained standing had been the kitchen. Drew and I leaned at the doorway, squinting to see inside. The door frames were skewed, the chimney cracked and falling, floorboards hanging broken into a half-filled basement, porcupine shit everywhere. Drew stepped inside gingerly, then I, testing what was left of the floor with the toes of our boots. In the corner, a trashed Glenwood stove lurked. Drew picked up a Scotch tape dispenser. "That really gets me," he said. "Anomalous."

The Homasote paneling had come down in stained, fibrous shreds, exposing fresh furring strips. Under a litter of leaves was a Nescafé label. The rear corner had rotted down into the earth a couple of feet. The back door was squashed to three-quarters height. Galvanized bucket, plastic trash can, home-made kitchen table upside down (its cedar legs rough and kicking at the air). Bottles and jars all a-tumble, a section of mirror that once had held the poet's image.

In the dooryard, such as it was, we studied a horseshoe-shaped basement, rotted floorboards fallen into it. Under the leaves and fallen branches we found wooden beams and the remains of an extensive stone foundation. Down the hill, Drew spotted three thick-boled and twisted yellow birches, eccentric. "Those weren't always in such dense woods," he said, forest detective. "That was a field down there, or a barnyard."

I took another long look into the remains of the house. One hoped for books. One hoped for volumes of poetry, notepads, sharpened pencils. But this was a considered flight, not Pompeii.

DAYLIGHT WAS SHORT, AND THEN SHORTER. WHILE JULIET rested upstairs, I'd sit in the kitchen and hold the baby, feeling my complicated feelings—love and dread, love and responsibility, love and anger (self-abnegation resented), purest love, joy. I listened to the radio till I couldn't bear it: we had a new president. And I read a great deal, changing diapers at chapter heads. I read master's theses. And in the warm cone of light from the standing lamp over the armchair by the wood stove, I read *Then and Now,* which is a retrospective of Theodore Enslin's work over six decades, newly published at the time. Looking up from the page, I thought of his house over the stream: that desolation had made me feel in some inscrutable way that I'd touched his life, whereas his poetry made me feel I'd touched his mind, a clatter of image and order and broken thoughts, wordplay unto roughhousing, all of it underlaid with a quality of somber judgment, a sense of futility inside plea-sure, each poem a mannerly painting.

Then one evening in the dark kitchen, with the baby happy on my shoulder, I got up my nerve and called him: he was part of Temple Stream history, after all, and with that connec-tion I might start a conversation. I'd gotten his phone number from a mutual Temple friend, the artist Jeanne Bruce. Ted's wife, Alison, quizzed me, vetting the call, then Ted himself got on the line, voluble and kind, nearly eighty. He was easy to picture—I had a clear memory of his face from our one meeting—thick beard, broad shoulders, high forehead, thin hair combed over the dome of his head, strong nose, eyes warm, lively, and a little intimidating, flannel shirt, wide hands, half-frame glasses: "Oh, yes," he said, "I lived up on Wood's Hill, in what I called the mountain house, there on the Natty Brook, as I called it. The house was built by Nathaniel Staples in 1792. I bought the place in 1950. The land was still more or less open, laid out pasture-orchard-pasture-orchard up the hill, with stone walls between each, all the way to the top. I simply spotted the place from the top of Potato Hill on a hike with a friend, inquired in town and was able to buy it im-

mediately from Mark Mitchell—eighty-five or ninety acres for
seven hundred dollars."

He visited sporadically until 1961, when he moved into the
house full-time. He had no vehicle: "I got to town by shank's
mare, year round. Snowshoes in the winter to the end of the
plowed road, which is at the other house, the Oakes house.
Then walk to town. I'd be up there weeks at a time—pretty
much of a recluse for several years. One time I spent forty-
three days straight up there. Someone in the village got worried and sent a boy up to see what was going on. And I saw this
boy coming and yelled, 'Who is that!' Because I hadn't seen
anyone for so long. I left that night. Went straight down to the
Lower East Side of New York for three months. Never lived
quite so reclusively as that, after. The idea of all the isolation
was that I wanted to know if I was as good as I thought I was
professionally. I had made all these claims for myself as a
poet—I thought I better put myself where my mouth was. And
I learned things about myself I didn't want to know."

We talked an hour or more, and when we were done I knew
I had to see the place again.

Juliet and I had a babysitter two days a week, and on one of
those days—Juliet on her first solo mission since the birth, a
belated baby shower with friends in town (and then a luxurious nap alone)—I made lunch, filled a water bottle, collected
the dogs, brought *Then and Now* up to the end of the pavement, carried it into the woods along the stream, past the year-
round people, past the hunting camps, past the We-Bite dogs
(Wally and Desi, with eyes cast down, allowed themselves to
be sniffed, stayed out of trouble by way of submission, then

hurried along behind me), past the quiet man's destroyed house, and to the turnoff where once a covered bridge had been. I inspected the bedrock down under the current bridge and found the bored holes Ted had mentioned in our phone call, anchor sockets for a portable shingle mill, he'd said, a machine the last wave of settlers had brought with them.

I don't know what I hoped to achieve, but I carried Ted Enslin's new book, his life of poems, to his old dooryard that perfect sunshine day. Potato Hill seemed taller and craggier than it really was, rose in spruce slopes from the high Temple valley to its bare top. I noticed a tin cup hanging on a peg jammed into a thick old tree near the ruin, took it down to the little feeder brook (Jessie Brook, issuing from Jessie Pond, Ted's Natty Brook), washed it out. Back at the remains of the house, the dogs sniffed and whined after porcupine scent, thankfully without result. I stopped at the door, knocked ceremonially, listened bemused for a greeting. What a mess the old place had come to, what a shipwreck! I'd thought to sit and read in there, but it was too chilly, damp. So I dragged the homemade old kitchen table outside and set it up in sunlight, placed the dented drinking cup at my spot. A settler's beam across stones made a bench. I sat down, put my elbows on the table, poured a little water, and read poems aloud, starting with "The Town That Ends the Road": *It is this place / that you look for, / and you find it: / well-watered by / a brook called stream— / almost, but not quite, / a river."*

The dogs wandered off, rooted in leaf litter down by the old yellow birches Drew had pointed out. Ted had told me he'd asked the logger he'd hired to leave them standing—they'd been at the side of the original barn, which he said had fallen in 1955. I could hear the stream as I read, lost track of the words on the page, heard Ted's voice, our phone call: "Yes, we bathed in the Temple, washed clothes in it. Later, down at the other house, we'd swim at a camp Chester Orem owned. Great swimming. The locals, you know, there was word out that Ted and his girl, Alison, skinny-dipped."

I'd asked him if he'd considered himself part of the back-to-the-land movement, and he'd bristled: "I came to Temple a generation earlier than the back-to-the-land people. I moved because I didn't want to live the way most people lived, the usual cubbyhole. I wasn't part of a movement; it was just something I wanted to do. I didn't like city living. I simply hacked out a life for myself, learned how to do things for myself. At first, when the back-to-the-land types started coming, I was delighted to see it. But some of the parts of that movement, the socializing, the mouthing of big themes, I couldn't take. I just wanted to write.

"Denise Levertov and Mitch Goodman—I brought them to Temple. I was the only one of my persuasion up there. I knew them down in New York. They pushed me about finding them a camp, and I did, a place called the red camp." Dramatic pause. "It was painted red." I laughed: the good jokes are simple. "An old logging camp, abandoned, but in pretty good shape. I found the owner, an ancient old soul named Charles John Prescomb, fellow had a lot of land. Asked him if he would rent the camp. So I called Denise and told her I'd found them a camp. And she said how much. I said, well, it's pretty cheap: two dollars a week. And of course they came.

"Denise Levertov also washed clothes in the stream. They spent the summer in the red camp, then found their house

down on Mitchell Brook there. Carruth came later, George
Dennison, Bob Kimber, Jeanne Bruce, any number of writers
and artists and musicians. The locals were fine with us, I
think. I had some very close friends among them. I was purposefully quiet about what I did. To them I was just the guy up
in the old house. The poet. And it got around that I was writing. 'Oh, yeah, he's up there writing dirty books, making a mint
a money!' These stories would get back to me. I heard that
Slim Hodgkins—he ran the store—said I was 'Peculiar as hell,
but a pleasant man to talk to.'"

I sipped water at Ted's table and read one more poem in my
loudest voice—"The Glass Harmonica"—letting the words
echo through the intimate valley: *"It snowed in far country /
North and / beyond the trees. / As I went through the mirror / My
breath froze / clouding it, / and they saw me no longer / in the vil-
lages of spring."*

The dogs heard me calling out and assumed it was time to
go, trotted back to my side. But I only ate my lunch and read
out loud till a bank of clouds came in and the air grew cold
around me. So I closed the book and tucked it in my rucksack
and put the table back in the kitchen havoc, upside-down as
I'd found it, hung the cup on its peg, walked away from the
fallen place, and down the old trail to Temple Stream.

Upstream Nine
Poet's House to Schoolhouse Pond

THE BABY CURLED IN THE REED-WOVEN BASSINET A FRIEND
had loaned us, then on my shoulder as she woke and fussed. I
couldn't settle her, and soon she wailed. Dog Desmond
skulked and moped, glowering: he did not like the new presence in the house. Wally, more philosophical, chewed on the
one Beanie Baby that he hadn't stolen and buried in the
woods. Juliet slept upstairs. I remembered the mail, took Baby
Girl in her blanket outside into the brisk evening, and the air
quieted her. Leaves blew down the road, forlorn. No sound of
a car. No sound but wind. I'd been writing letters to friends
and acquaintances and distant relatives, announcing our
daughter's birth, and had enjoyed the mail coming back, all the
humorous suggestions for names. One of the notes I'd written
was to Connie Nosalli, whom I hadn't seen for several years,
care of her post office box in Belgrade Lakes, the only address
she had ever deigned to give me.

And here in a mountain of mail was a letter back from her, postmarked Baltimore, of all places. In the kitchen I lit a candle for atmosphere and rocked the child and opened the letter, which was not from Connie at all but from a stranger also named Nosalli who turned out to be Connie's husband's younger brother. He offered his personal congratulations on the birth of our baby, then blunt news: Connie had died back in June after suffering a year from the effects of a serious stroke.

Shaken, I read the note again, patted the baby's back, held the stiff paper in my hands. The child didn't care for my emotion; she kicked and squalled. I rocked her, held her. When she'd settled down, I read the note a third time. Connie's mischievous laugh, the scent of her dusty perfume, a brief glimpse of her face fading irretrievably as I tore open envelopes in candlelight. A note from a graduate student suggesting we name the girl Derrida, ha-ha. I'd meant to write Connie back in the spring. Junk mail, galley proofs, magazines, a note from Juliet's mom, three or four bills, brochures. What had I expected? Connie was in her nineties. I should have known it was serious from her postcard of dunes: it was her nature to play things down. I kept at the mail.

Low in the pile was a ruined envelope—I recognized it immediately: one of my bottles. I'd forgotten that dreamish project utterly. The baby stirred, burped, knocked her little head against my chin, knocked again, settled back to kisses against my shoulder. The envelope was as mold-spotted as the last one had been, as curly, the flap carefully taped closed. What strange coincidences the mail carrier brings! It was as if I'd

opened the box and found the stream itself flowing there, as if
Connie had brought the bottle home.

Inside the envelope was my form, of course, filled out in a
shaky, feminine, old-school script:

1. As exactly as you can: where did you find
your bottle?
*ON THE BEACH AT FORT POPHAM, MOUTH OF
MERRYMEETING BAY, SEQUIN ISLAND LIGHT
DIRECTLY AHEAD, THE FIRST HARBOR BELL-
BUOY DIRECTLY LEFT. FOUND BOTTLE AND
NOTE IN THE SAND EXACTLY THERE.*

2. On what date?
LAST DAY OF SUMMER.

3. In what circumstances? That is, what were
you doing when you happened on your
bottle?
BEACHCOMBING.

4. Who are you? Your name and address are
optional, but I'd love to talk to you.
I AM ELYSIA MORGAN MARTIN.

5. Add any note or information or anything at
all you'd like.
I AM EIGHTY-EIGHT.

The last day of summer would have been September
twenty-first, the day our girl was born: fresh, bright, jewel-clear,
crisp and windy. I patted baby's tiny back and read the questionnaire again, picturing this Elysia Morgan Martin kicking at

a shard of beach glass, realizing it was a bottle, seeing the note inside. I stopped over her name. I liked the picture it evoked of the Elysian Fields, all those Greek shades communing there, lyres and robes, paradise.

Ms. Morgan Martin had not provided a return address. The postmark was not heaven but Rhode Island, faint ink, town obscured, zip-code partial. I examined every detail minutely: one of my bottles had made it all the way to the ocean, a miracle.

I blew out the candle.

"What is it?" Juliet said when eventually, in the dark, she came down, and I told her. She hadn't known Connie Nosalli. She patted my back as I patted the baby's and we drifted into our separate thoughts in the dark.

After a time, the baby woke and squalled. Juliet put on the light, took the girl from me squinting. I got to work in the kitchen, made a few halfhearted attempts at cooking something fancier, but settled on the previous night's good bean soup and bread, and we quietly ate.

"Okay?" Juliet said.

"I'm okay," I told her. "Just a lot to think about."

So she was surprised a little later when I laughed in the midst of silence. She eyed me warily. The baby eyed me too, had learned to focus. I held the moment for several beats, then announced: "I have her name." And I said it, and spelled it, then said it again, adding the middle name (which we already knew), then adding the last name. Juliet thought about it while we ate, unconvinced at first, but then she began to nod. I tried the name again. After a short silence, Juliet tried it too. We said it together a couple of times, then addressed the infant, and suddenly the child had a name.

Cleaning up later, I arrived at the idea for another note in a bottle—just one more foolish float-note to mix sorrow with joy the way Connie had always done. Later, past midnight, I'd walk down to the stream in moonlight and toss it in—a fragile blue old bottle I'd found in the settler dump upstream, stopped with a cork—watch it turn on the eddy and come back twice before a breeze would catch it and set it into the strong current past the autumn-busy beavers, farewell. I found a good piece of paper in Juliet's desk, retrieved my timeworn fountain pen, seldom used, ink that would just wash away when the bottle broke, however many miles downstream. I don't recall the words I used, but I remember what I wanted to tell my old friend: how sad I was about her death, of course, how guilty not to have answered her card. But I had news for her, too, news that had come to me forcefully as I'd searched the shed for the proper bottle: I was going to quit my job at Ohio State, tenure or no. And finally—almost an afterthought before I folded the note and stuffed it in—I let Connie be the first to know the new girl's name, wrote it out for the first time. I liked the look of it so much I wrote it twice:

Elysia Pearl
Elysia Pearl

I'D BECOME OBSESSED WITH FINDING SCHOOLHOUSE POND, which my old U.S. Geological Survey map—a tattered gift from Bob Kimber—plainly marked as the source of Temple

Stream. Impatient, I waited for our babysitter's next shift, which would come on the first of December. Headwaters Day, I called it for fun, a solo mission.

Years before, in our first Temple spring, just meaning to fish for trout in Schoolhouse Pond (which I'd heard was stocked), and following an old fishing map torn from a guidebook, I'd been up there and failed to find any pond, just a game path pounded into the forest floor by moose and deer and fox and coyote. I'd ducked through and come out suddenly at the foot of a long, curving basin, a quarter mile of glorious meadow maybe a hundred yards wide, lit golden in low October sun, the million blades of grasses and sedges glistening, milkweed and cattail floaters gliding overhead near and far like unmoored stars, large old cedars leaning at the inside of the bend, three boulders rolled there like marbles—that would have been the place to camp, if I'd been looking. At the outside of the slight bend, across from the cedars and the boulders, a spooky stand of dead spruce lurked, weathered gray, branches drooping, a hundred small trees in skeleton, all coming to points.

Clutching the fishing map, I'd followed the moose tracks further in, pulled up short at the edge of a defunct beaver canal, just a soggy track ending in a mud hole backed up by the remains of a rotted seven-foot-high beaver dam breached low with a section of ten-inch pipe: someone had intentionally drained the pond. (Why fight the beavers there? More acreage for tree growth?) In the mud around the large puddle before the defunct dam the animal tracks were as extensive as at some African watering hole, as if this were the last water on earth.

If this was Schoolhouse Pond, Schoolhouse Pond was dry.

So much for my fishing expedition. I doubled back on the bull-dozed logging road I'd come in on, stood over an urgent brook I'd seen earlier, studied the fishing-guide map—nothing quite right—decided by a kind of triangulation of faith that this sweet gurgle passing under the road through a galvanized pipe into watercress and cattails must be Temple Stream.

Later I told Bob Kimber that Schoolhouse Pond was dry. He barked out his distinctive laugh: impossible! Why, he'd been up there dozens of times, if not lately. He said that the logging roads shifted all the time; the maps couldn't keep up; that's all: I'd been fooled, gotten turned around. That water-cress brook was just one of the many that come down off Day Mountain. He pulled out one of his old U.S. Geological Sur-vey maps, showed me the correct Schoolhouse Pond at the top of the settler road, marked both road and pond, traced the blue stream coming out of the blue pond with the tip of his pencil, and without ceremony gave the map to me. As it happened— life intervening—I wouldn't follow up on the problem for years.

Headwaters Day: I parked the old truck where the pave-ment stopped at the end of the Temple intervale, let the dogs out, and, clutching Bob's survey map—I'd saved it carefully, consulted it often—hiked in on the old settler road, carrying my trusty rucksack. The air was clear and quiet and the shad-ows still carried the deep cold of the night. The dogs leapt and raced, paused over each excrescency, marked every hummock, urged me forward at speed. We passed the shy man's wrecked house, passed the turnoff over the stream to Ted Enslin's, kept going, burst through the abstraction called the Avon town line, and, with not so much as a sonic boom, left Temple behind.

A mile more and we crossed over a substantial brook on a steel-deck bridge dropped in place by loggers. This subtraction nearly halved our stream, but couldn't change its character. Soon again we crossed over the Temple on a bridge made of thick spruce trunks covered with heavy boards. Wally dove down the rocky bank, crossed through the water: never take a bridge. The stream switched sides, accompanied us now on the left, falling through boulders, pushing at snags of fallen timber, making ice-edged pools, mesmeric eddies, charmed isles no bigger than Pleistocene beavers. The trail climbed, the tracks narrowed. I pictured settler carts climbing behind horse teams, great loads of apples, children following cheerfully.

To our right, east, a dark hemlock forest grew on a high, steep bank, a hundred feet nearly vertical, old trees clinging. I stopped to inspect a curious hump, a diagonal ridge on the diving forest floor, slowly realizing that it was the huge trunk of a fallen hemlock, much decomposed, barely holding its former shape, looking like someone enormous sleeping under a thick quilt of needles. The tree was all but soil, and the soil it had become held the tree's old shape but vaguely. If it had been lying there seventy-five years (likely, according to Drew Barton's later estimate), and if it had been alive for two hundred twenty-five (a conservative guess given its softened girth), then it had been germinated around 1700.

Which gave me something to ponder as I tumbled back onto the road, more of a track at that spot, rocky and washed over in frequent floods, the strongest incline on the stream. I pulled out the survey map and calculated that from the Sandy River, eleven stream miles away, the Temple gained only about a thousand feet of elevation. In the final mile or so, ahead, it would gain nearly half that again. The map clearly showed dogs and man climbing onto a plateau under Mount Blue and Spruce and Day mountains. My eyes, by contrast, showed us climbing through late-autumn trees into high winter and the life beyond that.

And though I'd gotten a late start, and though daylight would end at four, I took a little detour, acting on a hunch. The dogs leapt ahead, bound for Schoolhouse Pond, but I started up a muddy twitch road that showed recent tire tracks. The dogs raced back, chagrined, always wanting the lead. Ten minutes up the shoulder of the mountain in truck-tracked mud, we reached a carefully obscured access road skidder-graded into the hillside, rudimentary, rough, three deliberately placed boulders as guards. I snagged Wally by his collar. Desmond, better trained, I simply ordered to heel. And the three of us slunk up the tracks quiet as hot air rising, crested a little hump on a turn, found ourselves gazing at a large clearing, bountiful sunshine, a small log house at the far end all adorned with moose antlers, maybe a dozen pair. Earl's truck wasn't there, nor his skidder, but I could see where both had been parked, and a titanic pair of overalls hung from a peg by the cabin door. The orange bandanna tucked in its rear pocket was a trademark of the man.

The clearing opened out over hundreds of birch stumps (that might explain my latest load of firewood) and straight to the edge of a steep drop, leaving a view of Mount Blue, frosted white, imposingly close. He'd recently cut the woods around the house, and cut them well, lots of good forms left in place, many species. Back behind the cabin I could see a huge garden plot bounded by the old granite sills of the barn that had once stood there, cornstalks fallen every which way, long line of leeks still in green, tomato stakes still stout and upright, plants quite dead, enormous compost pile on the far side crowned with the stiff arms of broccoli plants recently pulled. Around the corner of the house pecked a large red chicken, followed by several more and a rooster. The early December light was dazzling, slanting across the opening Earl had made in the forest, lighting the rough grasses of the clearing orange, highlighting the few stumps he'd left, the tidied stone wall, the old orchard cleared on the other side, a dozen of the venerable apple trees already tended to, cut way back, raw pruning wounds glowing white. Earl Pomeroy had reclaimed a settler's homestead.

I crept closer on the far side of the wall, drawn by Earl's presence, the sense of some secret to be found there. The house looked well made, hand fashioned. The door was a chain-sawed slab from a massive tree trunk, no more than that, with what looked to be moose hide for hinges and a chunk of deer antler carved to serve as latch and handle. The windows were reclaimed, sashes of the same type in my house, the same type in all the old houses, two tall panes each, bubbled and streaked.

Suddenly, the door opened. A woman came out, oblivious of me, long wool dress, oversized fur slippers, deep in her thoughts. I held Wally's collar tighter, put a hand in Desi's face: quiet. The woman—Dunya—trundled with a curious hop to the outhouse, pulled the door open, stepped up awkwardly, pulled herself inside. I tugged Wally by the collar and gave Desi a sign and we three backed away. I didn't want to be caught skulking. And I knew I wouldn't be able to restrain

Wally if Earl appeared: Wally loves an acquaintance. We hadn't gotten far when the outhouse door swung open again. Dunya used the door for support, let herself down the single stair, and I got a brief sight of the unmistakable off-pink of a prosthetic leg. At sight of her, Wally gave a short bark. The woman stiffened as if shot and hopped to the house in a hurry, no slight look in our direction, just rushed to the cabin and inside.

I let Wally go, turned on heel, ducked full speed along the wall, followed by the dogs, then sprinted down the hill—mortified, foolish, spooked too, scared of Earl—sprinted in the mud all the way to the settler road, where I let myself walk again. I continued upstream, breathless. The road was rocks there, overwashed by Temple Stream in recent floods—the road had *been* the stream, briefly. Where the stream crossed the road next it had washed it away entirely—down in the woods a corrugated pipe lay twisted, loggers' work undone. Further down, clay piping tiles were heaped in gravel: the work of settlers washed away long since. Why hadn't I just walked up to Earl's magnificent door and knocked like a normal person? Instead, I'd made a trespasser of myself, a ghoul, a stalker.

The dogs and I climbed, passed through a Maine Guide's hunting camp—no one present, though it was still bird season. Deer season had been over for a week, happily. The dogs sniffed at the ATVs in their open sheds, sniffed at the door of the plywood cabin, sniffed under the carcass tripod passionately, raced to catch me up as I forged ahead: the light wouldn't last. As the road climbed, the stream—back on the right-hand side now—dropped down into the woods. I kept my eye on it; the stream would not mislead me, as roads and maps had done.

In dense forest the road dipped, crossed several brooklets and rills that left Temple Stream incrementally more diminutive, but still urgent. The nameless subbrooks left mud in the trail, and in the mud were deep moose prints, fresh. Down in the forest the stream was gone. I clambered lower for a close look, and in a flash of bright, bare, tooth-stripped wood, it all came clear: beavers. The dogs rushed to the water, sniffing avidly, leapt in and swam, drew my eye to the dam, sad and sagging but wearing a crown of fresh branches. The flowage, grown over in a new edition of popple, had once again been flooded. All those hapless saplings were already up to their thighs: beaver food. Several new canals worked back through flooded tangles of old alder. Nearly hidden in there was the lodge, all bright sticks and patted mud, and near it I could make out the tips of a submerged forest of sticks—feed for the coming winter. I started down through the woods after the dogs, stepped promptly into a wet plunge hole near freshly bitten stumps, fell hard on my butt and yelled in surprise. Hallelujah: a new pair of beavers had found this old place!

While the dogs assaulted me with their rescue tongues and hot breath, I struggled back to my feet, remembering the phrase *keystone species*. If frogs lived in this pond, and turtles, and fish, it was because beavers had made it possible.

And what did people make possible? Up the hill, light flooded the settler trail, and between stone walls a quarter mile apart the forest had been ravaged. An impromptu skidder road took the route of a brooklet, tearing its former mossy bed down to bare rock. The loggers had left the requisite timber standing—just enough not to qualify as a clear cut—but it was all stubs, scruff, bad forms, lightning-blasted yellow birches, trees grown in failed arches, large-trunked sugar-maple wolves full of cavities and bearing but one or two branches,[1] a few blight-plagued beeches, two or three dwarfish, double-trunked specimens of oak: not a healthy tree in sight. The forest floor had been tracked and cratered and bulldozed everywhere. Thousands of birch saplings crowded inches apart had hardly found growth. No other species in sight. The loggers had followed the letter of the law, if barely: it would be twenty years before that stretch of woods would be productive again, forty before much diversity would return. Past the far boundary of that cut another logger had been at work more recently and responsibly—spirit of the law—had left a forest in place, seed trees and shelter wood, and already his cut was filling in nicely with diverse species. He'd taken some portion of his profits in the future of the forest, and not only board feet.

The dogs and I made the height of the trail, and there, as Bob had said it would be, was an eroded track leading down to a glint of water: Schoolhouse Pond. Wally smelled the H_2O, raced down, and leapt in—second swim of the chilly day—and by the time I got to the edge, he was already climbing onto the single ice floe out there, an acre of ice in the three-acre pond. His kinetic energy sent the huge pan gliding. Quickly, it reached the far shore, Wally's stop, apparently: he leapt off. Desmond, like me, doesn't care for icy water, stayed hard by my side.

This was it.

My dry pond was nearby, not far to the east, a quarter mile:

---

1. Wolves are big old open-field farm trees surrounded by younger forest grown up around them.

all those years past on my fishing expedition I'd been this close. Desi and I made our way around the high north end of the pond through white cedars dense in their bog, no outlet, no inlet. Over where Wally had disembarked from the ice shuttle the forest was mossy and old. Not even the settlers had cut trees there—their stone wall ended impressively in a six-foot buttress at a respectful distance from the water. A schoolhouse had stood here, somewhere—how the trout must have beckoned to the daydreaming kids, the cool swim, the skim on ice. Now there was nothing but a little tarpaper hunting camp hidden up there, left open, stack of hunting magazines neat on a bench inside, fireplace in the dooryard, truck-beaten road in. The dogs sniffed and clawed enthusiastically at corners: mice.

They followed me back down to the pond at a trot, and we explored the south end, another white cedar bog, beautiful old specimens with high roots forming knee caverns and grottoes, housing for elves. I looked for current, found none, followed one promising channel, then the next, but they all petered to nothing among old cedars. The dogs splashed, fully engaged in my search, whatever I might be seeking. And then the cedar bog simply ended. The land rose to a low ridge, dried out. I crossed back and forth twice, from elevation to elevation, but Schoolhouse Pond had no outlet, and despite its beauty and huge floe of ice and age-old cedars standing guard, this was not the source I sought.

Back on the settler road the dogs stuck close; dusk was upon us. Every scrabble in the leaves made me jump, move faster. I'd wasted too much time bog hopping and had achieved only disappointment. The trees were dark, the sky falling into deeper blue, first stars appearing in the cut of the trail, which was the only sky visible, a ribbon. Suddenly, Desi stopped in his tracks, Wally too, dead stop, listening. I stopped behind them. Shortly, there was a jangling sound off the road, down to the right, something hidden among the boulders and trees. The dogs didn't bark: they only bark when they know they're safe. And they didn't bark even when the figure appeared, a man charging out from behind boulders, a huge form bearing an old-fashioned double-bladed axe on a long handle, a medieval warrior in thick clothing. He pulled up short and mighty, took a heavy stance, blocked the trail.

I said, "Earl."

The dogs whimpered, edged behind me.

"So, it's *you*," he roared.

"I'm sorry," I said.

He bellowed: "Do you expect welcome in my home, when I am not welcome in yours?"

Now Wally barked, and that started Desi, and it was an awful lot of sound in the quiet that had fallen upon the forest. Brave Desi feinted at Earl, growling, barking sharply, but he didn't want to take more than a few steps away from me. Big Wally stood safely behind, giving tight, fearful barks. My face was hot, then hotter, my legs light. I had no words.

Earl shouted: "*Spying* on Dunya!"

"No, Earl."

He shook the fearsome axe at me, brandishing it with one hand, enormous strength, admonished me in a low rumble: "You gave her a wicked fright. She's a daughter of *war*."

"War," I called, oddly calm, trying to sound soothing. "I know."

He roared again: "I followed your yuppie footprints."

Vibram soles, he meant. "I'm sorry, Earl. I was just...
curious."

"*Curious!*" He marched at me, oblivious of the dogs, who
barked almost yipping, incapable of taking him on. I looked to
the ditch at roadside, thought to leap into the stream, cross it,
run into the forest, but I was frozen by the knowledge I'd be
caught. Earl's step quickened. I braced to be tackled, braced
for an axe blow, turned my head, put my hands up to my face.

But Earl stopped his charge two long strides away, abruptly
made a fighter's stance, something relievingly histrionic in it.
He wound up sidearm and swung his axe whistling in the air
between us—two, three, four mighty passes. The dogs feinted,
barked, were nothing to him. He'd chop them into pemmican,
and they knew it.

"Earl," I bawled. "Earl, please." The woods had gone dark
around us. "That's enough drama. I apologize."

"*Drama?*" he bellowed, but he'd sagged, just so. And then
he backed away, step by step, slowly backed his way down the
settler road far enough that the dogs stopped growling. He'd
exorcised his fear, made me pay, yet he couldn't simply walk
away.

It was night, but the dark wasn't dark. There was still a
trace of sunset to the west, the million stars sneaking out
above. Earl vaulted onto the verge of the settler road in the
shadows under a large beech tree. He slapped the trunk with
his open hand to make a gunshot, eyed me coldly. Desi rushed
back to my side, Wally still cowering behind. Earl spat on
his hands—theater, no doubt about it, but still my heart
pounded—spat on his hands, fixed me in his gaze, planted his
rough boots, lifted his woodsman's axe, and swung it mightily,

one chop down, flip the axe head, one chop up, flip it again, five sets of chops, loud, solid blows, the axe head spinning efficiently between, five sets only and there came a terrible cracking sound. One more down stroke and the huge tree lurched into the wedge he had made. Earl stepped back too casually, watched the mighty timber fall across the road. It crashed, shook the earth, bounced, settled.

The dogs went silent, pressed up to my legs for safety. My heart beat in my throat, my feet seemed to float off the road. Earl twirled the axe, caught its handle, pointed the head at me once more, held it unwavering for ten long seconds, colossal strength, held my eye coldly. "You are *cast out*," he cried.

At length, he turned and tromped down the hill biblically. We could hear his vest buckles jangling all the way to the turn for the log road that led to the boulder-veiled access to his place. I gave him another minute, then bid my feet move, rushed to the fallen tree, ducked under its thick trunk, ran downstream behind the dogs in the blackness of the new night till we were safely in our truck and rumbling home.

Winter Solstice

DOWN TO SOLSTICE CREPT THE SUN. ELYSIA PEARL HAD BEGUN to sleep longer and longer, and Juliet had been able to expand her painting hours. Dog Desmond, ten years our baby, eyed the infant with continuing jealousy, but managed somehow to keep a veneer of civility, at any rate didn't drag her from her crib. Wally, in love, sniffed her hand, licked her toes gentlemanly, stood guard. The boy who'd been hit by the car had come out of his coma, another miracle, and though perhaps he wasn't going to be the same again, he was alive, and thinking, and getting better daily, so said the *Franklin Journal*. We bundled Elysia to John Hodgkins's place to show her off and cut our yearly Christmas tree streamside. Nancy Prentiss wrote me a note to say that she had started to think that alien plant species weren't so awfully bad after all. Colleen Callahan, the little neighbor girl who'd found the first bottle (tall and bright, strawberry hair and freckles, buzzing with curiosity), stopped by our dooryard with a serious friend named Gagnon (dark hair and dimples, frank gazes), to see if I'd heard back from any other bottles and was thrilled to learn I had: "Three's the magical number," she said, wonderment in her eyes. Gagnon, impressed, thought there'd be one more: I still hadn't heard from Europe, she said, or places even farther flung.[1]

For my part, I did resign my tenured position on the graduate English faculty at Ohio State, a rash move. But I'd been asked to teach a class as a visiting professor at Colby College, near home, and had a journalism assignment or two, and with the additional buffer of scant savings the new little family wouldn't starve immediately.

One way to save some money was to continue the practice of making my own repairs around the house, starting with the broken shutoff valve under the kitchen sink. At the hardware store I spied Ms. Bollocks trying to avoid me—I'd know that shaved head and sunken posture anyplace—made some swift moves, cornered her near the power tools, let her know the news: we wouldn't be needing her services anymore, though of course we'd be glad to help her find a new situation.

First she shrugged—her roommate Briana had bought a farm, so all housing needs were covered—but then her face brightened with an idea even as her eyes went shrewd: "Well, that's all fine, Bill, but you people owe me twenty-four hundred dollars."

I didn't even blink, just waited for her logic, and soon it came:

---

1. There *was* one more, in August of 2001: an open and empty envelope, contents lost in the mail—failed seal, all that time in a moist bottle—no postmark, no return address: mystery.

"It's four hundred a month, right? Unless you were planning to raise it up this year, in which case let's say four-fifty. Six months, Bill, multiplied times four-fifty a month, that's twenty-seven hundred dollars, correct? And if you're just going to cancel out on me like this, then you can pay it to me right now."

"Well, no, no, see here, Ms. Bollocks," I said reasonably, playing country squire, "it's you who would be paying us."

"Not if I ain't there, Bill," she told me, condescending: clearly I just didn't understand higher mathematics.

I knew where the cycle of that argument was heading, decided to cut it off with even more formal tones: "But despite all, Ms. Bollocks, my wife and I would like to thank you for all the years you helped us out and especially for the kind gift."

Slowly, beaming, trying to keep the ingenuous face, she said, "My kind gift?"

Beaming myself—I couldn't help it—I said, "Yes, Ms. Bollocks, you know the box you left in my dresser drawer? My penis! It's almost as big as yours now!"

At that she let out such a bray of laughter that every head in the store turned our way. And I laughed too, and Ms. Bollocks and I laughed together, and took each other by the forearms— that close to hugging.

I'D CONFOUNDED BOB KIMBER WITH MY REPORT ON School-house Pond, and now he was bound to come with me, the search for the source of the Temple a minor adventure for an outdoorsman nearly seventy who was preparing even then for an expedition up the frozen George River to Ungava Bay, three hundred sixty miles by snowshoe in dead winter with a crew half his age, northern Labrador into Quebec, all of them towing sledges, shooting ptarmigan, dreaming caribou. But my little geographic conundrum mattered to him: this was his home turf. He was waiting for me in his driveway, red rucksack already on his back, trusty old cable-knit fisherman's sweater on his chest, familiar wool pants, vintage duck boots, watch cap on his head, white hair falling in his eyes. He greeted me shaking his head: hell of a morning to be out stomping around!

There'd been half an inch of wet snow overnight, and the tracks of every animal that had crossed the settler road were before us: squirrel, partridge, snowshoe hare, fox, coyote, deer, moose, mouse. We left only the prints of people: no dogs this trip. The solstice forest around us stood in bare bones; our boots crunched frost castles that had risen from mud in the night. Quickly—Bob's pace is prodigious—we reached the knocked-down house. Bob had known the shy man a little, and was dismayed at the ruin, vowed to ask after him in town. After that came the turnoff to Ted Enslin's mountain house. Bob had known him, too, of course.

Ted had told me about a milestone marked *A* and *key* at the Avon town line, dated as early as 1784, and we looked for it in the leaf litter where the line should have been—couldn't find it—another thing gone missing since the poet had lived there.

Bob at one time or another had known most of the people who'd lived up there. I asked if he knew Earl Pomeroy.

Bob thought a minute, eyeing me through fogged eyeglasses. "Doesn't ring a bell."

"A behemoth in overalls?"

He tilted his head. Deaf in one ear, he hadn't heard me, something I'd grown used to.

I crossed around to his good side as we marched, repeated myself.

"Ah! Well! Plenty of giants in these woods!"

We laughed, but I dreaded seeing Earl again, one of the reasons I'd invited Bob along. And I'd hesitated to tell Bob the story of my trespass and expulsion. My trepidation grew as we hoofed closer to Earl's turnoff, but there was no sign of him, no sound of a motor, no Sasquatch prints in the slight snow. So I kept the story to myself, even as we passed the spot where Earl had felled the large beech over the road. Not hard to do: the tree was gone. The stump had been cleaned up, too, chain-sawed neatly at the ground. The wood had been hauled. The remaining branches had been pulled carefully out of the stream and up into the woods in small pieces—thorough Earl, leaving no sign, wasting no timber.

Bob and I charged up the eroded hill between magical pools and fallen hemlock, waded through the stream where it had eaten the road, passed through the hunting camp with hellos—one of the guides was there, an elderly fellow with a florid nose, cheerfully cleaning house after his season—and into the forest. Just above the beaver pond Bob pulled up short. I couldn't stop, plowed into him. A moose stood in the road ahead, contemplated us calmly, brief standoff till he was bored and legged it slowly up into a sloppy cut, stepping over slash, working his antlers between the thousand saplings.

Bob said, "When Rita and I first came to Temple it was

heaven up here. We used to ski, snowshoe, take hikes. There were a lot more moose, for one thing, and there were no bulldozed roads up here at all, from the Temple side or the Avon side. It was just the sweet old settler road, like it is for a little still. The woods were in nice shape, a lot of pasture land still showing, still a couple of wrecky houses standing."

At the top of the next rise, Bob pointed to a white-painted cross someone had made out of leaf springs from a truck and had nailed to a black cherry tree at an opening in the stone wall. This was the cemetery from the Avon hill settlement. Some good person had come through and cut back the popple scrub, placed little American flags on the graves of the Civil War vets. But someone else had left ten very large stumps—had logged the graveyard, in effect, letting in the light that allowed the popples to grow. A few headstones were standing; many more were buried in the leaf litter and snow, some deeper than that, fallen to time or skidder tire, broken, strewn. We scraped the dirt out of old-fashioned names—Loretta, Marilla, Mehitable, Prudence, Asahel—grew chilly.

Below us down in the woods the stream tumbled—recent rain and the new melting snow had swollen it, and the flow was emphatic. We'd find the source easily with volume like that. The obvious way, of course, was to simply follow the stream uphill until we found its start. We clambered down off the settler road to the Temple through the thick young woods under the gaze of dead settlers and had a look. Ice knobs had formed on sedges dipping the current, and the multitude of rocks were coated with ice, a lovely, satisfying spectacle. After a minute, we started up through the woods alongside the water. The walking was easy enough around slash and through mixed-species saplings—these had grown at different rates under the shelter of canopy trees some good logger had left. But then we crossed a property line marked clearly and straight as a surveyor's laser by an impassable forest of birch saplings, no other species, no shelter wood, irresponsible logging, very difficult going.

In summer we might have used the stream itself as a right-of-way, but the ice made that too difficult. We hacked our way alongside it for a couple of hundred feet but gave up, turned north and deadheaded our way to a wide stone wall atop which we skipped, all the way to its terminus near a basement hole. We poked around those rocks briefly, found iron hoops from wagon wheels and the pothook from a hearth. From these things a farmstead rose before us, hard-won but productive, kids at chores, grown-ups tossing hay, old folks putting up preserves, animals grazing, views to mountains on all sides.

"Let's skip the scrub and start with the pond," Bob said. He still didn't quite believe me. Schoolhouse Pond had no outlet? This seemed impossible, and certainly countered the survey map, which we both trusted implicitly. Had I missed something? At Schoolhouse Pond, we watched the ice floe turn. It had shrunk to maybe a quarter acre in the relatively warm weeks since Wally had ridden it, but new ice was growing in lace at the margins of the water. A breeze rippled the surface, stirred the cedars, chilled my sweat. I pointed across the way to the high butt of the rock wall I'd seen last time.

Bob squinted, wanting to see the wall, pulled two different pairs of glasses from his various pockets, tried them on, squinted more. "I just can't make it out," he said ruefully. Still, he tried, muttering, "My vision was perfect till I was forty."

We worked our way quickly through the cedar bog. Just to prove it to himself—no insult implied—Bob crossed back and forth in the snowy leaf litter where the mixed-hardwood forest resumed: no brook of any kind. Together we crossed back and forth in long transects south of the pond: no stream. After a half hour, our morning disappearing, we reentered the birch scrub on a compass point south till we hit the stone wall, followed that west up to the settler road—no stream—then turned around reluctantly and followed the wall the other way, east, slim branches whipping the cold skin of our faces. When the wall ended, we kept going, pushing the slim trees aside, a difficult march. Suddenly, we poked out of the scrub onto the bulldozed road.

We'd just crossed the whole valley under Schoolhouse Pond from road to road: no Temple Stream. We looked up that logging road, down that logging road, and then we looked at each other. Bob frowned and said, "Where did that friggin' stream go?"

We pulled out three maps. The DeLorme *Maine Gazetteer*, meant as a road map, showed the stream just petering out on Day Mountain. The old fishing-guide map, my original evidence (which had fallen into two pieces at the crease), showed the stream crossing a road about where this road seemed to be and running to a large pond marked Schoolhouse: wrong. Bob pulled out the survey map: it showed the Temple issuing from Schoolhouse Pond, but at least it had the pond right, so mixed marks. Further, it showed a long pond where my beaver meadow had been, no doubt correct at the time the map was drawn, wrong now.

"We'll have to call these guys," Bob said.

We used our heels to mark the muddy snow where we'd come out of the forest, and I took Bob to my dried-up pond, just as beautiful as when I'd seen it last, those spruce trees ghostly at the bend.

"How'd I ever miss this?" Bob said.

It would have been the place for lunch, but a stiff southerly wind had come up (it would bring deep snow that night), damp and claw-cold in our faces. We thrashed up into a section of uncut woods and found a fallen balsam, broke lichened branches to make room to sit. My jeans and T-shirt and socks had gotten damp and I'd taken a terrible chill. In my rucksack, underneath lunch, I had dry socks and a T-shirt, but no trousers. Bob was decked out in wool, mostly, and was dry. His rucksack was heavier than mine, just his routine survival items, things I carried too—lunch, matches, knife, rope, clothing, compass, map—but also a hatchet, a large tarp, several packets of dried food, a first-aid kit, a roll of duct tape, mess kit, space blanket, and who knew what else. If anything went wrong, we had what we needed to live for a few days, depending on injuries. Bob taught by example. Not that that place was remote—we were only a few miles from home—but anyplace in the winter forest can become remote instantly in the event of a bad fall.

Bob put his folded tarp on the wet snow for me to stand on, gave a happy shrug. "Even half frozen on a soggy day, it's good to be in the woods," he said. I changed socks quickly as I could in the cold wind, stripped down to bare chest and put on a new undershirt. Dressed and more comfortable, but unrelievedly conscious of the damp legs of my blue jeans, I sat beside Bob and pulled out my lunch: that hummus sandwich didn't look big enough by half. My feet were freezing. Bob pulled out his own double-sized Swiss-cheese sandwich and something even more inviting: a thermos of exquisitely hot herbal tea. He handed me the cup first. That warmth, it was like God's touch, and it brought me life, radiated from my belly, warmed my heart, my blood, which quickly warmed my toes, another Kimber lesson.

We ate companionably, sharing the thermos, sharing bites of sandwich back and forth, grew voluble, switched places on the spruce trunk to put me on the side of Bob's good ear. Thinking of Earl (we'd have to walk down past his road on the way home) I asked Bob how he'd gotten along with people in Temple over the years.

He thought a minute, said, "There was a *lot* of tension. Especially around the antiwar stuff, which I was into, neck-deep. The thing that really sticks in my memory is the insularity of our little émigré community. In retrospect, I've got a very torn feeling about it. There's a lot I could have learned from the local community, but didn't. But after all these years, you know, it's like stones in the bottom of the brook, they rub against each other long enough and the sharp corners get rounded off, they start to fit together. Still, no matter what, even though Rita and I have been here thirty years, to our neighbors we're always going to be year-round summer people."

Bob recalled for me several hunting adventures he'd had in this basin, all the skiing he'd done before the logging began, even a few nights camping with Rita and their son, Greg. And he described again the dense woods he'd found there, days gone. He said, "Places like this don't have a chance. So many

people in the world, needing so much. But I guess I won't volunteer to die just yet."

We talked in that vein, everything an elegy in the woods in
late December. I pulled out four bonbons I'd liberated from a
Christmas box, and chocolate never tasted so good. As we ate,
we heard a raven squawking off in the forest, closer, further,
closer again, then I spotted it, several hundred yards west of
our bivouac, a huge black bird soaring just over the treetops,
clacking.

"Wolves," Bob said.

I knew what he meant. We'd both just attended a talk given
by a wolf researcher and learned that ravens like to travel with
wolves—they scavenge from wolf kills—and apparently the
two species have adapted to one another. In wolf country, up
in Canada, out west, ravens see the migrating herds of caribou
or antelope from the sky, show wolves where to go, join them
at the resulting kills. But wolves are extinct in Maine (if perhaps poised for a comeback via Quebec).

I howled and the raven wheeled, just like that, wheeled
back and flew over us in a big, cautious circle, cocking its head
to look down upon us. With a disappointed squawk (no wolves
to speak of, and the humans not dead enough to eat), the bird
flew off to look for other eyes to peck.

Now we were both getting cold. Thin clouds had veiled the
sun and robbed what little warmth it had offered; the air itself
seemed frozen. Time to run our engines. We packed up, made
our way back to the moose path and into the meadow, struck
off through the dried pond, hopping rocks and stumps through
the old beaver channel, making our way clear down to the

thickness of alders at the far end. We didn't need to battle through them: we could see an unbroken ridge of land beyond, maybe ten feet of elevation higher than even a full pond would ever attain, proof, it we needed it, that this wet beaver meadow had never been Temple Stream's source.

"A puzzle," Bob said.

We beat our way back to the bulldozed road, chugged to the spot we'd marked coming out of the birch scrub, scratched our heads, kept going. The road dipped down, and down a little more to where it crossed the watercress brook, which we found flowing with authority through its galvanized pipe under the road into cattails and ice knobs on sedges, sandy bottom, gold glints of mica, hearty flow, jubilant babble of rare languages, washed rocks cased in ice.

What if that little sprite really was the Temple?

Bob shook his head and said, "Wouldn't that be something?" meaning that we needed to keep a healthy skepticism, although here before us as we investigated was a brook of about the right size, a brook flowing about the right direction and in about the right place to meet and so be the stream we'd left for a walk on a stone wall just an hour and a half and a good lunch before. All we had to do to test the hypothesis was follow this brook downhill.

The sun found an opening in the high, thin cirrus: solstice three o'clock. Spruce Mountain was a jagged blue ridge, the snow of Day Mountain suddenly lit rose gold. We had something less than a half hour till sunset, just an hour after that of adequate light to get out. We'd have to nearly run to get to the car by dark; I'd done something like that before and seen an ogre, didn't want to see him again.

But our mission was clear.

We gestured politely for one another to go first, then plunged together into the scrub, pushed saplings from our faces, climbed over discarded limbs, crossed and recrossed the muscular little brook for advantage—the place we'd quit couldn't be a third of a mile downstream. We crossed a property line into open old woods where the walking got easy. The brook was wider—not a brook you'd miss, fell into a rocky slot noisily, two steep banks, large trees. Suddenly, looking to the woods on the other side, Bob spotted our own footprints in wet snow. He pointed up the hill to a stone wall. We scrambled up there on all fours in the bare wet snow, reached the wall, looked over the lip: Loretta, Marilla, Mehitable, Prudence, Asahel.

Incontrovertibly, the watercress brook was Temple Stream.

We beamed, turned without pause, and scrambled back down the slope to the water, stood in it ceremonially—waterproof boots—then followed our tortured path back up along its course to the bulldozed road. And there we posed for a long minute simply staring down into the watercress brook moving through its pipe under the road, cattails and glint of mica: Temple Stream.

The sun set fast over Spruce Mountain, leaving a pure pink in its wake, a bloody, deepening pink pulling at the dense clouds moving in from the south. East, a darkening periwinkle blue settled in behind Day Mountain. The first planets showed just beside her shoulder: Jupiter, Saturn. Along the northern horizon, around the edge of the bowl of the big sky up on that plateau, the delicate lavender of alpenglow rose, harbinger of night.

Still, we charged into the tangled raspberry brambles on the other side of the bulldozed road—thorns and needles—then into old scruff in a recovering cut, following the brook. Which made a sharp turn north immediately, paralleling the road for several hundred yards. At our feet and knees a mess of old branches draped in dead sensitive ferns hobbled us, but we wanted to have the water in sight. The brook steamed in the evening cold, our footprints in the snow made puddles. Bob remarked on all the green, a winter terrarium: Christmas ferns, equisetum, baby balsam trees making their way to sun, star mosses and staghorn mosses, brief glimpses of summer.

The brook got small, then smaller yet, meandering through the damp, damaged forest. Where old branches blocked our progress, we picked out a passable route that took us away from the flow, but fought our way back, found the stream, picked out another passable route, found ourselves on a rise. We worked our way back, but did not come to the stream. Ahead, the land got only drier, and we found ourselves on an old twitch road that had become a snowshoe-hare highway, bunny tracks thick up and down it in the snow.

To the north, the land fell away quickly. And down there in the failing light we could make out the alder bog at this end of the dried-up pond, the very alders we'd just avoided. We turned on heel, faced south. Bob pulled out the survey map. There was barely light to read it. The land fell away south, too, but more subtly: so subtly that no such topographical gradation was noted. But, in fact, the flattened ridge we stood upon marked a minor watershed.

"We're there," I said.

The slight snow cover made it easy for us to retrace our steps, and we did, both suddenly in a boyish hurry, tumbling over each other, making our way with difficulty back to the last place we had left the stream in all its diminutive insistence, a hundred yards only. We scrambled upstream, got separated by a few yards, then a few yards more, kept going, found the two sources of the Temple separately and simultaneously, gave shouts—two perfectly clear upwellings, two sweet fonts of water urging up out of the leaf litter, a spring with two mouths, the overflow beginning the long trip downhill in old skidder ruts nearly erased. Bob and I were thirty yards apart in the woods but hidden from each other by all the scrub and scruff. I looked into the depths of my urgent spring. Grains of sand danced in there, lavender-glinting mica.

"Walk it back down," I called. Our elevation was above the dry pond. So: the spring was artesian; the source was Day Mountain; water flowing underground from high above found daylight here. Temple Stream flowed from a logger's clear-cut at the head to a gravel pit at the mouth, from industry to industry, but it had flowed before industry, and when industry was gone it would flow on.

Bob and I both made our ways back downstream, making sure flow was evident at every step, called back and forth, delighted with the small discovery, these inch-wide brooks. Gradually, the course I worked on turned into a definite rivulet, two or three inches across. And Bob called that his had, too. Intently I followed mine. After a few focused minutes, Bob and I met, and our two brooklets met, and the trickles formed a brook, and the brook was Temple Stream, which would flow growing bigger and bigger past Bob's house first, then past mine—that old wreck of a homestead where my new daughter was doubtless sleeping a long solstice nap with her mother, my Juliet—would flow down to the Sandy and then in confluence with the waters of a dozen streams like it to the Kennebec and from there, conjoined, to a quiet marriage with the Androscoggin River at Merrymeeting Bay and thence to the Gulf of Maine and the endless ocean blue.

Appendix A

THE TOWN THAT ENDS THE ROAD
by Theodore Enslin

I.

It is this place
that you look for,
and you find it:
well-watered by
a brook called stream—
almost, but not quite,
a river.
            The stream, then,
Is the pulse of the
town-
        ship

including the village,
and certain outlying districts—
                most of them
abandoned
                except
for vicarious life
in the easier months.
The stream begins
above the town
                    lines
in a number of bog ponds,
carries down and out of it
a sediment
                almost unseen
until the dam
                    at the mill
fouls it and
                traps it,
and then releases its sludge
to another town
and a river.
It is the back
bone
of the place
now,
            though it
is no longer
                important
in the sense that it once was.

II.

There is the village
                   proper,
and a few fanning roads
which soon die
in the leaves—
                   overgrown
as the fields
             of the old men
who left themselves there—
sweat dried on the rocks
that still might lick salt,
if you knew how to find it.
Following the stream of water,
a stream of houses,
                     decaying
in most cases—
                   the barns
fallen in,
             and the chimneys
crooked
             and faulty.
The men who live here
take to the woods
                   early,
or disappear.
                   They are
crabbed in their survival,
gnarl early,

carry
themselves to their graves
in poverty
            and harshness.

III.

Above the town
lie its mountains—
ravaged by over-
cutting:
            dark growth
and hard wood,
But the mountains are open
In their sleep and
                        aloofness
They heal better
                        than men.
They contain bits
                        of the life
that sticks to them—
                        wild—
and the tame remnants—
cellar holes,
                        walls,
an axe-head
                        or two,
wagon-tires,
                        where deer
and other free lives
                        nose through them
for berries.

IV.

But the life of the men
casts a shadow
                    even
across the sun—
there is something
                    that bitters
even the best days.
                    It will not
rub out.
            When you first come here
you will not notice it,
then time
            drives it
home
        like a nail
into bone.
There is sadness,
and desperate
                    hatred
In the close-in
                of winter
It becomes
            unbearable.
The wind is a scream—
a pain
        that bears gossip—
that act
        of those men

who have nothing to do
except curse that same nothing.
It will pass.
                    There is brightness,
But the ache of the land
comes up
                    time
and time again.
You have found
                    the town
that ends the road,
but it finds you
                    as surely
In your love
                    of it,
you come close to its horror,
and cling there.
It will murder you
in the end.

Selected Bibliography

Arora, David. *Mushrooms Demystified*. Berkeley: Ten Speed Press, 1979.

Arseniev, V.K. *Dersu the Trapper*. New York: E. P. Dutton, 1941.

Bardach, John. *Downstream: A Natural History of the River*. New York: Harper & Row, 1964.

Bentley, W.A., and W. J. Humphreys. *Snow Crystals*. New York: McGraw-Hill, 1931.

Beston, Henry. *Herbs and the Earth*. Boston: David R. Godine, 1990.

Black, Peter E. *Watershed Hydrology*. Englewood Cliffs, NJ: Prentice Hall, 1991.

Black Elk, Nicholas, and John G. Neihardt. *Black Elk Speaks*. Lincoln: University of Nebraska Press, 2000.

Bourque, Bruce J. *Twelve Thousand Years: American Indians in Maine*. Lincoln: University of Nebraska Press, 2001.

Bunker, John, Susan Kiralis, et. al. Fedco 2002 Trees Catalog. Waterville, ME: Fedco, 2002.

Butler, Ben and Natalie Butler. *Porter and Russell Lived on a Hill.* Farmington, ME: Farmington Historical Society, 1969.

Butler, Francis Gould. *A History of Farmington, Maine.* First edition, 1885. Reprint edited by Gwilym Roberts. Rockport, ME: New England History Press, 1983.

Chapman, Frank M. *Birds of Eastern North America.* New York: D. Appleton and Co., 1929.

Chartrand, Mark R. *National Audubon Society Field Guide to the Night Sky.* New York: Alfred A. Knopf, 1991.

Coffin, Robert P. Tristram. *Kennebec, Cradle of Americans.* New York: Farrar and Rinehart, 1937.

Coleman, James M. *Deltas: Processes of Deposition.* Champaign, IL: Continuing Ed. Publication Co., 1976.

Collins, Henry Hill, ed. *Complete Field Guide to North American Wildlife.* New York: Harper & Row, 1959.

Davis, Marvin and Helen. *Bottles and Relics.* Ashland, OR: self-published, 1969.

Dennison, George. *Temple: From a Writer's Notebook.* South Royalton, VT: Steerforth Press, 1994.

Dickinson, Emily. *Collected Poems.* Philadelphia: Courage Books, 1991.

Dunne, Pete, et al. *Hawks in Flight.* Boston: Houghton Mifflin Co., 1988.

Emerson, Ralph Waldo. "The Over-Soul." *Nature and Other Writings.* Boston: Shambhala Library, 2003.

Enslin, Theodore. *New Sharon's Prospect & Journals.* San Francisco: Coyote's Journal #7, 1966.

————. *From Near the Great Pine*. Peoria, Illinois: Spoon River Press, 1988.

————. *Then, and Now: Selected Poems 1943–1993*. Orono, ME: National Poetry Foundation, 1999.

Garde, R. J., and K. G. Ranga Raju. *Mechanics of Sediment Transportation and Alluvial Stream Problems*. New York: Halsted Press, 1985.

Graves, Eleanor, ed. *Beavers and Other Pond Dwellers*. New York: Time-Life Books, 1977.

Grey Owl. *Pilgrims of the Wild*. Toronto: Macmillan, 1935.

Halfpenny, James. *A Field Guide to Mammal Tracking in North America*. Illustrated by Elizabeth Biesiot. Boulder, CO: Johnson Books, 1986.

Harrison, Hal H. *Birds' Nests* (Peterson Field Guides). Boston: Houghton Mifflin Co., 1975.

Kazmann, Raphael G. *Modern Hydrology*. New York: Harper & Row, 1972.

Kepler, Johannes. *A New Year's Gift, or On the Six-Cornered Snowflake*. Originally written in 1611. New York: Oxford University Press, 1966.

Ketchum, Richard M. *The Secret Life of the Forest*. New York: American Heritage Press, 1970.

Kimber, Robert. *Upcountry: Reflections from a Rural Life*. New York: Lyons and Burford, 1991.

————. *Living Wild and Domestic: The Education of a Hunter-Gardener*. New York: The Lyons Press, 2002.

Kirk, Ruth. *Snow*. New York: William Morrow and Co., 1978.

Klamkin, Marian. *The Collector's Book of Bottles*. New York: Dodd, Mead and Co., 1971.

Knight, Charles A. *The Freezing of Supercooled Liquids* (Van Nostrand Momentum Book No. 14). Princeton, NJ: D. Van Nostrand Co., 1967.

LaChapelle, Edward R. *Field Guide to Snow Crystals.* Seattle: University of Washington Press, 1969.

Leopold, Aldo. *A Sand County Almanac.* New York: Oxford University Press, 1949.

Leopold, Luna B. *Water: A Primer.* San Francisco: W. H. Freeman, 1974.

Levertov, Denise. *Selected Poems.* New York: New Directions, 2003.

Long, Kim. *Beavers: A Wildlife Handbook.* Boulder, CO: Johnson Books, 2000.

Ludlum, David M. *The National Audubon Society Field Guide to North American Weather.* New York: Alfred A. Knopf, 1991.

Mallett, Richard P. *The Early Years of Farmington: 1781–1860.* Wilton, ME: Wilton Printed Products, 1994.

Martin, Horace T. *Castorologia; or, the History and Traditions of the Canadian Beaver.* Montreal: Wm. Drysdale and Co., 1892.

Matthiessen, Peter. *Wildlife in America.* New York: Viking Press, 1959.

Matula, George J., Jr., ed. Research and Management Report 2001. Augusta, ME: Maine Department of Inland Fisheries and Wildlife, 2001.

Milne, Lorus J. and Margery Milne. *Audubon Society Field Guide to North American Insects and Spiders.* New York: Alfred A. Knopf, 1980.

Morgan, Lewis H. *The American Beaver and His Works.* Philadelphia: J. B. Lippincott Co., 1868.

Moyle, Peter B. *Fish: An Enthusiast's Guide.* Berkeley: University of California Press, 1993.

Newcomb, Lawrence. *Newcomb's Wildflower Guide*. Boston: Little, Brown and Co., 1977.

Ovid. *Metamorphosis*. Translated by Rolfe Humphries. Bloomington: Indiana University Press, 1955.

Parker, Thomas. *History of Farmington, Maine, from Its First Settlement to 1846*. Farmington, ME: J. S. Swift, Publisher, 1846.

Peterson, Roger Tory, and Margaret McKenny. *Wildflowers*. Boston: Houghton Mifflin Co., 1968.

Pierce, Richard Donald. "A History of Temple, Maine: Its Rise and Decline." Dissertation for Boston University Graduate School, 1946.

Pliny the Elder. *Natural History: A Selection*. Translated by John F. Healy. New York: Penguin Books, 1991.

Polak, Michael. *Bottles*. New York: Avon Books, 1994.

Preston, Richard J., Jr. *North American Trees*. 4th ed. Ames: Iowa State Univ. Press, 1989.

Rose, Guy E. *Trapping Maine Beaver and Fisher*. Augusta, ME: self-published, 1940.

Rue, Leonard Lee. *The World of the Beaver*. New York: J. B. Lippincott Co., 1964.

Ryden, Hope. *Lily Pond: Four Years with a Family of Beavers*. New York: William Morrow and Co., 1989.

Sandoz, Mari. *The Beaver Men*. Lincoln: University of Nebraska Press, 1964.

Schumm, Stanley A. *The Fluvial System*. New York: John Wiley, 1977.

———, ed. *River Morphology*. Stroudsburg, PA: Dowden, Hutchinson, and Ross, 1972.

Scott, W. B. *Freshwater Fishes of Eastern Canada*. Toronto: University of Toronto Press, 1954.

Sibley, David Allen. *The Sibley Guide to Birds.* New York: Alfred A. Knopf, 2000.

Smith, Douglas Grant. *Pennak's Freshwater Invertebrates of the United States.* New York: John Wiley, 2001.

Strong, Paul. *Where Waters Run: Beavers.* Minocqua, WI: Northword Press, 1997.

Thoreau, Henry David. *A Week on the Concord and Merrimack Rivers; Walden; The Maine Woods; Cape Cod.* New York: Library of America, 1985.

Venning, Frank D. *Wildflowers of North America.* New York: St. Martin's Press, 1984.

Voshell, J. Reese, Jr. *A Guide to Common Freshwater Invertebrates of North America.* Blacksburg, VA: McDonald and Woodward, 2002.

Warren, Edward Royal. *The Beaver: Its Work and Its Ways.* New York: Williams and Wilkins, 1927.

Wilsson, Lars. *My Beaver Colony.* New York: Doubleday, 1968.

Woodbury, Anthony C. "Counting Eskimo Words for Snow: A Citizen's Guide." University of Texas, Austin. Author's Web site, 2001.

Yalin, M. S. *River Mechanics.* New York: Pergamon Press, 1992.

York, Vincent. *The Sandy River and Its Valley.* Farmington, ME: Knowlton and McCleary, 1976.

Acknowledgments

Warm thanks to Erick Apland, John Atwood, Drew Barton, Meghan Bitterauf, Ms. Bollocks, Henry Braun, Elizabeth Colleen Callahan, Theodore Enslin, John Hodgkins, Juliet Karelsen, Roger "Sky" Kay, Bob Kimber, Rita Kimber, Pit Marcus, Elysia Morgan Martin, Wes McNair, Connie Nosalli, Fred Ouellette, Earl and Dunya Pomeroy, Nancy Prentiss, Gwilym Roberts, Elysia Roorbach, Tom Weddle, and Monica Wood, for their help and support in the making of this book.

To protect the privacy of some of the people in this book, I've taken the liberty of changing a few names and otherwise creating disguises that I mean to be impenetrable, including the construction of composite characters like Earl Pomeroy and Ms. Bollocks.

Many thanks, too, to the librarians of the Ohio State University science libraries, the Butler Library at Ohio State, the Maine State Library, the Bates College Library, the Camden Library, the Portland Public Library, the Colby College Library, and dozens of other libraries by way of interlibrary loan. And deep thanks to Jean Oplinger and her staff at the Farmington Public Library, and to the librarians of the Mantor Library at the University of Maine at Farmington, retired or not: Janet Brackett, Shelley Davis, Laurie MacWhinnie, Diane McNair, Sarah Otley, Frank Roberts, Joan Small, and Moira Wolohan. Special thanks to Zip Kellogg of the University of Southern Maine Library, and to the historians of Farmington, Temple, and Avon, Maine.

I received crucial financial help in the form of grants during the making of this book from the National Endowment for the Arts and from Furthermore: A program of the J. M. Kaplan Fund, also instrumental logistical help from Sarah Cecil and the Maine Writers and Publishers Alliance.

Warmest thanks to Susan Kamil, my editor at Dial, and to her assistant, Noah Eaker. And thanks to my editors at *Harper's*, where sections of this book first appeared.—Colin Harrison, John Sullivan, Lewis Lapham, and Mary Lamott. Finally, endless love to Betsy Lerner, my agent.

If you have remarked errors in me, your superior wisdom must pardon them. Who errs not while perambulating the domain of nature? Who can observe everything with accuracy? Correct me as a friend, and I as a friend will requite with kindness.

—Carolus Linnaeus

About the Author

BILL ROORBACH, recent winner of an O. Henry Award, is the author of *Big Bend,* winner of the Flannery O'Connor Award; a novel, *The Smallest Color;* and a memoir, *Summers with Juliet,* among other books of nonfiction. His short work has appeared in numerous publications, including the *Atlantic, Granta,* and the *New York Times Magazine,* and has been widely anthologized. Currently he holds the Jenks Chair in Contemporary American Letters at the College of the Holy Cross. *Temple Stream* flows from an article that first appeared in *Harper's Magazine.*